TAMING THE

WHAT TO EXPECT IN A LAWSUIT AND HOW TO
MAKE SURE YOUR ATTORNEY GETS RESULTS

LAWYERS

KENNETH MENENDEZ

MERRITT PUBLISHING,
A DIVISION OF THE MERRITT COMPANY
SANTA MONICA, CALIFORNIA

Taming the Lawyers
What to expect in a lawsuit and how to make sure your attorney gets results

First edition, 1996
Copyright © 1996 by Kenneth Menendez

For a list of other publications or for more information from Merritt Publishing, please call (800) 638-7597. Outside the United States and in Alaska and Hawaii, please call (310) 450-7234.

Library of Congress Catalogue Number: 96-075087

Kenneth Menendez
Taming the Lawyers
What to expect in a lawsuit and how to make sure your attorney gets results
Includes index.
Pages: 305

ISBN: 1-56343-133-5
Printed in the United States of America.

To Mom and Dad,

Who made it all possible.

And to Lisa, Steven, John and Mary,

Who make it all worthwhile.

Acknowledgments

No book is the product of one person. Even when the author writes the book alone, there are always scores of people upon whom the author must rely in order to take the book from pipe dream to finished product. The danger in trying to thank those people is that inevitably some people who ought to be thanked are accidentally omitted. I apologize in advance to those who will fall into that category. Your omission was wholly unintentional. The words and thoughts in this book are mine. Likewise, I must claim all of the mistakes.

With all of the caveats safely in the record, I would like to express my deep gratitude:

To Lisa, whose unwavering support and countless sacrifices made this book possible. It's easy to write a book about doing the right thing when you're married to someone for whom doing the right thing is a way of life. And to our children, Steven, John and Mary, for being a daily source of joy and a constant inspiration to strive for a better future.

To Donnie, for being the best brother, friend and adviser anyone could ever hope to have, and for undertaking the thankless task of reading the first draft of this book. If everyone in the world was like Donnie, the lawyers would be out of business.

To my sisters, Jane and Linda, for the love and laughter they bring to our lives. And to the memory of my brother, Michael, whose life was a testament to the power of love and the things which can be achieved through sheer courage and determination.

To the memory of my parents, for teaching us the importance of love, laughter and perseverance. Nobody was ever raised righter.

To Bill Thompson, for twenty years of friendship, for slogging through an early draft of this book and for helping me to make it less "lawyerly" (i.e., boring).

To everyone at Love and Willingham for their support during the writing of this book. To Daryll Love, who is the kind of lawyer all good lawyers would like to be. To John Gilleland, Allen Willingham, Hezekiah Sistrunk and Bob Monyak, my cohorts from the old days at the big firm. To Kim Woodland and Jane Sams, for enduring our political "discussions." To Mike Hannan for sharing the frustration of being a Braves fan. To Traci Green Courville, for graciously enduring a vociferous next door neighbor. To the staff, for their patience, assistance and friendship. And especially to Jackie Eaton, for typing the first draft of this book.

To Tricia Molloy, for her enthusiasm and creativity in publicizing this enterprise.

To Jim Walsh, Cynthia Chaillie and the team at Merritt Publishing, for their support and guidance.

To the loose confederation of Pass Christian boon companions—especially Cle Dade, Jim Harrison, Devan Ard, Cleave Ham, Bruce Frankenberg, Jeff Gould, John Boyle, and Bobby Bories—and the Atlanta contingent—Mark Riley, Tom Harper, Bob Berg, Chip Ingraham, and Jerry de Golian—for helping me keep life its own self in perspective.

And to all of the lawyers, for inspiring me (in one way or another) to write this book.

Ken Menendez
Atlanta, Georgia
March 1, 1996

Table of Contents

Introduction

This book is written for people who, either as a result of prudent career choices, bad grades in college or dumb luck, are not lawyers. In light of this, I have struggled mightily to avoid descending into the morass of legal technicalities and jargon which we lawyers seem to employ at a moment's notice. If you were interested in learning about such arcana as pendent jurisdiction, *res ipsa loquitur* and the Rule in Shelley's Case, you would have attended law school.

Nevertheless, a working knowledge of the components of a lawsuit is necessary in order to make full use of the strategies enunciated in this book.

This book will explain the civil litigation system and provide suggestions for functioning effectively within the context of the system. The civil litigation system is struggling to address most of the problems described above, but systemic change is slow and uncertain. Fundamental changes in the system and in the conduct of the system's participants are needed to address this situation. Many thoughtful commentators have suggested changes and some of those changes are currently being implemented. Until such changes are fully implemented, however, today's business person must learn how to function within the existing system in order to minimize the drag on his business.

A strategy for functioning effectively in the existing system must be predicated on an understanding of the litigation system and the ways in which lawyers operate in the system. This book will describe ways in which you or your company can avoid the system's pitfalls and use the system to your advantage. This book will also describe ways in which you can manage your lawyers and establish a mutually beneficial working relationship with those lawyers. This book will increase your knowledge of the system and enhance your ability to function in the system effectively. In this fashion, it is my hope and belief that the system itself will be improved.

The prospect of having to tame a lawyer would not bring a smile to the face of most sane people. Except, perhaps, people who are married to lawyers and those people, by definition, can't be classified as sane. Nevertheless, in a time and culture in which lawyers are as ubiquitous as indoor plumbing (and not always as useful), avoiding lawyers for any sustained period of time is close to impossible. Since your number will be up sooner or later, it's important to develop a strategy to keep your encounter with the lawyers as short, inexpensive and painless as possible.

I can show you how to do this. This is not because I am a genius or because I have been invested with special insight by a benevolent Deity. I am just a lawyer who has worked in the system and, like most lawyers, have seen good, bad, and downright awful ways to deal with lawyers.

Most people do a poor job of managing lawyers. Individuals who are confident and successful in their personal and business affairs are often tentative, hesitant or inept when it comes to dealing with lawyers. This may be due to a lack of familiarity with the law or a desire to let the expert (that is, the lawyer) make the decisions. Whatever the reason, when dealing with lawyers many people abandon the very principles which have contributed to success in their business and personal lives. Seeing this opening, lawyers just assume that they should take complete control of the situation. Letting a lawyer do this, especially by default, is a very bad idea. This book will show you how to prevent this turn of events.

The approach I will suggest is not complicated. Some of the principles will be familiar to you. You may already be using some of them. The value lies in applying these principles in an integrated and consistent manner.

This is not to say that implementation of this system is a snap. It requires time, effort, attention to detail and, perhaps most importantly, persistence. Put another way, the system is simple, but not easy. This is a distinction worth pondering for a moment. Stripped to their essentials, many systems are simple but not easy. For most people, for example, the system for losing weight is simple. Eat less and get more exercise. Period. Simplest thing in the world. But not easy.

Similarly, the system outlined in this book is, in a sense, simple. Implementation, on the other hand, can be quite challenging. You will face a variety of obstacles. Inertia. Sloth. A reluctance to set up more procedures or create more paperwork. A reluctance to change the arrangement you have been using with your lawyer and a hesitation to impose new requirements on the lawyer, who might interpret the new approach as reflecting a lack of faith or trust on your part.

The greatest challenge involves sticking with it. At some point, you'll get busy. You'll be swamped with other work. You'll become bored with certain recurring aspects of the system. You'll decide that it wouldn't hurt to omit a few of the steps. Resist these impulses. Unless you implement these principles consistently, this approach will not work.

If, on the other hand, you follow this system consistently, it will work for you and your business. And before you know it, your lawyer will be tamed.

TAMING THE LAWYERS

Chapter One

The Lawyer: A User's Guide

Any successful program for managing your lawyer must be predicated upon an understanding of your lawyer and his way of looking at the world. While a complete understanding of lawyers is unattainable—and perhaps undesirable—headway can be made by understanding the lawyer's point of view, how lawyers are trained, how they analyze problems and how they work.

The Legal Type

I'm sometimes asked a version of the old chicken-or-egg question about lawyers: "Does the law attract a disproportionate number of overbearing people, or is it the profession that makes them insufferable?"

In the great tradition of lawyers everywhere, I answer that question by stating that the answer is a little of each.

People who end up in the legal profession share a number of common characteristics, chief among them being that they have all excelled in their school work. Everyone remembers—not too fondly—the kid who sat in the front of the classroom, spent most of the class raising his hand, completed his assignments three weeks in advance and always reminded the teacher that she had forgotten to assign homework.

Chances are this kid went on to become a lawyer.

I have no empirical evidence to support this, but it is my firm belief that the ranks of lawyerdom contain a large number of first children, teacher's pets, honor roll veterans, student council presidents and hall monitors. These are people who are quite accustomed to being right most of the time and have felt this way ever since they won the spelling bee in the fourth grade.

When these people reached their senior year in college, they were faced with a dilemma—where could they next continue to dazzle the world with their intellect? Most of them having majored in interesting but useless subjects like English, History, Political Science and Ancient Civilizations, business was out of the question.

Besides, business is often illogical, sometimes rewarding people who never made the honor roll.

More school was the logical answer. Medical school was out because if lawyers could stand the sight of blood, they would have taken Organic Chemistry in their sophomore year and started the medical school career path. Besides, doctors don't usually get to be President.

A master's degree and a teaching career were possibilities—they offered lots of library time and continued summer vacations. But most members of the group noticed that teachers earned less than rickshaw jockeys and these people didn't plan on eating macaroni for the rest of their lives.

Enter the perfect solution: Law School. Three more years of school—often on Mom and Dad's tab—followed by a job where book sense—as opposed to business sense or common sense—is important and you get paid to read books, theorize and make speeches.

There are, of course, exceptions to this profile. Many lawyers put themselves through law school after trying other careers. Some lawyers were engineering majors or possessed skills other than reading and writing. Sadly, these lawyers are in the minority. Most lawyers are subject to the same criticism leveled by Indiana University basketball coach Bobby Knight against journalists: "Everybody learns to read and write in the second grade. Most of us go on to other things."

Clearly, then, law school attracts a certain type of person. But does the practice of law itself produce the characteristics displayed by lawyers? Put another way, is there something in the day-to-day experience of being a lawyer that produces aggressiveness, stubbornness, verbosity, arrogance and high blood pressure?

Well, yes. The practice of law is a demanding way to spend one's professional life. More importantly, there is an aspect of the practice of law that sets the law apart from most other ways of making a living. It is this peculiarity which I believe is at the root of many of the annoying traits displayed by many lawyers. The peculiarity is one of the cardinal rules to remember about the law:

NOBODY (ESPECIALLY THE LAWYER) IS QUITE SURE WHAT THE LAW IS.

The law is something that lawyers cannot ever fully know. There is simply too much law for any human being to master. There are too many statutes, too many cases, too many ambiguous decisions, too many learned commentaries, too many precedents, too many exceptions, and too many rules for any human being to even read, let alone comprehend.

Even the judges don't *know* the law. It is not uncommon for judges to have wildly different opinions as to what the law is, means and requires. Judge Smith thinks that the *Jones* case requires one result, while Judge Brown believes the *Jones* case requires the opposite result. Accordingly, judges in different states and jurisdictions often produce conflicting decisions, which in turn produce uncertainty and thousands of lawyer ulcers.

Even if one could read and comprehend all of the existing law, such a state of grace would be short-lived because, every single day, courts and legislatures in every state and in Washington crank out new decisions and new statutes. Every day, federal and state agencies produce new regulations and opinions interpreting existing statutes and case law. Every day, professors produce articles suggesting new interpretations of old cases and statutes. Every day, creative—or diabolical, depending on your point of view—lawyers craft new theories of law, citing heretofore overlooked footnotes in the dissenting opinions to cases decided in the nineteenth century.

In short, uncertainty is inherent in the system. This uncertainty breeds tension, which in turn produces or exacerbates unattractive qualities in your lawyer.

The lawyer becomes aware of this problem at an early stage of her career. The effect which this realization produces is not a positive one. The knowledge that she can never know all or even most of the law tends to make the lawyer very uncomfortable. In the past, the lawyer could always master a subject by reading all of the material three or four times. It makes the lawyer nervous to know she may have missed something essential to the case and downright panicked to think her opponent might not have missed it.

This impulse can reach excessive levels. The 1975 federal court case *In re: U.S. Financial Securities Litigation* demonstrates what can happen when lawyers—or their clients—decide to engage in "thorough" pre-trial discovery.

Lawyers for two real estate investors who had done business with U.S. Financial—and were co-defendants in the complex suit—served a set of interrogatories—written questions—that was "two inches high, 381 pages long, and contained 2,736 questions and subparts."

Additional copies were served on fourteen plaintiffs' attorneys, thirty-three other defendants' attorneys, fifteen defendants who were not represented by counsel, and five related and interested parties. Everyone was required to file written responses.

U.S. Financial moved for a protective order and claimed annoyance, oppression, and undue burden and expense.

The federal court in California sympathized with U.S. Financial's complaints, noting that:

> It was expensive to prepare, copy, and mail these interrogatories. Answering the questions would be much more burdensome. If an attorney takes ten minutes to answer each of the 2,736 questions and subparts, and charges $50.00 an hour, his fee would be $22,800. At three answers to a page the answers would fill 916 pages and measure six inches high. To mail copies to the sixty-seven parties on the service list, it would be necessary to reproduce a total of 60,192 pages. At $.03 a page, copying would cost $1,800. A conservative estimate of the total cost of answering is $24,000.

Those estimates pertained to one set of interrogatories. The litigation as a whole was much larger. Moreover, the lawyer's hourly fee today would be at least triple the $50 per hour quoted in this case.

The plaintiffs had served the defendants with a unified set of interrogatories. One of the major defendants had directed separate interrogatories to six groups of plaintiffs. Other defendants had served a unified set of interrogatories on thirty other defendants. The court, swimming in paper, complained:

> If every defendant proceeded to indiscriminately interrogate cross-claiming defendants the barrage of useless paperwork would be insurmountable.

> There are in excess of 300 cross-claims in this litigation. If 300 interrogatories of 381 pages are sent to each of the sixty-seven parties on the service list, the Xerox machines will have to grind out 7,535,800 pieces of paper which will occupy 3,768 linear feet of storage space.

> ...The threats of massive duplication, waste, and confusion are real.

No kidding. Happily, the court in this case ruled that the interrogatories were "unduly burdensome and oppressive" and struck—threw out—those interrogatories. Procedural rules adopted by state and federal courts since 1975 now place certain limits on the volume of discovery litigants are entitled to generate. Nevertheless, your opponent can still try to bury you in paper through creative drafting techniques or by asking the court to allow additional discovery.

The Dilemma of Too Much Information

Lawyers respond to the dilemma of too much information in a number of ways. Some lawyers turn into drudges, spending twenty hours a day reading everything available in a vain attempt to master all of the material or at least enough of the material to cut down on their heart palpitations. Other lawyers restrict their area of practice to substantive areas of the law so narrow that they cannot converse with confidence about anything other than Subchapter 4635 of the Internal Revenue Code.

Depending on which cranny these lawyers select, they become either rich, destitute or law school professors.

Many lawyers cannot or do not wish to restrict themselves in this way. Accordingly, these lawyers must develop a way to deal with the nagging insecurity produced by the awful knowledge that they no longer know it all or even most of it. The solution for many is to adopt a pose of confidence which, given even a small opportunity, often segues into arrogance.

Experienced lawyers know that even if you're not sure about a position you're taking, it helps a lot if you sound and act as though there is no possibility whatsoever that you could be wrong. Lawyers discovered long ago that sounding right is almost as important as being right. Moreover, there is a good possibility that the other people in the room—clients, lawyers and even the judge—are even less sure of their position than you are of yours.

The result of all this is that lawyers learn early on that they must advocate their position forcefully against all comers. Any sign of hesitation, timidity, indecision or ignorance provides your opponent with an opening into which he will drive his sword.

It's impossible to determine whether the adoption of this pose produces any results. In most instances, no one knows why a judge or jury entered a particular verdict. There is no way to tell whether the lawyer's behavior influenced the result. In light of this, the lawyer assumes that his performance had a positive effect. If the lawyer wins, he assumes that his forceful presentation carried the day. If the lawyer loses, he assumes that he lost because the law or facts were against him, but he would have lost even worse had it not been for his forceful presentation.

Certain day-to-day aspects of the practice of law also play a role in producing the not-so-sunny disposition displayed by most lawyers. Lawyers are pulled in various directions by a diverse cast of characters. The client wants to win, but doesn't want to spend much money doing it. The client believes that the lawyer's fees are outrageous and pays the fees sporadically and only after much complaining.

The opposing lawyer's sworn duty is to assail the lawyer in every way possible, make the lawyer look foolish, deride his every statement, and run him out of town on a rail if possible. The judge has no patience with the lawyer, sets impossible deadlines and demands consistent obeisance.

Back at the office, the lawyer faces all of the challenges of running a business. The various bar associations prod the lawyer to join committees and perform *pro bono* work, in addition to monitoring the lawyer's conduct to ensure that he has not run afoul of the Canons of Professional Ethics. All the while, the specter of a malpractice claim hovers over the lawyer with Damoclean menace.

There is also, as the psychologists might say, the learned behavior of the peer group. Lawyers spend most of their time with other lawyers. Seeing that their peers are aggressive, competitive, self-confident and high strung, neophyte lawyers tend to take on these qualities, either in self defense or because it seems to be the accepted way of behaving.

All of this is not in defense of—or apology for—lawyers. We chose this profession and, compared to the way the majority of people make a living, it's a pretty cushy deal. Nobody has a gun at our heads forcing us to remain lawyers. This is, rather, an attempt to acquaint the business person with the mind set of many lawyers. A familiarity with attitudes which may be held by your lawyer will help you to work more effectively with your lawyer.

How Lawyers Are Trained

It is axiomatic that law school plays a central role in fashioning lawyer outlook and behavior. Much has been written about the institution of law school and whether it prepares students to be effective lawyers.

Law school is, first and foremost, a hotbed of competition. At most law schools, the vast majority of the law students have always been at the top of their respective classes throughout their entire academic career. Arriving at law school, they find themselves in a class comprised of other academic hotshots with transcripts every bit as impressive as their own.

These would-be lawyers know that their success in the job market will depend almost entirely on their academic performance and class rank. All of which means that they have to beat the brains out of the person sitting next to them, not just for the sake of pride, but for career advancement. The amount of pressure and competition varies from law school to law school, but it is present in some degree at every law school. This atmosphere affects the law student's personality, work habits and general view of the world.

Then there are the teachers. Law school is taught by law professors who are, by and large, bright individuals who are either unwilling or unable to function as practicing lawyers.

While every law school has adjunct professors who are practicing lawyers and full professors who are former practicing lawyers, most law school instructors are creatures of the academy or government.

Most law professors I have known would benefit from a healthy dash of reality borne of service in the private sector. The people who are training tomorrow's lawyers—and who trained your lawyer—are people who have spent most, if not all, of their careers insulated from the realities of the business world.

Many law professors employ the Socratic method of instruction. This approach has been dramatized in countless books, films and television programs—usually inaccurately. The Socratic method involves the law professor asking a series of questions rather than delivering a lecture.

When employed by a skilled professor, the Socratic method can be a wonder to behold. Unfortunately, the number of law professors who can skillfully use the Socratic method is dwarfed by the number of professors who employ it badly. In the hands of a not-so-skilled professor, the Socratic method produces little more than mass confusion. In such classes, the students learn very little law. Instead, they spend most of the class period hoping they won't be called on by the professor and wondering why they didn't go to business school.

As for the curriculum itself, most law students receive instruction in courses such as Contracts, Torts, Civil and Criminal Procedure, Constitutional Law, Property Law and Legal Writing. Much of the instruction in these subjects focuses on legal theory, as opposed to the hard and fast rules of law. Some law school curriculums are more theoretical than others. Certain law schools are proud of their mission to teach their students how to "think like lawyers" without getting bogged down by the specific statutes and case law.

Such details are given cursory attention by many law schools. One of my Civil Procedure professors spent an entire semester discussing three appellate cases. The Rules of Federal Civil Procedure remained undisturbed while our professor spent two months discussing the nuances of the case of *Pennoyer v. Neff*.

A charitable observer would suggest that there was hidden value in this exercise which the callow law student was too inexperienced to detect.

The less charitable observer would suggest that the semester was wasted while a professor exalted theory and esoterica over substance.

In any event, many law schools do not focus upon the practicalities of the law or law practice, choosing instead to use the classrooms as testing grounds for the theories which the professor hopes to use in his next law review article. While clinical programs and the realities of the tightened job market for lawyers have led law schools to pay more attention to practical training in recent years, most law students graduate from law school unprepared for the practice of law.

There are, of course, certain things which law schools do well. Many law schools are quite successful in teaching their students how to "think like lawyers." What does this mean? It means teaching the law students how to identify the question which lies at the heart of a dispute or controversy. In conjunction with this, law students are taught how to distinguish relevant facts and questions from irrelevant facts and questions.

A majority of lawyers would cite the ability to think logically, spot issues and identify the relevant facts as the most important and useful skills they acquired in law school—in addition to the ability to function on three hours of sleep each night.

Upon completion of law school, the aspiring lawyer must obtain her license to practice law. This is accomplished by passing the bar exam, which is administered by the bar association of the state in which the student wishes to practice law. The bar exam is an excruciating hurdle for lawyer wannabes. Having already invested three years and countless thousands of dollars to learn the law, the law student is now required to demonstrate that she has in fact learned the law—or some part of it—by taking a two- or three-day exam which is administered twice each year.

Adding to the challenge is the fact that most law schools focus on teaching their students broad theories and "how to think like a lawyer" rather than the specific rules which the students will need to know in order to pass large portions of the bar exam. Consequently, law students spend additional time and money to take bar preparation courses which identify the subjects and questions most likely to appear on the exam.

When and if the student passes the bar exam, the second phase of the lawyer's training begins. A young lawyer's post-law school training usually begins with a period of apprenticeship under the tutelage of an experienced—or at least a more senior—lawyer. This system is haphazard at best and grossly inefficient at worst.

Due to the circumstances of their practice or position, some senior lawyers are able to devote a great deal of time to the training of young lawyers. In far more cases, however, the senior lawyer is too busy to devote much time to training the young lawyer. Instead, the senior lawyer delegates to the younger lawyer those tasks for which the senior lawyer lacks time or interest. The young lawyer is left to teach himself how to handle those tasks.

While there is something to be said for hands-on training, in many cases the young lawyer is overwhelmed and confused. The results can run the gamut from excessive bills to the client, who ends up paying for the young lawyer's learning process, to full-fledged prejudice to the client's case.

Many law firms—both large and small—have formal training programs for young lawyers and many of them function quite well. Other law firms have never given much thought to the training of young lawyers other than a vague notion that (1) young lawyers should start their careers doing legal research, to be followed by a gradual allocation of responsibility for more complicated tasks, and (2) the training received by the young lawyers should mirror the training received by the senior lawyer. The underlying assumption is, "I turned out to be a crackerjack lawyer, so the training I received must be the proper training."

The result is that some lawyers are trained very well and other lawyers train themselves as they go along. This is important to the business person because it helps to explain why lawyers approach problems the way they do. It also represents fair warning to business persons that some lawyers are undertrained for certain tasks which you may ask them to undertake.

How Lawyers Analyze Problems

An important facet of managing your lawyer is understanding how lawyers analyze problems. Lawyers are trained to identify the issue at hand and focus on the facts relevant to that issue. By definition, this requires a focused and often narrow analysis. It is important for a business person to remain aware that the lawyer is analyzing the problem in this fashion. There are advantages and disadvantages to such an approach.

The advantage involves the lawyer's ability to hone in on the relevant facts. Most good lawyers can assess a dispute or controversy and strip it to its essential parts. The lawyer typically does this in a focused and objective fashion. Such objectivity may be difficult for the business person whose money, pride and livelihood are enmeshed in the controversy. The lawyer's focused approach often distills the controversy to its essence, thus defining the real problem faced by the business person.

Unfortunately, there are a number of disadvantages to the lawyer's approach. First, the lawyer's focused approach may produce a narrow, single-faceted view of a situation. By focusing on the issues and only those facts which are pertinent to those issues, the lawyer sometimes fails to consider the larger context in which the dispute has occurred. Such tunnel vision can prevent the lawyer from achieving an accurate perspective.

The second problem involves another cardinal rule:

LAWYERS ARE TRAINED TO IDENTIFY PROBLEMS RATHER THAN SOLUTIONS.

The lawyer's approach focuses on problems rather than solutions. This is perhaps the principal difference between the approaches employed by lawyers and non-lawyers. By nature, training and experience, the lawyer tends to identify problems, while the non-lawyer focuses upon the desired goal and ways to bring that goal to fruition. Lawyers spend much of their professional lives looking for problems, such as the flaw in a particular argument or the points on which parties disagree.

The ability to identify areas of conflict, lapses in logic and other inconsistencies is highly valued in the practice of law. Consequently, lawyers are trained to see and articulate why things won't work rather than to identify ways to make things work. Many lawyers become habitual naysayers, willing and able to identify a dozen reasons why any plan, deal, strategy or argument won't work.

The lawyer's approach is reflective of two traits found in most lawyers:

1. a basic conservatism and

2. an almost manic resolve not to overlook anything.

The histrionics of certain high-profile lawyers notwithstanding, lawyers are an inherently conservative breed. Evidence is the lodestar. Emotion and speculation are untrustworthy and, most damning, not relevant. Accordingly, most lawyers are conservative in their analyses and risk-averse in the advice they offer.

This is not necessarily a bad thing. The lawyer's function is often to ground the client's flights of fancy and to temper the client's hopes with a bracing dose of reality. Nevertheless, the client must be cognizant of the conservative mind set possessed by most lawyers and guard against allowing the lawyer's inherent conservatism to convince the client that any and every course of action is sure to end in disaster.

It is often said that a lawyer could draft a foolproof contract which would protect the client from any and all potential problems, but that the contract would be worthless because no one would ever agree to its terms. The client should realize that it is the lawyer's nature— and duty—to anticipate problems and advise the client of those problems.

Second, lawyers are intent upon—if not obsessed with—not missing anything. A lawyer's greatest fear (other than having to find gainful employment as something other than a lawyer) is that there is a piece of relevant information out there—a statute, a case, a document, a fact—of which she is unaware and which would alter a legal situation completely. This fear is a product of the aforementioned enormity of the law, as well as the paranoiac personality of many lawyers.

In her quest to ensure that she has reviewed every pertinent sliver of information, the lawyer will research every matter which could have some bearing on the problem at hand. If this means staying up all night to review obscure law review articles or plow through warehouses full of documents, so be it. The lawyer is indefatigable in her quest to acquire 100 percent of the relevant information before issuing an opinion or taking a course of action.

The problem with this approach, of course, is that it is never possible to acquire 100 percent of the relevant information regarding any issue. Even if it were possible to acquire 100 percent of the relevant information, the cost of acquiring 100 percent of the information—especially the cost of acquiring the last 20 percent of the relevant information—is often prohibitive.

This is one of the many points at which the lawyer's approach diverges from the non-lawyer's approach. Non-lawyers are often comfortable making a decision on the basis of a reasonable amount—say, 80 percent—of the pertinent information. The lawyer, on the other hand, focuses not on the 80 percent of the information in her possession, but on the 20 percent of the information which she does not have. The absence of that last 20 percent of information often leads the lawyer to advise inaction or an attempt to acquire the last 20 percent of information.

The lawyer's desire to investigate every potentially relevant piece of information is also a function of external forces. Chief among these external forces is the fear of being sued for malpractice. If, for example, the litigator fails to assert a particular defense and the client loses the lawsuit, there is always a possibility that the client will find another lawyer who will argue that the original lawyer botched the case by failing to assert that defense.

Recognizing this possibility, lawyers often conclude that the best way to insulate one's self from such allegations is to do everything. Raise every defense. Depose every witness. Research every possible theory. Review and copy every document. Deny every allegation. Raise every possible objection.

In addition to complicating and lengthening the litigation process, such conduct by the lawyer is expensive. It behooves the client to remain cognizant of the lawyer's inclination toward overkill.

Finally, many lawyers tend to analyze disputes with a cynical, suspicious, often pessimistic eye. Although inherent personality traits can contribute to this attitude, the lawyer's experiences play the major role in forming this jaded attitude.

Lawyers—and especially litigators—tend to see people at their worst. A litigator's day is spent dealing with situations gone bad. At best, the conflict or dispute is the result of people failing to meet their respective obligations. In many instances, the controversy involves lying, duplicity, treachery, misrepresentations and other venal conduct.

The 1993 New York state court case of *John Doe v. Mary Roe* is a good example of this sort of behavior. The facts of the case were outlined by the court in its decision.

> In the fall of 1988, Doe and Roe began an intimate relationship which lasted to approximately November 1991. Doe testified that during this time he engaged in sexual activity only with Roe. He did not use a condom during this relationship since Roe used other forms of birth control.

> Doe testified that he received a call from Roe advising him that she had a medical problem, and that he should seek an examination. Doe visited his physician and was diagnosed as having Chlamy-

dia. He was put on a ten-day regimen of antibiotics. His physician advised if Doe observed no other signs, he would be considered cured. He incurred a doctor bill of $52 and a prescription bill of approximately $13.

Doe testified that while he engaged in sex before his relationship with Roe began, he always used a condom. Roe testified that she called Doe as soon as she found out about the problem....Roe further testified regarding the harassing and abusive phone calls and letters which began after Doe was diagnosed with Chlamydia. Roe also submitted photographic evidence of the obscenities painted on her car.

A number of Roe's friends [supported her statement] that Doe repeatedly called and harassed them about her. Although none of them saw Doe deface Roe's vehicle, one witness did observe Doe near the location of Roe's car on [the same night].

Doe sued Roe claiming that she caused him bodily injury by infecting him with Chlamydia. He claimed damages for medical treatment, mental anguish, and "loss of capacity for the enjoyment of life," totaling $2,000. Roe countersued for the same amount and claimed intentional infliction of emotional distress based upon the threatening and abusive phone calls Doe allegedly made to her in December 1991, and the alleged vandalizing of her car during the same time period.

The court ruled that there was insufficient proof that Roe knew of her condition and intentionally transmitted it to Doe. Roe notified Doe as soon as she knew she had a problem, following a physical examination, which was after the last time they had sexual relations. "Roe acted properly when she discovered her problem by letting Doe know within a reasonable time," the court ruled. A clear finding of negligence was not possible "since the testimony reveals that it is just as likely that Doe could have been carrying this disease and transmitted it to Roe."

Doe had sued Roe for $2,000 when his expenses amounted to no more than $65, consisting of his medical and prescription bills. He

Chapter Two

A Legal System Gone Haywire

If asked, many people would summarize the problems with the American legal system succinctly: Too many lawyers (probably preceded by a few defamatory adjectives).

Asked to elaborate, many would complain that lawyers generate too many lawsuits, require compliance with too many regulations (most of which were written by lawyers), force companies to spend inordinate amounts of time on non-revenue producing activities and in general represent a powerful drag on business.

This characterization contains a good deal of truth and begs a host of qualifiers.

The proliferation of lawyers is an undeniable fact of modern life. In 1965, total enrollment in law schools accredited by the American Bar Association was 54,265. In 1995, there were 134,784 students enrolled in ABA-accredited law schools. ABA-accredited law schools graduated—or disgorged, depending on your point of view—42,581 lawyers-to-be in 1994. In the same year, 49,135 aspiring lawyers passed state bar exams and were therefore allowed to begin the practice of law.

In 1994, the American Bar Association recognized 176 law schools in the United States. In addition to the accredited law schools, there are scores of law schools which have not yet obtained accreditation. All told, there are over 200 law schools at work training tomorrow's lawyers.

As of March of 1995, there were 896,140 lawyers in the United States—roughly one lawyer for every 310 people. By the end of the decade, the United States will be home to over one million lawyers. California, where trends tend to develop earliest and most radically, has 111,640 lawyers. Put another way, one of every eight lawyers in the United States lives in California.

If you're thinking about doing business in California, you've been warned.

The question of whether we need so many lawyers is beyond the scope of this book. I believe that America is the freest and fairest nation in the world (to steal a phrase from Peggy Noonan), so it isn't surprising that we have more lawyers than any other country. It's terrific that we have enough lawyers to insure that almost everyone who needs a lawyer—as well as plenty of people who really don't need a lawyer—has a reasonable chance of finding one. Still, I'll concede that we appear to have gone overboard in our production of lawyers.

In the end, I have great faith in the free market. We are already in the midst of a market correction which will impact what we do with so many lawyers.

More Law Means More Lawyers

Over the past thirty years, our legislatures and courts have been busy creating lots of new rights for the benefit and enjoyment of the citizenry. Whenever a new right is created—either by a legislature or, more dangerously, by a judge—there is an inevitable domino effect which follows.

For example, when Congress or a state legislature passes a law, the statute itself may be short—but the statute is just the beginning. As with most laws, the statute will be subject to different interpretations by different people and their lawyers.

Rare indeed is the law that is so clear and well-conceived that every interpretation has been anticipated and addressed in the statute itself. In most instances, the statute raises as many questions as it answers and is subject to interpretation and misinterpretation by lawyers and regular people alike. Moreover, such pesky details as how the law will be administered, who will be in charge of administering it and whether there are any exceptions are not usually addressed in the statute.

To fill this void, legislatures and bureaucrats often promulgate regulations to clarify and facilitate implementation of the statute. Like the statute itself, these regulations can be ambiguous, confusing and subject to varying interpretations by people...and their lawyers.

The regulations are often voluminous. In 1992, the Code of Federal Regulations was 125,331 pages long. To put this in perspective, the CFR had 43,118 pages in 1966. Between 1988 and 1992 alone (under a Republican administration, no less) the CFR grew by 7,851 pages.

In addition to the laws enacted by Congress and the legislatures, industrious judges have been creating new law at a dizzying pace. The body of law derived from the rulings of trial and appellate judges is referred to—without irony—as the common law. The expansion of the common law has increased the sheer volume of law to which we are all subject.

Being somewhat old fashioned, I believe that the drafters of the Constitution had a pretty good idea in assigning legislatures the task of writing the laws. But judicial activism is an issue for another discussion. For the purposes of this book, it will do to say that the courts have played a major role in increasing the framework of laws within which citizens must operate.

Once in place, these new laws must be read, understood, explained, argued over, challenged, modified, amplified and, ultimately, followed. In order to accomplish these tasks, society calls upon lawyers.

A Reflection of Social Upheaval

The expansion of the general body of law over the past thirty years has created a need—and I use that word advisedly—for more lawyers to administer the system. Reacting in part to that need, universities everywhere expanded the size of their existing law school classes or started law schools from scratch.

The increased demand for legal education has been reflected in the rising number of law school applicants. In 1965, the number of people taking the Law School Admissions Test (a prerequisite to law school) was 39,406. By 1995, that number had more than tripled to 127,905. Although law school applications have declined somewhat since their peak in 1991, the effects of the explosive growth will be felt well into the next century. There are more lawyers than ever. And they all need something to do.

Anecdotal evidence suggests that the increased interest in law school was reflective of, and partially created by, the social upheaval which occurred in the United States in the decade between 1964 and 1974. During this period, students were in no great rush to complete their studies and graduate to Vietnam or the real world. The flower of the nation's youth was much more interested in social revolution than in getting started in the advertising business.

The perceived gray flannel suit existence of their parents was anathema to large numbers of this generation. Those numbers—and I was one of them—preferred careers where we could make a difference, work for justice and change the world without selling out.

Capitalism was a dirty word and, to many, the pursuit of the dollar seemed a crass, shallow and unacceptable way to spend your life.

What to do, then? Faced with the end of their college careers (and, for the men, their student deferments from the draft), never having held an adult job, possessing few marketable skills beyond the ability to write term papers and filled with an often sincere desire to create positive social change, our generation opted for law school in unprecedented numbers.

Law school seemed like the perfect solution. In the short term, it offered three more years of school, thus delaying entry into the real world and full-fledged adulthood. In the long run, it would provide us with the skills with which to transform the nation and bring justice to a society which seemed to need plenty of it.

In addition to increased demand from college campuses, a growing number of people began to enter law school after having actually held real jobs. The expansion of community law schools, many with night programs, made it possible for people working full-time jobs to obtain law degrees. Attracted by perceived higher pay and better working conditions, thousands of people already in the work force enrolled in law schools. This group added to the already burgeoning cadre of law students.

Society's Perception of Lawyers

While lawyers are not held in great esteem by the public at large—often ranking below politicians and bill collectors in opinion surveys—the media and the popular culture portray the law as a desirable vocation. The law and lawyers have been seeping into the general public consciousness with increasing frequency over the past thirty years.

Although you could choose a number of points of origin of this trend, the decade of the 1960s saw an increase in the number of stories about lawyers in popular books, magazines, television and films. The exploits of Louis Nizer, Edward Bennett Williams, F. Lee Bailey, Richard "Racehorse" Haynes and others gave the profession a measure of drama and romance. The exploits of television lawyers such as the venerable *Perry Mason* and its progeny heightened the public's interest in lawyers, as did feature films such as *To Kill a Mockingbird* and *Anatomy of a Murder*.

In the midst of this trend appeared Watergate. Everyone involved in the scandal seemed to be a lawyer—the heroes, the villains, even the innocent bystanders. While there was enough wrongdoing by lawyers to stain the profession for several hundred years, the enduring images seemed to be of the good lawyers whose mission was to find the truth and bring the conspirators to justice. Judge John Sirica, Sam Ervin, Archibald Cox, Leon Jaworski, Elliott Richardson, even the Supreme Court—all represented to many the ultimate examples of the use of a law degree for the power of good.

Even the presence of so many lawyers among the conspirators conveyed the message that a law degree was the ticket to power.

In any event, Watergate spawned enormous interest in the law, which in turn manifested itself in another surge in law school applications. One of Watergate's legacies was convincing large numbers of students to become lawyers and journalists (and sometimes both), which surely secures the scandal's place in history's hall of infamy.

During the 1980s, television—and in particular the long-running series *L.A. Law*—depicted lawyers as leading exciting, challenging, lucrative and socially useful lives.

On television and in the movies, every case involves clear-cut good guys and bad guys, every witness is beautiful or handsome and attracted to the fearless lawyer, every client pays his bill, every trial is televised, every lawyer is able to promote social justice while pulling down a six-figure income, every lawyer lives in a beautiful house overlooking the city and spends two or three months a year vacationing in Aruba.

The fact that reality is not within shouting distance of this image has had little effect on the public's perception of lawyers.

Even the disheartening spectacle of such recent legal embarrassments as the trials of O.J. Simpson and the Menendez brothers (no relation to the author, thank goodness) seems to have done little to alter the notion that the law is a desirable career. To many people, being a lawyer seems like a swell way to make a living.

Reality isn't so simple. Lawyers need something to do all day. And they aren't immune to the lottery mentality that affects certain potential litigants. Many lawyers fantasize about hitting the jackpot with the next case that walks into their office.

Accordingly, more lawyers generate more lawsuits. And some lawyers are awful when it comes to telling prospective clients that they have no case.

There's an old lawyer story about a small town with only one lawyer. The lawyer had very little business and was on the verge of going bankrupt until a second lawyer moved into town. One year later, both lawyers were rich.

Economics from a Lawyer's Perspective

While the myth of the wealthy lawyer is exaggerated, it is true that, compared to society at large, most lawyers do well. While lawyer compensation spans a very broad range, it is undeniable that it has steadily—and sometimes spectacularly—increased over the past twenty-five years.

The median starting salary in private practice for 1995 law school graduates was $53,700. Entry-level salaries at large law firms are even higher, averaging approximately $66,000 and reaching as much as $85,000 in that hotbed of fiscal excess, New York City.

It's not unusual for good lawyers to make six-figure incomes while they're still quite young. Compensation usually increases as the lawyer gains additional experience, justifying—in the lawyer's mind—ever higher billing rates. At the top of this cycle, partners at large law firms in major cities often make over half a million dollars each year.

The boom in lawyer compensation has been fueled by a number of factors. The increasingly complex legal framework in which businesses and individuals must function has created an increased demand for legal counsel and services. Clients are required to pay larger sums to lawyers in exchange for an ever-burgeoning array of legal services.

Competition among law firms for the best law school graduates led to a bidding war of sorts in which the starting salaries for first-year lawyers increased substantially. This pressure from the private sector caused an associated, if less dramatic, increase in compensation for government lawyers.

The inflation of the 1970s triggered steep increases in the rates charged by lawyers. All told, increases in lawyer compensation outpaced the increases in many business sectors. People began enrolling in law school in order to secure a comfortable—often very comfortable—financial future.

The Litigation Explosion

The dramatic increase in the number of lawyers has produced lots of lawsuits. While varying state reporting systems make accurate tallies difficult to obtain, the National Center for State Courts reports that a total of 19.7 million civil cases were filed in the United States in 1992. An additional 273,000 civil cases were filed in federal courts. Although a large number of those cases involved non-commercial cases (divorces, the probating of wills and small claims court cases), the number remains staggering.

Whether as a party, employer, insurer or otherwise, businesses bear a substantial portion of the cost of all civil litigation. Those costs are often passed on to the consumer in the form of higher prices for various goods and services.

The litigation explosion has been fueled in part by some of the factors involved in the increase in the number of lawyers. In addition, other factors have contributed to the increase in litigation.

The body of law, both statutory and common law, in the United States has expanded over the past thirty years. As the law expanded, lawyers were asked to perform increasingly esoteric tasks which required additional training and cost more.

More requirements, more prohibited acts, more rights—all of these are fertile breeding grounds for lawsuits. For example, the Americans with Disabilities Act did not exist prior to 1991. In the first year of its existence, the ADA generated more than 12,000 complaints to the Equal Employment Opportunity Commission. Many of these complaints will lead to lawsuits. This is not to say that the ADA does not address certain very real needs; it's simply to say that each new statute, each new right or requirement created by legislatures or judges, leads to greater opportunities for lawsuits.

Changing Social Attitudes

We have become in large part a nation of whiners and victims. A disturbing and dangerous proclivity has taken hold of large numbers of Americans—the tendency to blame every misfortune on others or on society as a whole. Taken alone this trend would be disturbing enough, but the deleterious societal effect is increased when large numbers of individuals use the courts to rail against life's inequities.

Even more dangerously, the courts in many cases allow themselves to be used in this way.

Of course, there are many instances of wronged individuals rightfully using the courts to address their grievances. Many horrible situations which would not have been addressed by the law fifty years ago can be and are addressed today.

Let's stipulate that it is a good thing that people with legitimate grievances have forums in which to air and seek redress for those grievances.

Unfortunately, the expansion of the law to address legitimate grievances has also provided access to the court system to a vast number of illegitimate litigants. The courts are cluttered with thousands of specious lawsuits filed as a result of nothing more than an unwillingness to accept responsibility for one's own conduct, a desire to require other members of society (often businesses) to absorb the cost of such conduct, and a stubborn refusal to accept the fact that life is often unfair and it's nobody's fault.

Examples of spurious lawsuits are legion. You tripped over your own feet and broke your arm? It couldn't have been your fault. It must have been the city, which made the crack in the sidewalk too deep or the slope of the sidewalk too steep. Maybe it was the owners of the nearby office building, who built a fountain which sprayed water on the sidewalk, making it slippery. Maybe it was the hot dog vendor, who shouted too loudly and distracted you. Maybe it was the bus that ran late that morning, forcing you to walk more quickly than usual. One thing is certain—it wasn't your fault.

There's another thing that is certain—somewhere out there exists a lawyer who will take your case.

Much of the blame for spurious lawsuits lies with lawyers—legislators, judges and practicing lawyers. Legislatures have expanded the rights and protections to which citizens are "entitled" so prolifically that they seem bent on creating by legislative decree a utopian society devoid of risk, injustice and misfortune.

When the current law doesn't cover a particular situation, creative lawyers file lawsuits which seek to expand the parameters of the protection and liability established by the existing law. Judges often refuse to throw such cases out of court, because they are in sympathy with the alleged victim, because they believe the law *should* provide a remedy, or because they prefer to let a jury rule on the merits of the case (or the lack thereof).

Relaxed Rules Encourage Litigation

It is much easier to sue someone today than it was thirty years ago. The rules of civil procedure—the technical rules governing lawsuits—have been liberalized over the past thirty-five years. One of the most significant changes involved the adoption of something called notice pleading.

In days of yore, lawsuits had to be worded very specifically in order to survive. The rules required something called issue pleading, which meant that in its initial complaint, the plaintiff in a lawsuit carried the burden of identifying the issues and advising the defendant of a large number of the facts involved in the claim.

A wide array of technical requirements had to be met in order for the lawsuit to remain in court. Failure to meet those specific and demanding requirements could—and often did—result in lawsuits being thrown out of court on the basis of what would no doubt now be called technical errors.

To be sure, the system sometimes resulted in rough justice and the dismissal of a number of legitimate cases. Just as surely, the system put a premium on good lawyers, required both the lawyer and the party to put a great deal of thought and preparation into the filing of a lawsuit and cut down on the number of frivolous lawsuits. Notice pleading changed all that.

Notice pleading means, more or less, just what the name implies. If a pleading (the complaint which kicks off the lawsuit) contains sufficient information to put the defendant on notice (in a broad and very general nature) of the allegations that are being made against the defendant, the pleading is sufficient.

Notice pleading is in large part the product of the notion that under the old system certain meritorious claims were dismissed due to technical defects in the pleadings. This was true. What's more, there was the amorphous belief that notice pleading would be fairer—a tricky concept in legal circles.

The drafters of the new rules realized that notice pleading would increase the number of lawsuits filed, but they may have reasoned that this was a small price to pay in order to ensure that meritorious cases were not dismissed due to technical defects.

The new rules mean that almost any lawsuit can be filed with nothing more than a bare allegation that one party has injured another party in some way. By making it easier to file lawsuits and to keep them in court until trial, the new rules have contributed to the increase in the number of lawsuits.

Judges

The conduct of judges has played an important role in the litigation explosion.

Let's stipulate that most judges are honest, intelligent, hard-working public servants who attempt to carry out their duties in the fairest possible fashion in accordance with existing law.

Having said that, it's undeniable that some judges do not do their job very well and, therefore, have some complicity in the litigation explosion. Simply put, judges too often allow cases which should be dismissed to stay in court.

Federal and state rules of civil procedure contain provisions pursuant to which judges may dismiss a lawsuit at an early stage if, after having been given a reasonable opportunity to do so, the plaintiff is unable to demonstrate the existence of a genuine issue of material fact.

If the plaintiff has not done so, the defendant may—and often does—file a motion entitled a Motion for Summary Judgment, which asks the court to dismiss the case. This is an important juncture at which judges may exercise their discretion to dismiss spurious cases. Unfortunately, most judges don't like to grant motions for summary judgment.

Motions for summary judgment are serious matters because to grant one denies the plaintiff her opportunity to argue her case to a jury. Accordingly, judges should—and do—treat such motions as serious matters which should be granted only when the facts, when viewed in the light most favorable to the plaintiff, compel such a result. Nevertheless, there are many instances in which such a ruling is justified by the facts or the lack thereof.

Unfortunately, judges seldom grant such motions. This hesitation flows from several sources.

First, it is always safer and easier for a judge to deny a motion for summary judgment. While such a denial may be appealable in some instances, appellate courts rarely reverse a denial of a motion for summary judgment. Judges concerned about their reversal rate know that the denial of a motion for summary judgment is always the safer course.

Second, many judges are reluctant to deny a party his day in court. These judges believe that little harm can result from denying a motion for summary judgment, while real harm might result from granting such a motion. The grant of such a motion might result in a meritorious claim being forever banned. By denying the motion, no meritorious claim is excluded. If the claim is without merit, the jury can so pronounce it. In effect, the denial seems a no-lose situation, but there is a hidden cost.

The reluctance to use motions for summary judgment to dispose of meritless cases increases the cost of litigation for all litigants by allowing baseless cases to remain in court, consuming judicial resources and resulting in settlements being paid not because the claim has merit, but only to avoid the greater cost of taking the case to trial and risking a large jury verdict.

Economic Extortion

I considered using a euphemism of some sort here, but extortion is the right way to say what I mean. Some lawsuits are filed for the sole purpose of pressuring the defendant into settling the case in exchange for a cash payment. In such instances, the absence of demonstrable legal liability on the part of the defendant is of little consequence.

Unscrupulous litigants, aided by lawyers who are equally unscrupulous, philosophically motivated or hopelessly naive, often file lawsuits with the express purpose of obtaining a settlement. At some point, the plaintiff's lawyer will regale the defendant's lawyer with a list of all of the things the plaintiff plans to do in the course of the litigation—exploring every aspect of the defendant's business or personal life, requesting the defendant's tax returns, causing the defendant's employees or family members to spend hours responding to discovery requests, obtaining a list of the defendant's customers and contacting those customers, generating unfavorable publicity, and forcing the defendant to spend unpredictable amounts of money in legal fees.

The plaintiff's lawyer will say that the plaintiff has little to lose because the lawyer is working on the basis of a contingent fee arrangement. This pitch usually ends with the plaintiff's lawyer stating that despite the obvious strength of his client's case and the righteousness of his cause, in the spirit of cooperation the plaintiff is willing to settle the case in exchange for a lot of money.

This practice occurs in part because the rules allow—and even encourage—it to occur. Although the rules provide for sanctions against people who file frivolous lawsuits and, in certain rare instances, their lawyers, these sanctions are imposed infrequently.

In much the same way that the crafters of the criminal justice system have determined that they are willing to let guilty defendants go free in order to avoid convicting an innocent defendant, the crafters of the civil litigation system have constructed a system which, in its effort to provide honest litigants with every opportunity to present their case, has left itself open to abuse by the unscrupulous litigant.

Most unscrupulous litigants—and their lawyers—are well aware of this fact.

Highly Publicized Damage Awards

Never underestimate the bandwagon effect. Newspapers and television are quick to publicize large damage awards imposed by juries. Such damage awards are almost always imposed against businesses.

The media consider it news when a big company is forced to pay millions to a small individual. Word of such verdicts permeates society and fosters the notion that the civil justice system is just another government-operated lottery eager to shower untold millions on the next lucky winner.

One of the most widely-heralded recent awards stemmed from the 1994 case of *Stella Liebeck v. McDonald's Restaurants, Inc.*

The case arose out of an incident which occurred in February 1992 at an Albuquerque McDonald's. Ms. Liebeck, a retiree, was severely burned by a cup of scalding hot coffee that she had purchased from the McDonald's drive-through. She had placed the cup between her legs to steady it and attempted to take the lid off to add cream. The coffee, which she spilled on her, was very hot—between 180 and 190 degrees Fahrenheit.

Liebeck suffered second and third degree burns on six percent of her body. She was hospitalized for eight days, had skin grafts and suffered from "scarring and disability."

Liebeck attempted to settle with McDonald's a number of times to gain compensation for the medical bills and the pain which she had suffered. When McDonald's refused and tried to offer her only $800 to cover her medical expenses, she took the company to court. Among other things, Liebeck sued McDonald's for breach of the implied warranties of merchantability and fitness for a particular purpose— legal jargon for "the coffee was too hot."

The case was tried before a jury. Experts at the trial admitted that coffee was too hot for consumption between 180 and 190 degrees. McDonald's claimed that it was company procedure to brew the coffee at high temperatures to enhance its flavor.

The jury rendered a verdict against McDonald's, awarding Liebeck $160,000 in compensatory damages, $2.7 million in punitive damages, and her attorney's fees. Specifically, the jury ruled that the product—the coffee—was defective and that McDonald's had breached its implied warranties. This was legalese for, "We agree. The coffee was too hot."

The case became an instant example of excessive legal awards and a rallying-cry for advocates of tort reform.

The trial judge later reduced the award for punitive damages to $480,000. The case was appealed by both Liebeck and McDonald's. Eventually, the two parties settled out of court for an undisclosed amount.

In the day-to-day reality of legal matters, such large verdicts are the exception rather than the rule. Plaintiffs often lose their cases, but the press is less likely to publicize a verdict in favor of a corporate giant like McDonald's. As basketball great Wilt Chamberlain once said, nobody roots for Goliath.

Still, the societal perception is that there is always a chance that a jury will be touched by a plaintiff's tale of woe. And this is often a good bet. If it works, the plaintiff can look forward to a multimillion dollar award and an appearance on *Oprah*. This notion contributes to the increase in the number of lawsuits filed each year.

The Costs of All This Suing

The dramatic increase in the number of lawyers and lawsuits poses a serious challenge to businesses and individuals alike. The ability of American business to compete is hampered by litigation, the threat of litigation, the cost of litigation (including legal fees, settlements and judgments) and the cost of attempting to prevent litigation. The effect is both global and local. For larger corporations, the foregoing costs reduce profitability. For smaller businesses, such costs can threaten the very existence of the company.

Large and small companies alike are inhibited from engaging in certain types of potentially profitable activities by the specter of litigation. Likewise, individuals can seldom afford to engage in protracted litigation, regardless of the merits of the dispute.

Some people argue that it is only the fear of litigation that keeps businesses from running roughshod over the rights of their customers and employees, endangering the environment and engaging in unfair (if not illegal) business practices. It is undeniable that some business people might do some of these things in the absence of a civil justice system which provides a forum in which such conduct can be identified and punished. But the current system inhibits legitimate businesses along with the potentially dishonest ones.

The result is a system of commerce hamstrung by a civil litigation system which has become overburdened and inefficient. The system often drains vitality, investment and productivity out of our businesses.

There is a more subtle—but nevertheless very real—negative effect produced by the current climate. Many businesses today have become reluctant to try new things, to fire unproductive employees, to conduct business aggressively because they are afraid of a lawsuit. This leaves businesses vulnerable to economic blackmail by unscrupulous employees, dishonest competitors and customers who refuse to meet their contractual obligations.

Problematic individuals are well aware of the costs associated with a lawsuit. They know that a business is often likely to settle a claim— even a baseless claim—rather than become ensnared in the civil litigation morass.

In my career as a commercial litigator, I have seen many instances of businesses forced to write off money which was owed to them because the cost of recouping the money was too great. In other instances, companies on the receiving end of baseless lawsuits pay to settle the case in order to avoid protracted litigation.

This situation can be illustrated by the following scenario. Assume that a company has been sued by a disgruntled former employee for wrongful termination. The record reflects a history of poor performance by the employee and the claim is baseless. The former employee seeks damages in the amount of $500,000. Shortly after the lawsuit is filed, the plaintiff's attorney offers to settle the case for $75,000.

The president of the company discusses the offer with his lawyer. The lawyer tells the president that he is confident that if the case goes to trial, the company will win the case. Nevertheless, it will take two to four years for the case to get to trial. In the meantime, the company can expect to spend between $75,000 and $150,000 in legal fees. It will have to allow the plaintiff's lawyers to delve into the company's business practices, hiring practices, revenues and corporate policies. At least half a dozen employees will be deposed by the plaintiff's lawyer.

The company also risks unfavorable publicity regarding the alleged discrimination. When all of that is completed, the lawyer believes the company will prevail at trial, but of course cannot guarantee it. Even if the company prevails at trial, it is unlikely that the company can recover any of its attorney's fees, but very likely that an adversary will appeal.

On the other hand, the company's lawyer says, the plaintiff's lawyer is offering to settle the case for $75,000 today. The lawyer believes that he can reduce that figure through negotiation to $60,000. In exchange for the $60,000, the case will be over immediately, no further funds will need to be expended, the company will not endure any negative publicity, there will be no further disruption of the company's work, there will be no risk of a large adverse jury verdict, the terms of the settlement will be confidential, and there will be no intrusion into the company's finances or past hiring policies.

The disadvantage, says the lawyer, is that the company will be paying $60,000 to someone who doesn't deserve a dime.

Faced with this choice, the majority of businesses would consider settling the case for $60,000. Some people would argue that settlement is the only logical course and that it is a defensible business decision. Others would characterize settlement in such a situation as the payment of blackmail.

No doubt, certain business persons would consider the payment of a settlement under these circumstances unacceptable and would direct the lawyer to defend vigorously against the baseless allegations ("millions for defense, but not one cent for tribute").

Many businesses don't have the luxury of adopting this position. The disadvantages—and, in particular, the cost—of protracted litigation far outweigh the cost of settlement.

TAMING THE LAWYERS

Chapter Three

The Mechanics of a Lawsuit

Legal disputes take many forms. The most common disputes include:

- contractual disputes with people who don't deliver the goods or services they promised;
- tort disputes over injuries caused by someone's alleged negligence;
- disputes with customers regarding the price or quality of a product;
- financing deals which go awry;
- disputes with employees regarding promotion, discharge and general working conditions;
- product liability disputes;
- trademark, patent and intellectual property disputes; and
- plain old garden variety disputes over money—what were the rights and obligations of each party and did those parties meet their respective obligations?

Any and all such disputes can form the basis for a lawsuit. In this chapter, I will discuss the basic mechanics of how a lawsuit begins, progresses and concludes. At each stage, a variety of complications can occur. While you can't predict how any particular lawsuit will develop, you can anticipate likely outcomes.

The natural and logical response to a dispute is an attempt to resolve the dispute without any lawyers. This is sensible, advisable and, in many cases, possible. Here is another of the cardinal rules of the legal world:

IF YOU CAN RESOLVE YOUR DISPUTE WITHOUT THE LAWYERS, DO SO.

In almost every case, it is better to settle your dispute without resorting to litigation or other formal methods of dispute resolution. Litigation is expensive, time-consuming, emotionally draining, distracting, and seldom leads to a satisfactory result. Litigation requires the investment of several years and tens—if not hundreds—of thousands of dollars.

Your lawsuit will probably settle prior to trial; 94.6 percent of civil lawsuits do. And, if you do get to trial, your legal fees will increase precipitously.

Except in cases involving egregious or fraudulent conduct by your adversary, any award by the jury in your favor will probably not include attorney's fees—unless you are dealing with a specific statute which provides for the award of such fees. So, even if you win the case, you may find that after deducting your legal fees you have recovered a negligible amount.

There are a few qualifiers to the cardinal rule of resolving disputes.

First, your informal resolution of the dispute must not run afoul of any existing laws. You can't decide to burn down the warehouse to collect the insurance.

Second, any resolution must make financial sense. Any dispute can be settled if one side is willing to surrender unconditionally.

Third, the resolution should not set an unfavorable precedent or constitute any admission of liability or wrongdoing which might pose a future threat to your business. Caving into the demands of one unscrupulous competitor may embolden other unscrupulous competitors to make similar demands.

Finally, and most importantly, the settlement must not violate your company's fundamental principles or your personal moral code.

There are some instances in which your adversary is trying to steal your money just as surely as if he appeared at your door with a mask and a gun. In other instances, you may feel that a settlement constitutes an admission of wrongdoing or a vindication of your adversary's position and therefore you are unwilling to settle the case. While a settlement may be advisable from a financial point of view, your sense of right and wrong may not allow you to make the settlement. In such instances, you shouldn't settle the case.

As long as you are aware of the consequences, financial and otherwise, of proceeding with the litigation and are willing to accept those consequences, you should never agree to a settlement which forces you to compromise your core principles. Trust your instincts.

The Complaint

Civil cases (a misnomer if there ever was one) are disputes between private entities—as opposed to criminal cases, in which the government charges a private citizen with wrongdoing.

A civil lawsuit is typically initiated by the filing of a Complaint in the appropriate court. The party filing the Complaint and seeking action by the court is called the plaintiff. The party against whom the Complaint is filed (the alleged transgressor) is called the defendant. Plaintiffs and defendants can be individuals, businesses, associations, governmental entities or groups of individuals.

Lawsuits may be filed in a variety of different courts. We have in our country a system of parallel—and sometimes overlapping—court systems, each of which have subject matter jurisdiction over certain disputes.

While there are certain specialized courts which adjudicate specific types of disputes (Bankruptcy Court, the United States Court of Claims, or Probate Court), the two primary court systems are the federal and state court systems.

The federal and state court systems handle both criminal and civil cases, but our discussion will be limited to civil cases.

Generally, the federal court system adjudicates disputes involving federal law, as well as cases involving citizens of different states. The state court system adjudicates disputes involving state law, disputes which occurred in that state and disputes between citizens of the same state. In some situations, citizens of different states can adjudicate their case in state court.

You can be sued in your individual capacity in the county or state where you live or, in some instances, in the place where the act which is the subject of the lawsuit occurred. Your business or company can be sued in any state in which it is located, has an office, or is incorporated.

Due to jurisdictional statutes referred to as *long-arm statutes*, your business may also be sued in any state where it transacts business—as that term is defined by the courts of the state in question.

Don't be lulled into a false sense of security by the fact that you don't have an office in California. The absence of an office or resident employee in a particular state does not necessarily insulate your business from being sued in that state.

State rules of civil procedure usually allow a plaintiff to file suit in the county in which the defendant business is located, transacts business or where the dispute occurred.

In order to file suit in federal court, a plaintiff must be able to establish a specific basis for federal jurisdiction, such as diversity of citizenship or a question of federal law. Federal lawsuits must also involve a disputed amount in excess of $50,000.

How You Know You've Been Sued

In addition to filing the Complaint with the court, the plaintiff must ensure that the defendant is physically presented—or served—with a copy of the Complaint. Federal and state rules of procedure pertaining to the service of the Complaint differ from jurisdiction to jurisdiction.

In some jurisdictions, a sheriff or marshal must serve the Complaint; in others, it may be served by any competent adult.

If you are being sued in your individual capacity, the plaintiff is usually required to have a copy of the Complaint personally served upon you. The rules typically require that the Complaint be served upon a company's registered agent for service of process, the company's lawyer, an officer of the company, or some other competent adult whom the plaintiff can reasonably infer to be an individual with the authority to make decisions on behalf of the company. There are also procedures for service by filing the Complaint with the Secretary of State's office and by publication in certain legal periodicals.

The service of a Complaint can sometimes be a tricky thing. Lawyers have been known to argue for months over whether a Complaint was served upon a defendant in a proper fashion. Businesses sometimes find themselves in default on lawsuits because the business has been served in accordance with the appropriate rules of procedure, but the lawsuit has been misfiled or has languished on the desk of an employee who did not recognize the necessity of filing a formal response to the lawsuit within a certain period of time.

The law can be very strict regarding failure to respond to a lawsuit within the prescribed period. Failure to do so can result in a default, in which the plaintiff wins without having to do anything. This may require the defendant to pay everything the plaintiff is seeking.

While defaults can sometimes be reconsidered, there are many instances in which they cannot. For this reason, it's imperative that businesses develop an internal monitoring system to ensure that no lawsuit is delivered and not acted upon.

The Complaint describes—often in the broadest and most ambiguous terms—the dispute, the conduct of the defendant about which the plaintiff is complaining and the relief sought by the plaintiff. Civil lawsuits involving businesses usually seek the award of money damages, but may also ask the court to impose equitable or injunctive relief. In such instances, a court orders a party to take certain action (such as reinstating a discharged employee) or enjoins a party from taking some sort of action (such as forbidding a business to use a particular trade name).

The damages sought by a plaintiff can fall into a number of categories:

- **Actual or Compensatory Damages**

  This is the money that the plaintiff claims it lost or is entitled to as a result of the defendant's allegedly wrongful conduct.

- **Punitive or Exemplary Damages**

  The big enchilada of damage awards. Punitive or exemplary damages have no relation to the money lost by or allegedly owed to a plaintiff. Rather, they are intended to punish the defendant and to discourage the defendant from engaging in the wrongful conduct again. The amount of such damages is limited only by the "enlightened conscience of the jurors." This means you could be in very big trouble.

- **Attorney's Fees**

  These are not generally recoverable by either party in commercial cases, except where allowed by specific statute or when a party engages in egregious bad faith or fraud in the inception of the business relationship. Translation: Don't plan on recovering your attorney's fees.

- **Expenses of Litigation**

  Litigation expenses are the costs of the litigation, excluding attorney's fees. Litigation expenses typically involve such items as deposition expenses, filing fees, expert witness fees and copying charges. The chances of recovering litigation expenses are only slightly better than the chances of recovering attorney's fees.

- **Sanctions**

  The federal system and many state systems allow recovery of additional damages against your adversary—and sometimes even your adversary's lawyer—if you can prove that the lawsuit was filed in bad faith and without any basis. Although lawsuits are often filed in bad faith without any basis, these sanctions are infrequently imposed.

The Answer

The federal and state rules of civil procedure require the defendant to file a written Answer in response to the Complaint within twenty (federal) or thirty (most states) days of the service of the Complaint. In its Answer, the defendant is required to admit or deny the allegations contained in the Complaint.

This is the first juncture at which delay can begin to occur. It is common practice for lawyers to grant one another extensions of time for the filing of pleadings and responses to discovery requests. In most instances, no permission of the court is required to obtain such an extension. It is a matter of agreement, custom and practice between the lawyers. Consequently, a defendant may obtain numerous extensions of time before filing an Answer. This delays the progress of the lawsuit.

This is important because it leads to another cardinal rule:

THE LONGER A LAWSUIT LASTS, THE MORE MONEY IT COSTS.

Think of your lawsuit as a giant taxicab meter with the handle stuck in the on position. The longer the lawsuit lasts, the more money it will cost you. The amount it will cost you will vary from month to month, but there will never be a month during the life of your lawsuit in which the lawsuit doesn't cost you some amount of money.

Anything you can do to expedite the progress of the lawsuit or to bring it to an early demise will save you money. The only possible exception to this rule is if you surrender unconditionally on the first day the lawsuit is filed and pay the plaintiff every cent he demands. Even then, the amount of money you pay on that first day may well be less than the amount of money you will spend if you take the lawsuit to trial.

In its Answer, the defendant is also permitted to make allegations of its own against the plaintiff or against other as yet unnamed parties. While the terminology differs from jurisdiction to jurisdiction, the following are the primary vehicles for raising such allegations.

The Counterclaim

Counterclaims are allegations made by the defendant against the plaintiff. The rules of procedure typically require a counterclaim to contain allegations that are related in some way to the subject matter of the original Complaint.

This means that if you're being sued for breach of contract, you probably can't file a counterclaim alleging that the plaintiff has failed to make his alimony payments. Counterclaims are often used as a strategic weapon to try to force settlement of the case by raising the plaintiff's potential cost of pursuing the lawsuit. The counterclaim may also allege that the plaintiff filed the lawsuit in bad faith.

Cross Claims and Third Party Complaints

If the plaintiff has sued other defendants and you believe that one or more of the other defendants is responsible for all or part of what the plaintiff is alleging, you may make your own claim against that defen-

dant. You may also bring an independent claim against that defendant, so long as your claim is related to the subject matter of the
lawsuit. These claims are called cross claims.

Cross claims tend to complicate the litigation and also tend to undermine any effort by the defendants to establish a united defense
against the plaintiff's allegations, but they are sometimes necessary.

If you believe that an entity not in the lawsuit is responsible for some
or all of the things alleged by the plaintiff, you may be able to bring
that entity into the lawsuit as a third-party defendant—assuming the
court can obtain jurisdiction over that entity. This is accomplished
by filing a pleading known as a Third-Party Complaint.

In that pleading, you are taking the following position: "I don't believe that I am liable to the plaintiff, but if I am liable to the plaintiff,
then this other party is liable to me."

Crowds Create Expensive Complexity

As you can see, a lawsuit can get crowded in a hurry. The more parties involved, the more complicated, expensive and time-consuming
the lawsuit becomes. In addition to the obvious reasons why more
participants lengthen a lawsuit, there is the very real problem of bringing more lawyers into each and every aspect of the case. Instead of
two lawyers examining every witness, you have five or six lawyers
examining every witness—often repeating the same questions asked
by a previous lawyer.

There is, however, a silver lining. The presence of additional parties
can facilitate a settlement of the case. Parties to a lawsuit—and their
lawyers—are forever searching for solvent entities who can be brought
into the fray to help pay the freight in some way.

Sometimes, cases involving multiple defendants settle when the defendants decide to pool their resources to generate a settlement offer
which is acceptable to the plaintiff. In such instances, each defendant bleeds a little bit, but none of the defendants bleeds to death.

This is, of course, only a skeletal description of the initial stage of the lawsuit. Numerous other issues often arise at this stage, dealing with such matters as whether the plaintiff has filed suit in the proper court, whether all of the parties necessary for a complete resolution of the dispute have been brought into the lawsuit, whether the Complaint is legally permissible and various other legal questions guaranteed to demand the attention of your lawyer and add to your legal fees.

For example, some suits can be filed in either state or federal court. If such a lawsuit is filed in state court, the defendant may decide that it is to the defendant's advantage to remove the lawsuit to federal court. This is a simple task which is accomplished by filing the appropriate pleadings in both the state and federal courts in question. The fun begins when the plaintiff decides to resist removal to federal court, typically claiming that the federal court does not have jurisdiction over the case. The resolution of this particular squabble can take months.

If it is a close legal question which merits review by an appellate court—or if one of the parties is intent upon delaying the progress of the lawsuit—the resolution of this question could take a year or more, all the while delaying the progress of the lawsuit.

Tired yet? Remember, everything we've covered to this point constitutes nothing more than the opening salvos. The Complaint and the Answer in a lawsuit are tantamount to the scenery in a play. They establish basic parameters and set the stage for the protracted drama to follow.

Discovery

After the Answer has been filed, the lawsuit lurches into the labyrinth known as pre-trial discovery. For those blissfully unaware of this dimension, pre-trial discovery is the period of the lawsuit during which the lawyers are allowed to discover just about any and everything about you, your company, your customers, your business plan, mistakes you've made in your business and personal life, your company's relationship with the IRS, those nasty allegations made about you in that lawsuit ten years ago and everything your ex-spouse said about you during the divorce.

Discovery is the period of litigation most responsible for delays, intramural squabbling between the lawyers and massive disruption to your life and your business. It's also the period during which the lawyers make party hats out of your bank account.

Like many aspects of the civil litigation system, discovery was born of noble intentions. Before the adoption of current rules of procedure, lawyers weren't allowed to—and as a practical matter, didn't bother to—engage in much discovery. While this had the salutary effect of getting cases to trial more quickly, it also had a number of negative consequences.

The first problem was that the dearth of discovery led to lots of surprises at trial. Under this system, neither side knew much about the other side's case until they showed up in court for trial. This resulted in what lawyers refer to as "trial by ambush."

In addition to elevating the blood pressure of the parties and their lawyers, this also meant that neither party could do a comprehensive job of preparing for the trial. You never knew when the other side was going to drag up the surprise witness everyone thought was dead or the incriminating document nobody knew existed.

While this made for some dramatic moments at trial and provided lots of cheesy courtroom scenes in movies and on television, most experts argued that justice wasn't being served very well. It seemed more fair (that troublesome word again) to give both sides a chance to obtain all of the relevant—and lots of irrelevant—information prior to trial.

The second problem with the old system was that neither party got a clear picture of the relative merits of their case and their opponent's case. A litigant and his lawyer can whip themselves into a frenzy of overconfidence about the strength of their case if they spend all of their time just talking to each other. Their view of the case might change if they knew that their opponent planned to call as a witness the former president of the company, who will testify about all of the document shredding that took place a few years ago.

Other than causing hypertension among the lawyers, is it really so bad not to have a clear picture of your adversary's case? You bet it is. If the various parties are all living in a fool's paradise, the chances of settling the case prior to trial are greatly decreased.

As a general matter, the more you know about your opponent's case, the more realistic you are about your chances for success at trial.

Assuming both sides have good knowledge and the lawyers for both sides assess the case in roughly the same way—admittedly, some big assumptions—the lawyers should be more likely to guide their clients to a realistic evaluation of the lawsuit. In theory, this should lead to more settlements.

Following this theory, legislators adopted new rules of procedure intended to improve the system by allowing the parties to discover more information (in other words, everything under the sun) about their opponent and their opponent's case prior to trial. This was intended to eliminate trial by ambush, to make the legal system fairer and to promote settlement of disputes.

The Tools of Inquisition

The new rules give lawyers the right to delve into just about anything that is even arguably related to the lawsuit. The standard for determining whether a party can be required to provide certain information is broad enough to embrace just about anything a lawyer might want to ask. Specifically, parties are entitled to ask any question calculated to lead to the discovery of admissible evidence.

The question does not have to seek information which would be admissible at trial. The question need only be reasonably capable of producing information which might lead to more questions which at some point down the line might elicit information which would be admissible at trial.

What does all this mean as a practical matter? It means that your adversary's lawyer can ask you just about any question he pleases. For example, you can be asked—and be required to answer under oath—whether you have ever been convicted of a crime. You can be required to produce your corporate and individual income tax returns. You can be required to disclose information concerning your hiring practices, your business plan, your financial strategy, lawsuits which have been filed against you or your company, and a host of other private matters.

Lawyers use a variety of tools to discover such information.

- **Interrogatories**

  Interrogatories are written questions drafted by your adversary's lawyer. You are required to answer these questions in writing under oath. Your lawyer will usually prepare the responses to the questions based upon factual information which you provide to your lawyer. Interrogatories typically request factual information regarding your company and the subject of the lawsuit. After conferring with you, your lawyer will draft responses to the questions and make objections to those questions he believes are not allowed by the law. The lawyer will then ask you to confirm that the answers are true and to sign an affidavit saying so. The responses are then sent to your adversary's lawyer. At this point, acrimony often breaks out. Your adversary's lawyer begins to argue with your lawyer about whether your answers are complete and whether you are entitled to make the objections which your lawyer made for you. Your lawyer responds by arguing that the questions themselves are improper. If the lawyers cannot resolve their differences, they go to the judge for a ruling on this squabble. The judge, who loathes discovery disputes, settles the squabble at some point. In the meantime, more time and legal fees have been consumed.

- **Requests for Production of Documents**

  These pleadings are very similar to interrogatories, except that they require you to produce or make available for copying every piece of paper in your possession which might have anything to do with the lawsuit. Requests for production of documents generate even more lawyer acrimony than interrogatories. One side is always asking the other side to produce documents which the other side claims they do not have to produce because the requested documents are confidential, irrelevant, protected by law, or just plain embarrassing. Once again, the lawyers troop down to the court house, fuming and spewing invective at each other. Once again, the judge wonders why he didn't go to medical school, but settles the dispute anyway. Once again, your legal fees fund this exercise.

- **Requests for Admissions**

  Designed to identify the things to which the parties can agree and eliminate the need to haggle at trial, requests for admission are drafted by lawyers and sent to their opponent's lawyer for answers. They usually involve items like "Admit that Exhibit A is a true and correct copy of the contract between the parties," but every now and then you'll see something tantamount to "Admit that your product was defective, that you are a congenital liar and that your accounting department planned the Brinks job." Lawyers don't expect you to admit anything juicy. Often they are just trying to get you to lie under oath so they can embarrass you later when they obtain proof of your mendacity.

- **Depositions**

  Depositions are the 2,000-pound gorillas of discovery. They are the most important, time consuming, dispute-producing, money-draining aspect of discovery. A deposition is an oral question and answer session conducted by your opponent's lawyer. Your deposition often resembles the least pleasant aspects of your most recent physical examination, is about as much fun, and costs more.

  On paper, the deposition is intended to give your adversary's lawyer the opportunity to discover what you know about the case through a series of well-honed questions which you are required to answer under oath in the presence of a court reporter who transcribes everything—and I mean everything—that comes out of your mouth. In reality, the deposition will also be used by your opponent's lawyer to evaluate your effectiveness as a witness, to pin down your testimony so that it can be used to impeach you at trial, to set traps for you, to rattle and intimidate you if possible, to test your memory, to embarrass you by forcing you to testify about every mistake you or your company has ever made from the beginning of time to the end of the world and to convince you that settling the case at any price would be preferable to having to go through this experience again at trial. Your lawyer will be there to "protect" you, but in truth there is very little she can do to prevent your opponent's lawyer from asking all sorts of questions, so long as the lawyer doesn't go overboard.

Depositions are sometimes taken for the preservation of evidence and for the possible presentation of that evidence at trial. This occurs when the lawyers believe that the witness will not appear at trial. In such instances, the lawyers may read the deposition at trial, which is guaranteed to put most of the jurors into a deep and impenetrable sleep.

The Costs of Discovery

There are a number of significant costs associated with discovery. Discovery can be time-consuming. Rules of procedure attempt to limit the length of the discovery period. The parties are allocated a period of time, usually four to six months, from the date of the filing of the last Answer to complete their discovery.

Unfortunately, discovery is completed within the prescribed period about as often as the Chicago Cubs get to the World Series.

There are a number of reasons why this almost never occurs, most of them related to the fact that it's up to the lawyers to initiate, agree upon, conduct and complete the discovery.

First, most lawyers are born procrastinators.

Second, most lawyers have a number of cases going on simultaneously and therefore have to juggle the discovery in a number of cases.

Third, it's tough to get opposing lawyers to agree on anything, especially who ought to be deposed, when, where, and for how long.

Fourth, delay is often part of the strategy of one of the lawyers.

Fifth, some lawyers delay because they are disorganized, lazy or dishonest.

Sixth, it's difficult to track down all of the witnesses and schedule their depositions. Lawyers always seem to find a new witness after the discovery period is over.

In light of all this, lawyers often ask the judge for extensions of the discovery period. It is then up to the judge to decide whether to grant an extension. A majority of judges grant one or two extensions as a matter of course. Other judges refuse to grant extensions without a showing of *good cause*—a legitimate reason why discovery needs to be extended—by the lawyers. Some judges rigidly enforce the discovery period, while others ignore it. Rare indeed is the case where the lawyer for one of the parties does not end up begging the judge for an extension of the discovery period.

Judges use their power during the discovery period in a variety of ways. Some judges never grant any extensions, hoping that the prospect of going to trial without that last bit of discovery will convince the party—or, more likely, the party's lawyer—that the case should be settled. Other judges allow parties to conduct every bit of discovery they wish without regard to the discovery period, believing that this will either promote a settlement or at least make for a smoother trial.

Some judges follow the discovery process closely, even checking with the lawyers before the end of the discovery period to make sure that all necessary discovery is being conducted. Other judges ignore the parties during the discovery period, taking the position that lawyers are adults—chronologically, anyway—and should be able to conduct the necessary discovery within the parameters established by the rules.

The discovery period is also the time when a lawsuit can grow like kudzu. As the lawyers obtain more information, the possibilities for expansion of the lawsuit are endless.

One of the parties may, for example, obtain information which suggests that another entity not currently in the lawsuit may bear some responsibility for some of the damages. If so, the rules allow the lawyers to ask the court for permission to add that company to the happy group of litigants. Unless this request is made at an unreasonably late stage—like the day before the trial is scheduled to begin—judges are inclined to grant such requests in the hope that bringing all of the parties which might be liable into the lawsuit will (1) ensure a just resolution of the dispute, (2) eliminate the need for piecemeal resolution of the dispute in a series of lawsuits, and (3) increase chances of a settlement.

If the judge adds new parties to the lawsuit, the discovery period is generally extended to give the new party and its lawyers a reasonable discovery period. This is but one of the many things which can extend the discovery period. Other culprits include such things as the unavailability of key witnesses, pre-trial motions and the judge's vacation.

Before we end our discussion of discovery, you may be wondering whether the new rules have achieved their purpose. There is little doubt that the availability of substantial pre-trial discovery has eliminated most aspects of trial by ambush. Today's lawyers are less likely to be confronted with surprise witnesses or documents at trial. This probably makes for fairer trials.

It is more difficult to say whether the expansion of discovery has produced more settlements. One major obstacle involves differing evaluations of the same case by the opposing litigants or their lawyers. Assume that your lawyer takes the deposition of your opponent's chief executive officer, who will be your opponent's key witness at trial. During the deposition the CEO comes across as a combination of Captain Queeg and the Mad Hatter. Seeing this, you and your lawyer assume that the other side will soon be approaching you with a settlement offer because they realize that the CEO would be a disastrous witness.

Much to your surprise, two days later your lawyer reports that your opponent's lawyer has just increased his settlement demand and spent twenty minutes on the telephone talking about how well his witness performed at the deposition.

How could this be? There are a number of possible explanations:

- Your opponent's lawyer is bluffing. He knows how poorly his witness performed, but can't admit it, lest the settlement value of his case plummet. He's trying to put the best face on the situation and hope that other factors will cause you to settle the case.

- He's out of touch with reality. It is possible that your opponent's lawyer and the CEO both believe that the CEO performed swimmingly and will be a credible witness at trial. Depositions sometimes resemble Rorschach tests. It's possible that this lawyer is seeing a silk purse where the rest of the world views a sow's ear.

- He's trapped. It is altogether possible that your opponent's lawyer, being a non-fool, realizes that his client put on a disastrous performance and that few jurors over the age of four will believe a word he says. Unfortunately, the CEO thinks he did a swell job and it is the CEO who is paying the lawyer's fee. It may not be wise for the lawyer to share the awful truth with his client because if he does so, he risks losing a client (which to many lawyers is a lot worse than losing a case). Besides, if he loses the case, the lawyer can always blame it on the jury.

Finally, your reaction to the deposition may also scuttle a settlement. Assume that your opponent and his lawyer both recognize that your opponent performed terribly. In light of this, your opponent makes a reasonable settlement offer. So far, so good. But now, you and your lawyer are full of vinegar because you believe that you have your opponent's shoulder blades in close proximity to the nearest wall. Thus emboldened, you reject the reasonable settlement offer and hold out for unconditional surrender. Unfortunately, unconditional surrender is not acceptable to your opponent and therefore no settlement is reached.

This is how human nature sometimes thwarts the system's attempts to encourage settlement. The new discovery rules may have increased the number of cases which settle, but the human element keeps the increase from being a substantial one. Accordingly, the costs associated with expanded discovery may outweigh the benefits.

Pre-Trial Motions

Before, during and after discovery, lawyers may ask the judge to make certain rulings regarding the law as it applies to the facts of your lawsuit. The vehicle for such requests is a formal motion made in writing and supported by legal briefs citing the authority for the request and the reason why the law should be applied in a certain way.

The number of motions available to the lawyers are legion. Lawyers can request that the judge throw the case out of court (Motion for Judgment on the Pleadings, Motion for Summary Judgment), that the judge make the other party state its claim with greater specificity (Motion for More Definite Statement), that the judge throw out part of the other side's claim (Motion to Strike, Motion for Partial Summary Judgment), that the judge allow an amendment of the original Complaint or Answer (Motion to Alter or Amend), that the judge rule that one or more parties are not properly in—or out—of the lawsuit (Motion for Joinder or Severance), or that the lawsuit be consolidated with another pending lawsuit (Motion to Consolidate).

Had enough? There's more.

Lawyers can request that the judge rule that a witness' deposition must be taken (Motion to Compel) or cannot be taken (Motion for Protective Order), that certain documents must be produced or cannot be produced. They can also ask the court to impose a fine upon a party or a lawyer for not doing what was required by the rules (Motion for Sanctions).

While this list is not exhaustive (we haven't even gotten into such items as Motions in Limine, Motions for Substitution or—one of my favorites—Motions to Require Physical Examination), you get the picture. Although motions can be important, they can also serve no purpose other than to delay the resolution of the case while costing the client large sums of money.

Consider the life of a typical motion. The moving party drafts the motion, writes a brief supporting the motion, files it with the court and serves a copy on the opposing party. The opposing party is given a specific period of time (typically thirty days, but it varies depending on the court and the type of motion) to file a response to the motion.

Lawyers often request and obtain extensions of the time within which the response to the motion must be filed. In addition to responding to the motion, the opposing party may also file a motion of its own along with its response.

After the response and any cross motions are written and filed, the moving party—that is, the party who started the whole thing by filing the original motion—is often given a period of time within which to reply to the non-moving party's response. In some instances, the law even allows the non-moving party to file a response to the moving party's reply to the non-moving party's original response to the moving party's original motion.

After all the briefs, responses and replies have been filed, the bundle is deposited in the lap of the court. The judge must rule on all of the various motions and cross motions filed by the various parties. Sometimes the judge will want to hear oral arguments on the motions. Oral argument gives the lawyers an opportunity to come into court and try to explain the arguments they have already explained so meticulously in all of those briefs, responses and replies they have filed with the court.

You may be thinking that this sounds redundant. An increasing number of judges agree with you. Judges are slowly but surely reducing the number of motions on which they will hear oral arguments. Nevertheless, many motions are still argued orally.

The Importance of the Calendar Clerk

Before the motion can be argued, however, the parties have to obtain a hearing date on the judge's calendar, which is a lot like trying to find a date as a college freshman. Hearings on motions are scheduled by the judge's calendar clerk, who possesses only slightly less power than the Pope or the President's wife.

Lawyers have sullied countless nine-hundred dollar suits groveling before a calendar clerk trying to get a hearing scheduled. The calendar clerk must select a time which does not conflict with trials being conducted by the judge, other motion hearings or the judge's tennis game. Needless to say, sometimes it takes close to forever to obtain a date on which the motion can be argued.

Depending on the type of motion and the anticipated length of the argument, the motion may be scheduled for a particular time or, much more likely, as part of a motion calendar. A motion calendar is a nifty device used by the court to hear lots of motions in one morning or afternoon. The calendar clerk will schedule a large number of motions—anywhere from ten to seventy, depending on the court and the type of motions—to be argued one after another on a particular day, beginning at a particular time. The calendar clerk sends out rosters called motions calendars to all of the lawyers. On the roster, each motion is assigned a particular number.

Let's assume your motion is the ninth motion scheduled to be heard on a motion calendar beginning at 9:00 a.m. on a Monday morning. Not knowing how long each argument will take, the lawyers involved in all of the motions listed on the calendar show up at 9:00 a.m. and then spend the rest of the day waiting for their turn. This system is inefficient and expensive for everybody except the judge. You get to pay your lawyer to sit in court for hours listening to arguments in other cases that have nothing to do with you.

The lawyer can't risk leaving the courtroom, however, because there is always the chance that some of the motions ahead of her won't be argued—either because the lawyers aren't there or because the case has been settled—and the judge will then be looking for your lawyer. Consequently, your lawyer has to sit in court all day and you can be sure that she is billing you for that time.

The Judge Rules on Motions

At some point, your lawyer will have an opportunity to argue your motion or argue against your opponent's motion. This is the point at which the lawyers discover a few things about the judge to whom the case has been assigned. Some judges will be prepared for the motion. They will have read all of the briefs, considered all of the arguments, and will have prepared incisive questions on the sticky points. In such instances, the judge may have one or two questions to ask and that's it.

At the other end of the spectrum, some judges will have no idea why you are in court on that particular day. Such judges will not have read the motions or the briefs and may not even know what the case involves. There are few things more frustrating to a lawyer, or to the client who has paid for the whole thing, than to spend countless hours writing a series of voluminous briefs explaining the complicated facts and law of a dispute only to have the judge stroll into court and say "All right. What's this case all about?"

After oral argument, the judge may or may not rule on the motions. The judge can, of course, rule from the bench—that is, decide the issue at that time. It is more likely, however, that the judge will "take the issue under advisement."

Roughly translated, this means "I'll think about it and get back to you when the spirit moves me."

This period of judicial contemplation can last days, months, or, in some egregious cases, even years. The judge may ask for additional briefs on points raised at the hearing, or he may tell the lawyers that he has enough information on which to base a decision. There is virtually nothing a litigant or his lawyer can do to force a judge to rule on a pending motion—at least for the first year or so.

There are lots of reasons why a motion can languish for months in a judge's chambers. The judge may be swamped with other cases. He may be cautious, indecisive, overwhelmed, lazy, confused or just plain slow. The judge may want the parties to submit additional briefs, may want to discuss the case with other judges, or may be waiting for an appellate court to issue a decision in an identical case.

Whatever the reason, your motion can fester in the judge's chambers so long that you will wonder whether it has spontaneously combusted and disappeared from the face of the earth. Aside from a few timid inquiries to the judge's law clerk, most lawyers are loathe to press the judge for a ruling. They are aware of the old lawyer maxim: "He who pesters the judge for a ruling may well get a ruling he wishes he never saw."

All the while, your lawsuit is on ice.

Eventually, the judge will make a decision. In most—but not all— instances, one side will get some or all of what it requested and the other side will either comply or will consider an appeal.

Depending on the type of motion and issue involved, the losing party may have the absolute right to appeal the judge's ruling to the appropriate appellate court. In other instances, an appeal can be taken at that point only if the judge allows such an appeal. In either case, if the losing party appeals the judge's ruling on the motion, the lawsuit often cannot proceed until the appellate court rules on the appeal.

The process of appealing the judge's ruling resembles the original motion process, except it often takes even longer.

Appellate briefs, response briefs and reply briefs must all be written. A hearing date must be obtained. You must wait your turn. Litigants from the entire state or federal circuit are also seeking review of other lower court decisions. Oral argument is held and then, because appellate courts almost never rule from the bench, you have to wait for the appellate court's written decision. This process usually takes two or three months—and can sometimes take up to a year or more to complete. All the while, the lawsuit remains stagnant but very much alive.

When the appellate court rules, the issue is resolved and the parties pick up the litigation where it stopped three years ago—unless there is another appellate court to which the issue can be appealed. If so, the process can be repeated at the next appellate level.

Of course, not every motion is as involved as this scenario suggests. Some motions are resolved quickly by the trial judge, no appeal is taken and the case is back on track in a short period of time.

Nevertheless, the more complex scenario does occur with some frequency. All the while, you will be paying your lawyers to run the legal maze.

Pre-Trial Orders and Conferences

At some point, discovery is completed, all pre-trial motions have been disposed of and the case stands on the eve of trial. Prior to making it to the trial calendar, however, the parties are usually required to submit to the court a jointly prepared document called a pre-trial order.

The pre-trial order is intended to distill all that has occurred up to this point in the lawsuit—the pleadings, the discovery, the various motions and rulings—into a brief document which tells the court what the parties allege and how they intend to prove it. Each party lists such things as the issues which they believe should be presented to the jury, the witnesses they might call to testify at trial, how long they think the trial will last, what exhibits they plan to offer into evidence and whether they think there is any chance to settle the case.

Lawyers for the opposing sides are supposed to work together to present the court with a consolidated pre-trial order. Sometimes this actually occurs.

Other times, there is sufficient disagreement that each side submits

its own version of the proposed pre-trial order to the judge. Like most facets of litigation, this process consumes both time and money.

Once the parties have submitted a proposed pre-trial order, the all-powerful calendar clerk schedules the case for a pre-trial conference. The pre-trial conference is a meeting between the judge and all of the lawyers. The pre-trial conference is sometimes scheduled immediately before the case is scheduled to go to trial. In other courts, judges want to hold and complete the pre-trial conference before placing the case on a trial calendar.

In either event, the pre-trial conference gives the judge an opportunity to resolve any outstanding issues between the parties and to try to browbeat the parties into settling the case.

Some judges don't believe in pressuring parties to settle the case. Others believe it is part of their job and pursue settlement in a vigorous fashion. While this judicial pressure can be—and often is—applied at various junctures in the case, it is at the pre-trial conference that many judges become most active in their settlement efforts.

I once participated in a pre-trial conference at which the judge told the lawyers to settle the case or he would keep all of the parties in his chambers over the Fourth of July weekend to negotiate. The case settled quickly.

Trial Calendars, Special Settings and Trial Prep

If no settlement is reached, the case is then scheduled for trial. Your case will be scheduled for trial in one of two ways. The majority of cases are scheduled by placement on a trial calendar, which is a lot like a motion calendar, only worse. The calendar clerk will schedule a number of cases—say, fifty—for trial in a particular one or two-week setting.

Each case is assigned a position. At the beginning of the week, a *calendar call* is held, which is an en masse court appearance by the lawyers involved in all fifty cases to confirm that those lawyers will be ready to try their respective cases when and if the court reaches that case. Everybody knows that the judge won't get to all fifty of the cases in the two-week period, but nobody knows how far the judge will get.

In light of this, lawyers have to exercise their judgment—i.e., guess—about whether their particular case will be reached.

The days preceding the calendar call are marked by lawyers calling the lawyers whose cases are ahead of theirs on the calendar trying to find out if those cases are going to trial. There are also numerous last-minute pleas to the calendar clerk by lawyers trying to get off the calendar.

In the days immediately preceding a calendar call, cases can disappear from the calendar at warp speed. It's not unusual for a case that was number twenty-eight two days before the calendar call to find itself in the number two position on the morning of the calendar call.

The calendar call itself is a cross between a draft board hearing and your negotiations with your eighth grade English teacher when she called on you and you hadn't done your homework. The judge goes down the list looking for cases to try. The lawyers scatter everywhere trying to avoid being caught.

A number of cases will have been removed from the calendar prior to the calendar call and others will be removed during the calendar call. After a while, the judge will find a number of cases that seem to be ready for trial and will create a new calendar for the trial period. The rest of the cases which remain on the calendar will either be released—which means, "You don't have to worry about being forced to try the case during this two-week period. We'll put you on a future calendar"—or told that they are on standby.

Standby is the litigant's version of purgatory. You don't believe you'll be reached in the two-week period, but there is an outside chance you might be reached, so you have to remain ready for the whole two-week period.

This is one reason why trials are so disruptive and why it is this particular stage of the lawsuit when many people are least pleased with the legal system. The typical exchange between lawyer and client during this period goes something like this:

CLIENT: So, when will our case go to trial?

LAWYER: We're on a trial calendar for June 3.

CLIENT: What does that mean?

LAWYER: It means that our case and fifty others might be called to trial sometime during the two weeks beginning June 3.

CLIENT: So will we go to trial or won't we?

LAWYER: I don't know. We're number eleven on the calendar. We might be reached and we might not be reached.

CLIENT: When will you know?

LAWYER: Anywhere from one day to four hours before we have to start.

CLIENT: This is crazy! What am I supposed to do for that two-week period? What about all the witnesses who are supposed to testify? What are they supposed to do?

LAWYER: Clear your schedules, don't go out of town, stay near a phone and be ready to drop everything and come down to the courthouse on very short notice.

CLIENT: What if we're not reached?

LAWYER: Then we'll be placed on a future trial calendar and you'll get to go through this whole process again in a few months.

CLIENT: How much did you say it would take to settle this case?

There is an alternative to all this guesswork. Your lawyer can request that your case be given a "special setting." This means that instead of being placed on a trial calendar, your case will be given a specific time and date of its own for trial. The all-powerful calendar clerk will tell you that your case will be tried beginning at 9:00 a.m. on June 14 and the judge will clear his calendar just for you.

Upon hearing of this option, you tell your lawyer that you think that this sounds more efficient and civilized. Let's do that, you say.

Unfortunately, there is a problem with this approach. Judges don't like special settings and for a very good reason. Let's assume your case is specially set for June 14. You've told the judge that your case will take a week to complete and the judge has cleared his calendar for the week of June 14. The judge is all yours for that week. Then, on June 13, you and your adversary settle the case. This leaves the judge with nothing to do all week except wonder why he was stupid enough to agree to a special setting. This is bad for the judge and bad for a court system trying to process cases.

Lawyers and litigants, on the other hand, love special settings. Special settings provide certainty and if the litigants settle the case and the judge has nothing to do, well—that's the judge's problem.

These diverging points of view create some degree of tension regarding special settings. Lawyers are always asking for special settings and judges rarely want to set a case specially. The cases with the best chances of being specially set are (1) cases that will require so much time to try that the judge has little choice but to specially set them and (2) cases dependent upon out of state lawyers, out of state witnesses or witnesses who can only be available on a particular date.

But even the scheduling problems of key witnesses do not always ensure that a judge will be convinced to specially set a case.

The last month or so before the trial is a period of intense activity for you, your lawyer and your bank account.

A lawsuit progresses in fits and starts. Long periods of inactivity are followed by sporadic outbursts of intense, sometimes frenzied, activity. The period preceding trial is one of these frantic periods.

Immediately prior to trial, your lawyer will have to engage in a series of tasks, all of which will consume your money and some of which will consume your time. Your lawyer or her assistants will have to assemble and make copies of all of the documents to be used at trial, either as exhibits or otherwise. Any demonstrative evidence (models, charts, films, mark-ups) will have to be finalized and presented to the court and opposing counsel. Expert witnesses will at long last be required to finalize their opinions. Your lawyer will have to prepare memoranda regarding legal issues which are likely to arise during trial, questions to be asked of the prospective jurors during jury selection, proposed legal instructions for the actual jurors, subpoenas for non-party witnesses and examinations and cross examinations of all witnesses and potential witnesses.

Your lawyer will also have to prepare the witnesses who will be called in support of your case. Preparation is the sine qua non of successful trials. While preparation does not guarantee success, lack of preparation guarantees failure. Your witnesses will have to spend hours with your lawyer reviewing their testimony and preparing for opposing counsel's cross examination. Unfortunately, such preparation will take you and your employees away from your primary task of running a business.

The Trial

Due to its frequent depiction in films, books and television programs (including recent gavel-to-gavel coverage of certain high-profile—and usually lurid—trials), the trial is the aspect of the litigation process with which non-lawyers are most familiar.[1]

The trial begins with the selection of a jury, as lawyers attempt to fill the jury box with individuals who the lawyers believe will be sympathetic to their respective cases. Volumes have been written about the central role an unbiased jury plays in our system of justice.

---

[1] A comprehensive examination of a civil jury trial is beyond the scope of this book. Accordingly, I will not review the trial process in great detail. Rather, I will briefly describe the primary elements of a civil jury trial.

While society at large may desire an unbiased jury, no competent trial lawyer ever seeks an unbiased jury. The trial lawyer is trying with all of his might to fill the jury box with individuals who are biased in favor of his client.

The process by which a jury is selected is referred to as voir dire. Prospective jurors are questioned by the lawyers or, in some courts, by the judge. The questions seek to elicit information regarding the background of each of the jurors, as well as the opinions of the jurors regarding issues involved in the case at hand. The lawyers are also attempting to use the jury selection process to begin to educate the jurors about the case and to try to engender sympathy from jurors for their respective clients. Upon completion of the examination of the jurors, the lawyers try to agree upon the jurors for the case. Each side is given a certain number of "strikes" which can be used to prevent certain members of the jury panel from becoming jurors.

Jury selection is regarded by some commentators as the single most important aspect of the trial. Without question, it is one of the most important elements of a trial. Parties often associate special assistant counsel—extra lawyers—for the sole purpose of assisting in the selection of the jury. Such lawyers are often local lawyers who have extensive knowledge of the community and, by extension, the pool of prospective jurors.

Some civil trials are held before a judge rather than a jury. There are a number of strategic reasons why you might want a judge rather than a jury to decide your case. The case might be extremely complicated or involve facts which would inflame a jury, rendering them less likely to decide the case on its merits. Both sides must agree to a non-jury trial. If either side requests a jury trial, then a jury trial will be held. In most cases, one of the parties believes that it would be to their advantage to have a jury decide the case. Accordingly, it is likely that your case will be tried before a jury.

After the jury is selected, the lawyers for each side make opening statements to the jury in which they attempt to frame the issues and the evidence in the light most favorable to their respective clients.

The plaintiff then presents its case, submitting evidence in the form of the testimony of witnesses and the submittal of documents and other physical evidence. The defendant's lawyer is given an opportunity to cross-examine each of the plaintiff's witnesses upon completion of direct examination.

When the plaintiff has presented all of its evidence, the defendant typically asks the court to rule that the plaintiff has failed to prove its case (Motion for Directed Verdict). If the judge agrees, the case is over and the defendant wins, subject to the inevitable appeal by the plaintiff. If, as is more likely, the judge denies the defendant's request, the defendant proceeds to present its evidence and witnesses. The plaintiff's lawyer now has the opportunity to cross-examine the defendant's witnesses.

When the defendant completes the presentation of its evidence, both the defendant and the plaintiff ask the court to declare them the winner. In most instances, the court denies both motions. The lawyers then make closing arguments to the jury, once again attempting to characterize the evidence and law in the manner most favorable to their respective clients. Closing arguments contain much hyperbole, some common sense and, on a few occasions, a bit of eloquence.

Contrary to the impression created by certain recent televised trials, most closing arguments don't last for weeks. In most cases, the judge allocates each party a limited amount of time in which to complete its closing argument. After completion of the closing arguments, the judge instructs the jury on the applicable law and sends them out to deliberate.

Juries: The Great Unknown

What goes on in a jury room is one of the great mysteries of the law. You never know what fraction of the week's testimony might have caught a juror's attention. Speaking with jurors after a trial is always enlightening, often frustrating and sometimes downright scary.

As you might guess, jurors decide cases on the basis of all sorts of things, only some of which have anything to do with the evidence presented in the case. In many instances, the factors cited by jurors in support of their decision have nothing to do with the facts of the case.

Jurors are forever telling lawyers after the case that they ruled in a certain fashion because one side's main witness resembled the jury foreman's cousin Ed, who is the most honest guy in town.

Jurors decide cases because they didn't like one side's lawyer, because they were sued once and didn't like it one bit, because the weekend was approaching and they needed to reach a consensus, because they felt sympathy for a witness or anger toward a witness or any of a thousand other things that have nothing to do with the evidence in the case. Whether all of this results in justice is anybody's guess.

Jurors often reach the right result for the wrong reasons. In any event, the jury system is superior to most of the alternatives—star chambers and trial by combat, for example.

Sometimes the jury cannot agree on a verdict. The dreaded hung jury causes the judge to declare a mistrial, which means you have to start from scratch and try the case again in front of a new jury. In most instances, the new trial will not be held immediately. Your case will go back into the hopper and will appear on another calendar at some point in the future.

Assuming the jury reaches a verdict, the judge announces the verdict and dismisses the jury. The losing lawyer then asks the judge to disregard the jury's verdict and rule in favor of his client anyway (Motion for Judgment Notwithstanding the Verdict) or to modify the jury's verdict (Motion for Additur or Remittitur).

The judge seldom does this, but in some cases the judge decides to exercise this option. Prominent in the pantheon of lawyer nightmares is to have a jury award your client a million dollars and then have the judge rule that the verdict was contrary to the weight of the evidence and reduce the award to $25 or throw it out altogether.

The Appeal

Neophytes and optimists may assume that the end of the trial signals the end of the lawsuit...or at least the beginning of the end. Unfortunately, this is often not the case.

Once the verdict is entered as a judgment, the losing party has a statutorily imposed period of time—usually thirty days—in which to file an appeal. During this period, the gamesmanship continues. The lawyers for the losing side often approach the lawyers for the winning side with a proposition that goes something like this:

> We know those lunatics in the jury box awarded you $300,000, but the trial was so compromised by countless errors by the moronic judge that the verdict is certain to be overturned on appeal. We both know that an appeal can take anywhere from six to eighteen months, at which point the appellate court may well order a new trial—if they don't throw you out of court altogether. You know the appellate court is crazy and liable to do anything. During this six to eighteen month period, your client will have to continue to pay you money to fund this exercise.

> In light of this and in light of the fact that you have no case and we will force you to spend at least $60,000 on the appeal, we think you'd be wise to settle with us right now. In a spirit of cooperation and in an attempt to keep our own legal fees down, we're willing to pay you $50,000 to settle the case. Otherwise, we'll file the appeal.

You may be thinking that this proposal smacks of extortion and contains substantial amounts of bluff. You are right.

Nevertheless, there are grains of truth in the proposal, especially the parts about how time-consuming and expensive an appeal would be and the unpredictable nature of the appellate court.

A substantial number of cases are settled for an amount less than the amount of the verdict in exchange for the losing party's agreement to forego an appeal. The avoidance of continued legal fees and the elimination of the risk of losing on appeal play a major role in a party's decision to settle the case for less than the amount of the verdict returned by the jury.

If no such settlement is reached, an appeal is likely to follow. There are three reasons why appeals are taken so frequently. First, it is all but impossible for a judge to conduct a trial of any length without making a number of decisions which could be characterized as errors by an appellate court.

During the course of a trial, a judge makes hundreds of rulings on such matters as what evidence may be presented to the jury, what instructions should be given to the jury, the conduct of the lawyers and the witnesses, and the way in which the law should be applied to the instant case. In addition to this, a judge will have made a number of pre-trial and post-trial rulings on motions, some of which may also be the subject of an appeal.

While many of these rulings by the trial judge could be ruled harmless error (the law's version of basketball's "no harm, no foul" rule), others may be important enough to warrant a reversal or vacation of the jury's verdict.

Second, lawyers know that appellate courts are capable of reversing any case, often for reasons that have very little to do with the specific errors raised by the losing party. Appellate courts are comprised of human beings who possess the biases and opinions of all human beings. If, upon review of a case, an appellate court decides that justice was not served, they can almost always find a basis upon which to reverse the case.

In some instances, the appellate court may believe that the jury rendered an unjust verdict. In other instances, an appellate court may be seizing an opportunity to modify or change the law as it deals with a particular aspect of the case on appeal. In either instance, appellate courts can be quite creative in establishing a basis for reversal of a jury's verdict. The party which lost at trial often views an appeal as simply another step in the litigation process which offers that party an opportunity to prevail.

Third, as I've suggested, an appeal can provide the losing party with a degree of leverage in post-trial settlement negotiations. Even if the winning party doesn't agree to a settlement immediately after a jury returns a verdict, the case can always be settled at some point in the future. The prospect of an appeal gives the losing party something with which to bargain.

The procedure for appealing the verdict or judgment of a trial court is similar to the procedure used in the appeal of a trial court's ruling on a motion. The losing party—now called the appellant—has a set amount of time in which to notify the appellate court of the appeal. Then the brief writing begins.

The appellant writes its brief. The winning party—now called the appellee—is given an opportunity to respond. After the appellee's response is filed, the appellant is often given a chance to reply to the appellee's response brief. Oral argument is scheduled, the lawyers present their arguments to a panel of the appellate court and then the parties sit back to await the ruling from the appellate court. Some jurisdictions require the appellant to post a bond to protect the appellee during the appeal.

At some point, the appellate court announces its decision. The appellate court can reverse or uphold the entire verdict or certain of its component parts. If the trial court's decision is affirmed, the case is over—unless, of course, the losing party has the right to file an appeal with a higher appellate court. If, on the other hand, the appellate court finds any basis for reversal of all or part of the trial court's judgment, the appellate court may send the case back to the trial court for another trial in front of a new jury.

At this point, the client considers (1) physically assaulting every lawyer in sight and (2) settling the case.

TAMING THE LAWYERS

Chapter Four

Alternatives to Litigation

One of the best ways to reduce your legal costs is to avoid litigation. Fortunately, there are a number of alternatives to litigation which may be utilized to resolve a dispute.

In almost every instance, you should try to resolve a dispute through negotiation before resorting to litigation or other formal dispute resolution methodologies. Such negotiations typically involve only the parties and eliminate most of the costs associated with formal dispute resolution options.

In my experience, the most successful negotiators enter the negotiation with a clear idea of their ultimate goal and the amount they are willing to compromise in order to achieve that goal.

Remain receptive to creative solutions which may develop during the course of the negotiation. Don't embarrass your adversary; many times he is simply trying to save face, so give him a way to concede gracefully. Negotiate only so long as it appears that there is a reasonable chance to reach a negotiated settlement.

Prior to the start of formal negotiations, obtain a clear agreement as to whether statements made in the negotiation will be admissible as evidence if a lawsuit follows. Remember that in the absence of such an agreement, anything you say in the course of the negotiation may be used against you in a subsequent lawsuit. For example, in the course of the negotiation you may concede that your employee made certain mistakes. Unless you have agreed that statements made in the negotiation are confidential and protected from discovery, your admission may find its way into the lawsuit which follows.

Such confidentiality agreements need not be complicated. You and your adversary need only agree that any statements made during the negotiation are made in an attempt to settle the dispute and are therefore privileged, confidential, and not subject to discovery or admissible in any lawsuit which may be filed in the future.

It is imperative that you reduce this agreement to writing. It is best to obtain the signatures of both parties on the agreement, but a confirming letter will suffice if it is written correctly.

A confidentiality agreement is often a predicate to a successful settlement negotiation. Freed from the fear that their statements will be used against them in the future, the parties can engage in a candid discussion of the problem. This candor usually increases the chances of reaching a settlement. In the absence of a confidentiality agreement, the negotiators may be reluctant to speak freely or make the sorts of admissions which often form the basis of a successful negotiation.

Should your lawyer be involved in the negotiation at this point? In most cases, the answer is no.

The presence of lawyers transforms the tenor of the settlement negotiations—and not for the better. The whole point of early settlement negotiations is to attempt to solve the problem in such a manner which will eliminate the need to call in the lawyers.

If one party brings a lawyer to the negotiation, one of two things will happen, neither of them good. The other party will either (1) suspend the negotiation until he can bring his own lawyer or (2) alter his negotiating posture, becoming less candid and more aggressive. We lawyers often have that effect on regular people.

If you want to use your lawyer at this stage of the proceedings, restrict the lawyer's activities to coaching you in preparation for the negotiation. If you are unsuccessful in negotiating a settlement, your lawyer will have plenty of chances to negotiate in the future.

Even if the original settlement negotiations are unsuccessful, keep in mind that you may negotiate a settlement at any point in the proceedings until the final appeal is exhausted. Negotiation often represents the most cost effective means of resolving your dispute. Engage in negotiation the way certain Chicago politicians advise their constituents to vote: Early and often.

Unfortunately, in some instances even a supposed final settlement doesn't end the case. Consider the 1995 case of *Rodriguez v. Missouri Pacific Railroad.*

Rudy Rodriguez sued his former employer, Missouri Pacific Railroad Company, for damages for back injuries allegedly sustained during a railway accident. Before filing suit, Rodriguez had been terminated from Missouri Pacific because he failed a drug test. Rodriguez claimed that he lost seniority, vacation rights, fringe benefits, and income as a result of the termination.

On the morning of the trial, the court was advised by Rodriguez's lawyer that the parties had agreed on a compromise. The court entered a sixty-day order of dismissal. On September 1, 1993, Rodriguez executed a "Settlement, Release and Indemnity Agreement" with Missouri Pacific.

About fifteen months later, Rodriguez filed suit against the railroad again. He wanted the same trial court to enforce a local labor board's opinion ordering Missouri Pacific to pay him back pay, vacation pay, and benefits accrued between July 1992 and January 1995, the day of Rodriguez's formal resignation.

Not surprisingly, Missouri Pacific sought a dismissal on the ground that Rodriguez's lawsuit was barred by the September 1993 Settlement Agreement. Rodriguez countered that the Agreement applied only to the first lawsuit—it released Missouri Pacific only from his claims related to injuries sustained as a result of his accident but not from its obligation for back pay, fringe benefits or vacation time.

The court agreed with the railroad:

> The Settlement Agreement provided that in return for Missouri Pacific's agreement to pay Rodriguez $215,000 plus miscellaneous medical expenses, Rodriguez settles, compromises and forever acquits any and all causes of action, claims or rights of any kind which he or anyone else who claims through him had in the past, has in the present, or may have in the future against Missouri Pacific....

> Rodriguez also executed, as an express condition of the Settlement Agreement, an "Agreement Not to Return to Work" in which he agreed not to go back to work for Missouri Pacific, effective as of September 1, 1993. That undertaking also explicitly served as Rodriguez's resignation effective January 1, 1995.

Rodriguez's "Agreement Not to Return to Work" and Missouri Pacific's agreement to purchase months towards Rodriguez's retirement benefits eligibility would have been uncalled for had the parties not intended that the Settlement Agreement would preempt the labor board's decision. The court ruled as a matter of law that Rodriguez's second suit was barred.

The good news was that the court held Rodriguez to the terms of the 1993 Settlement Agreement. The bad news was that Missouri Pacific had to spend seven months and thousands of dollars to enforce that Agreement. Missouri Pacific asked the court to require Rodriguez to pay its attorney's fees—but the request was denied.

Early Neutral Evaluation

As the name suggests, early neutral evaluation involves obtaining an assessment of a dispute from an unbiased third party at an early stage of the dispute. This approach is typically utilized before the parties resort to more formal dispute resolution methodologies such as mediation, arbitration and litigation. If negotiation fails to produce a settlement of the dispute, the parties may choose to present their respective positions to a neutral individual who is acceptable to both of the parties.

The evaluator listens to the presentations of the parties—often asking questions—and then informs the parties of his evaluation of the dispute. The process is intended to lead to a settlement, the hope being that the neutral evaluation will convince one or both parties that a compromise or other settlement is warranted. Keep in mind that the evaluator does not have the authority to impose a settlement. Rather, the evaluator seeks to facilitate a voluntary settlement by showing the parties how an independent third party would respond to their respective positions.

Mediation

Mediation is the current rage in the area of alternative dispute resolution. Wary of the cost of litigation and the uncertainty of arbitration, private parties are flocking in droves to hundreds of newly formed mediation services. Burdened by ever-increasing case loads, courts everywhere are requiring parties to engage in mediation as a prerequisite to litigation. In short, mediation seems to have become everyone's favorite option for the resolution of private disputes.

There is a substantial amount of confusion regarding mediation and what it entails. Mediation is generally defined as the process pursuant to which two or more private parties engaged in a dispute utilize the services of an impartial third party in an attempt to resolve the dispute. The parties present their respective cases to the mediator, who then attempts to guide the parties toward a mutually acceptable settlement of the dispute.

The cardinal feature of mediation is that the mediator has no authority to resolve the dispute or impose a settlement on the parties. In this regard, mediation is quite different from litigation or arbitration.

The mediator can be just about anyone, provided that the parties agree on the mediator. Mediators may be retired judges, lawyers, professors, government employees or business people. Many mediators work full time for private mediation services. Other mediators serve on a part-time basis.

In the typical mediation, the mediator begins by meeting with the parties simultaneously. Each party is given an opportunity to explain its position to the mediator, usually in the presence of the other party. During these presentations, the mediator may ask questions regarding the dispute. Although some mediators wish to hear testimony from various witnesses, many mediations involve nothing more than narratives given by the principals or their lawyers.

Mediation is informal in nature. Rules of law—including rules of evidence—do not apply. The parties usually provide the mediator with documents in advance, but few mediations involve substantial use of demonstrative exhibits. Lawyers often participate in mediations on behalf of their clients, but some mediators prefer that the lawyers stay home. This question should be resolved by the parties and the mediator prior to the start of the mediation.

After the mediator has heard the presentations of each party, she will meet individually with each party. In this private segment of the mediation, the mediator probes each party for candid assessments of the strengths and weaknesses of their case, their willingness to compromise and their openness to a settlement.

During these private sessions, the mediator will often give each party her assessment of the relative strengths and weaknesses of each party's case. At this juncture, a mediator is attempting to facilitate a settlement by, among other things, letting each party know her reaction to the case.

At this stage of the proceedings, the mediator may engage in a kind of shuttle diplomacy, holding numerous individual meetings with each party in an attempt to forge a mutually agreeable resolution to the dispute.

The tenor of the mediation is often affected by the ability of the mediator. A skilled mediator can facilitate a settlement using flattery, scare tactics, cajoling, economic arguments, emotional appeals, bare-knuckle threats or apocalyptic predictions. The mediator may tell Mr. Smith that his chances for success are located somewhere between slim and none, while telling Mr. Jones that Mr. Smith has a strong case. The approaches employed are as numerous as the mediators themselves.

This process sometimes produces a settlement of the dispute. If so, the parties reconvene and execute a short agreement outlining the terms of the settlement. The mediator collects her fee and everyone goes home relatively happy.

If, on the other hand, no settlement can be reached, the mediator may reconvene the parties and reveal to the parties her assessment of the dispute. In such instances, the hope is that although the parties cannot agree on a resolution, the mediator's remarks may spur the parties to reconsider their respective positions. Such a reconsideration could result in a settlement at some point in the future.

The parties may choose to make mediation a formal part of the settlement process. This can be accomplished by utilizing a variation of the so-called "Michigan Mediation Rule." This rule utilizes the mediator's decision as a benchmark against which the ultimate resolution of the dispute is measured. The Michigan Mediation Rule provides that if a party, after receiving a mediator's recommendation, does not better its position by 10 percent or more, that party will be required to pay all attorney's fees and litigation expenses incurred by its opponent from that point forward. This approach invests the mediator's recommendation with greater weight and increases the risk of ignoring the mediator's recommendation. This approach tends to increase the likelihood that the parties will accept the mediator's recommendation.

Some Benefits Even Without Settlement

Mediation can be valuable and productive even when it does not result in a settlement. The exercise of presenting one's case to a neutral third party can be enlightening. People involved in legal disputes tend to focus on their own version of the events. They are often surrounded by like-minded individuals who share their perspective.

Mediation can expose this person to a comprehensive presentation of his adversary's position. This can be a worthwhile experience which triggers a reconsideration of that person's position.

Second, each party receives the benefit of a neutral third-party's re-action to their respective positions. As a commercial dispute devel-ops, business persons can become convinced of the rightness of their own position. "We're right," thinks Mr. Smith. "Any intelligent per-son would see the merit of our position, as well as the weakness of my lying opponent's position."

What a surprise, then, when the mediator tells Mr. Smith that his case is a weak one and that, if she were a juror, she would rule in favor of Mr. Smith's opponent. This experience can be both cathartic and productive. Fresh from this surprising brush with reality, Mr. Smith may well decide it is time to settle the case.

There are certain disadvantages associated with mediation.

First, the mediator cannot impose a settlement on the parties. A party is free to—and often does—ignore the mediator's assessment and advice.

Second, some business people dislike mediation because they believe it forces a party to reveal the strengths, weaknesses and strategy of its case to their opponent. While this may happen, your opponent can obtain this information during the discovery phase of a lawsuit. It's unlikely that there is any information which would be obtained in a mediation which could not be obtained in a lawsuit or through some other source.

Nevertheless, this concern causes some parties to engage in token participation in a mediation. These parties prefer to hold their real arguments and key facts in reserve for use at a trial. Needless to say, such a strategy undermines the mediation process and usually ensures that the mediation will not produce a settlement.

Third, there is the time factor. Mediation can in some instances delay the ultimate resolution of the dispute. Assuming the mediation doesn't produce a settlement, it adds another step to the dispute resolution process.

Finally, mediation can add to the cost of the dispute resolution process. In some instances, the mediator's fee is paid by the parties involved in the mediation. In major urban areas, mediators often charge between $100 and $150 per hour per party, in addition to administrative fees and expenses of the mediation.

More significantly, participation in a mediation can increase a party's legal costs. Even if your lawyer doesn't participate directly, you will usually employ your lawyer to prepare you for the mediation. If the lawyer participates in the mediation, the additional legal fees are even more substantial.

The additional cost must, of course, be weighed against the possibility of settling the case. In my opinion, such a possibility (which would eliminate the need for future legal representation) more than justifies the marginal increase in legal costs.

On balance, mediation is a worthwhile process. The mediation sometimes produces a settlement. Even if it doesn't produce a settlement, the mediation can force a person to assess his case realistically.

Moreover, mediation can serve as a useful dress rehearsal for trial. It gives the parties an opportunity to test theories, evaluate potential witnesses and estimate their financial exposure. These exercises can produce a settlement or, at the very least, a more realistic assessment of one's case. Judicious use of the mediation process can reduce your legal costs.

Arbitration

Arbitration is the most prevalent—and the most controversial—form of alternative dispute resolution available in modern legal circles.

Proponents laud arbitration as an efficient, inexpensive and rational method of resolving private commercial disputes. Critics decry arbitration panels as unpredictable kangaroo courts presiding over a process which is devoid of the protections of the rule of law. The truth, of course, lies somewhere between the two.

Prior to discussing arbitration's merits and shortcomings, an understanding of the process itself is essential.

Arbitration is the submission of a private dispute to a neutral third party for resolution. It is a voluntary dispute resolution mechanism conducted pursuant to the agreement of the parties. The parties to an arbitration agreement define the nature, purpose and parameters of the arbitration.

Arbitration can be binding or non-binding, depending on the terms of the arbitration agreement. If the arbitration agreement states that the arbitration is binding, however, there is no appeal or recourse from the decision of the arbitrators—absent fraudulent conduct on the part of the arbitrators.

There are two cardinal principles regarding arbitration. First, you cannot be required to arbitrate your dispute unless you agree to do so. Second, if you agree to arbitrate, you will be required to arbitrate and, if the arbitration is binding arbitration, you will be bound—often without opportunity for an appeal—by the decision of the arbitrator.

The Federal Arbitration Act and the arbitration statutes which exist in the vast majority of states have been interpreted as requiring parties who agree to arbitrate to honor that agreement. The Federal Arbitration Act applies to any case in which interstate commerce is involved. In today's world, almost every commercial dispute involves interstate commerce of one sort or another. All of which is to say, if you agree to arbitrate, it is all but certain that you will be required to arbitrate.

It is possible for parties to agree to non-binding arbitration. Private parties sometimes establish non-binding arbitration as an interim dispute resolution methodology which must be completed prior to the institution of litigation. Numerous courts around the country have also adopted programs requiring civil litigants to participate in non-binding arbitration prior to trial.

However, the non-binding nature of an arbitration must be stated within the body of the arbitration agreement in order to be effective. In instances where there is ambiguity concerning whether the arbitration is binding or non-binding, courts are inclined to construe arbitration agreements as binding.

In general, courts view arbitration favorably. Given the chance, a court will almost always uphold the enforceability of an arbitration agreement. The reason for this is very straightforward: Every private commercial dispute which is resolved through arbitration is one less case that the courts have to handle.

Today's courts are inundated with cases in general and criminal cases in particular. The Constitution requires the courts to handle all criminal cases, and to do so in a timely fashion. Accordingly, if private disputes can be resolved in another forum, the judges have more time to devote to the criminal cases.

The current support represents a revised approach on the part of the courts. When arbitration first developed, some courts were almost hostile to it—viewing arbitration as an encroachment on the jurisdiction of the courts. In recent years, however, the increasing case load of courts and the proliferation of arbitration seems to have altered the view of arbitration exhibited by most judges.

Arbitration Clauses and Agreements

Private parties should take great care to avoid agreeing to arbitrate in instances when they don't intend to do so. This can occur when a company signs an agreement or contract which contains an arbitration clause. The arbitration clause, for example, may be included in supplemental documents which are incorporated by reference into the agreement. If so, you will be deemed to have agreed to arbitrate. Yet another reason to read the fine print.

The parties to an agreement to arbitrate establish the rules concerning the arbitration. You can establish whatever rules seem logical to you, so long as your adversary agrees to those rules.

If the arbitration is administered by a private dispute resolution service, that entity may have rules which apply to all of its arbitrations. If so, you will be bound by those rules.

For example, the American Arbitration Association (AAA) has established specific rules for arbitrations involving commercial disputes and more specific rules for such industries as the securities industry and the construction industry. I will use these AAA rules as a guide to a discussion of the procedure followed in most arbitrations.

The arbitration process is initiated in whatever way your arbitration agreement requires. In most instances, one party is required to file a Demand for Arbitration. The Demand for Arbitration usually provides very little information concerning the substance of the demanding party's claim. The responding party may or may not be required to file a formal response to the Demand for Arbitration.

The next step involves selection of the arbitrators. The arbitration agreement will usually identify either (1) the specific individuals who will serve as the arbitrators or (2) the process through which the parties can select the arbitrators. In most cases, the parties have to agree upon the arbitrators.

If the arbitration is being administered by the AAA, the local AAA office will distribute lists of potential arbitrators to the participants. The participants then have the opportunity to eliminate from consideration any individuals whom, for one reason or another, they do not wish to have as arbitrators. This process sometimes takes a fair amount of time to complete. If the parties cannot agree upon a panel of arbitrators, the AAA will appoint the panel.

The arbitrators will often hold a preliminary meeting with the parties to discuss the procedures to be employed in the arbitration. In many instances, the discussion is limited to determining a time and place for the arbitration, establishing the procedures to be followed during the arbitration and setting the fees to be paid to the arbitrators.

One of the most important differences between arbitration and litigation is that arbitration does not typically involve any pre-hearing discovery. This is either an advantage or disadvantage, depending on your point of view. In any event, unless the parties agree to do so, they usually do not have an opportunity to conduct any formal pre-hearing discovery.

The arbitration hearing is held at a mutually agreeable site. Arbitrations often take place in rented conference rooms at hotels or at the office of the agency which is administering the arbitration. The hearing is much less formal than an in-court hearing. The rules of law do not apply, unless the parties agree that such rules will apply. Lawyers often participate in the arbitration, but there is no requirement that they do so.

The arbitration hearing proceeds roughly in accordance with the procedure used in a civil trial. The complaining party is allowed to present its case, using witnesses, documents and exhibits. Upon completion of the testimony of each witness, the opposing party is given an opportunity to cross-examine the witness.

After the complaining party has presented its case, the defending party is given the opportunity to do the same. Upon completion of both cases, the lawyers or principals make some sort of closing statement.

The arbitrators then decide the case. In most instances, the arbitrators will not issue a decision on the date of the hearing. The arbitration agreement establishes how quickly the arbitrators must make a decision. In many instances, there is a thirty-day time limit.

Unless the arbitration agreement limits them, arbitrators have wide latitude in making their decisions. Some arbitrators will write lengthy opinions regarding their decisions. More frequently, the arbitrators will issue a one-sentence decision awarding a certain amount of money to one party or deciding the issue in question.

Unless the arbitration agreement states otherwise, there is virtually no appeal from the decision of an arbitration panel. In most states, courts will only overturn an arbitration decision on narrow procedural grounds—fraud, arbitrator partiality, an overstepping of authority by the arbitrator or failure to follow prescribed procedure. Although some courts have hinted that completely ignoring the evidence constitutes a violation of due process, most courts refuse even to consider this argument.

So, the fact that the arbitrators' decision may be devoid of logic and ignores all of the facts is of no import. This may sound like rough justice, but that's what arbitration is all about.

If the losing party refuses to comply with the arbitrators' order, the winning party can go into court and have the court enforce the arbitrators' order. In the overwhelming majority of cases, the court rubber stamps the arbitrators' decision.

There are a number of alternative forms of arbitration. The most familiar is often referred to as *baseball arbitration* due to the fact that it is used to settle salary disputes between major league baseball players and team owners.

In this form of arbitration, each side submits to the arbitrator a proposed result—usually in the form of a dollar amount to be awarded. The arbitrator then conducts the hearing. At the conclusion of the hearing, the arbitrator must choose one of the proposed results submitted by the parties.

This is an all or nothing scenario which restricts the arbitrator's ability to render a decision which is reflective of all of the evidence.

Another form of arbitration can be conducted pursuant to a high-low agreement between the parties. In this proceeding, the parties establish financial parameters on the award before the arbitration. Assume, for example, a dispute in which ABC Co. claims that XYZ Co. owes it $100,000. XYZ concedes it owes some amount to ABC, but believes the amount to be much less—say, $20,000.

In order to limit their respective exposures, the companies agree to the following high-low agreement: They will submit the dispute to an arbitrator for a decision. If the award is in the $20,000 to $60,000 range, the award will be accepted by both parties. If the arbitrator awards less than $20,000, they agree that XYZ will pay $20,000. If the arbitrator's award is greater than $60,000, XYZ will be required to pay only $60,000.

This approach reduces some of the uncertainty present in arbitration. ABC Co. is assured of recovering at least $20,000. XYZ Co. is assured that it will pay no more than $60,000.

Advantages of Arbitration

Proponents of arbitration characterize it as a speedy, inexpensive alternative to litigation. As is the case with most generalizations, this statement contains a kernel of truth at its core.

The first advantage of arbitration is that it offers a way to resolve a private commercial dispute more quickly than civil litigation.

Arbitration is faster than litigation for a number of reasons, chief among which is the fact that the parties to an arbitration don't have to wait for their turn in court. Civil litigation cases are heard by a finite number of judges—and those judges have other items on their plate.

Arbitration participants don't face this problem. They agree upon certain private individuals to act as arbitrators, select a convenient date and hold the hearing. In effect, arbitration allows the participants to rent their own judges. This will almost always produce a hearing long before an analogous hearing could be obtained in court.

Arbitration is also quicker than litigation due to the absence of pre-hearing discovery. There is considerable debate as to whether this absence is an advantage or disadvantage.

While it is true that arbitration generally proceeds more quickly than litigation, there are a number of factors which can delay resolution of a dispute through arbitration.

The selection of the arbitrators can delay the process. Unless the arbitrators are identified in the arbitration agreement, the parties must identify and agree upon specific individuals to act as arbitrators. Human nature being what it is, agreement is sometimes difficult to achieve. Even when the agency administering the arbitration is allowed to break a stalemate by appointing a panel, the process can drag on for months while the parties review lists of prospective arbitrators.

Scheduling the arbitration can also lead to delay. The arbitrators, aware that their fee is being paid by the parties, are reluctant to establish a date and order all of the parties to be there on that date. They generally defer to the parties with regard to the setting of the date of the hearing. If one party is very busy or intent upon delaying the resolution of the matter, that party can delay the hearing for a substantial period of time.

The second advantage of arbitration is that it is usually less expensive than litigation. The reduced expense is a function of the shorter amount of time needed to resolve the dispute and the absence of pre-hearing discovery. Most lawyers still work on the basis of an hourly fee, so in most cases your legal costs rise in direct proportion to the amount of time required to resolve the dispute. Because arbitration takes less time to complete than litigation, the legal costs incurred by a company will typically be less in arbitration than in litigation.

The absence of pre-hearing discovery is perhaps the most important factor leading to a more expeditious—and less expensive—completion of the process. Without having to wade through a slew of interrogatories, document productions, depositions, motions and the like, the parties to an arbitration are usually able to resolve their dispute much more quickly than parties in litigation. The reduced time results in lower costs.

Arbitration does involve certain expenses which are not present in litigation, though. Arbitrators are paid on a daily basis for their services. In major metropolitan areas, it is not unusual for arbitrators to receive between $500 and $1,000 per day for their services.

In addition, the parties must pay for all expenses associated with the arbitration. These items can include such things as the rental of the room where the arbitration takes place, the arbitrators' travel, meal and hotel expenses—if any—and the court reporter.

The third advantage of arbitration is that the dispute can be resolved by business people familiar with the industry in question. Many people believe—with some reason—that lay juries are unable to grasp the complexities of many civil disputes.

While jurors possess tremendous reserves of common sense, they are not experts in a given field. For example, it is unreasonable to think that jurors who have never used computers can grasp the subtle business aspects of software development in the course of a two-week trial. You couldn't do it and neither could I.

Invariably, one of the parties in a lawsuit thinks that he can gain an advantage by filling the jury box with individuals unable to grasp the complexities of the case at hand. This is something the lawyer can usually accomplish. The result may be a jury filled with people who have never heard of a municipal bond trying to decide whether a broker made a sufficient disclosure about the riskiness of an offering.

In arbitration, on the other hand, the arbitrators will almost always have some knowledge of the industry or business at issue in the dispute.

In the securities industry, the arbitrator is often a broker by trade. In construction disputes, the arbitrator will often have a background as an owner, contractor, architect or subcontractor.

Arbitration proponents argue that this decreases a party's ability to mislead the decision maker with lots of technical jargon in an attempt to divert attention from one's own misdeeds. Of course, this sophistication can cut both ways. Experts may carry biases formed from their experience in the industry.

So, while arbitrators possess expertise, they may also possess attitudes or perspectives which may predispose them to be more sympathetic to one of the parties. In the end, this is a trait which they share with lay jurors.

Disadvantages of Arbitration

There are certain disadvantages associated with arbitration.

Arbitrations do not usually allow the consolidation of claims or *joinder of parties*. Most arbitration agreements restrict participation in the arbitration to the parties to the arbitration agreement.

Put another way, unless you're a signatory to the arbitration agreement (or to the specific contract containing the arbitration agreement), you cannot be compelled to participate as a party to the arbitration.

In a practical sense, this means that in order to obtain complete relief, a party may be required to participate in more than one arbitration.

Because arbitration panels are not bound by the decisions of other arbitration panels, a party may obtain inconsistent results from different arbitration panels regarding a single dispute.

The classic example of this situation involves a construction dispute between an owner and a contractor. Assume that an owner has separate contracts with his contractor and architect, each of which contains an arbitration clause. If the contractor files a demand for arbitration with the owner—claiming that the plans prepared by the architect caused delays on the project which in turn entitle the contractor to additional money—the architect cannot be made a party to that arbitration.

While the owner may be able to persuade the architect to appear on his behalf to defend the plans, the architect cannot be subjected to liability in the original arbitration. If the arbitrators determine that the plans were defective, no award can be entered against the architect because she was not a party to the arbitration.

Instead, the owner—on whose behalf the architect prepared the plans—will be found liable.

If the owner then decides to seek compensation from the architect, he will have to institute a new and separate arbitration proceeding against the architect. The new arbitration panel will not be bound by the decision of the original arbitration panel. The architect can, however, offer as evidence the testimony of the owner defending her plans during the first arbitration.

So, it's quite possible that the second arbitration panel could find in favor of the architect.

Facing this prospect, the owner would prefer to resolve the entire dispute in a single arbitration in which all of the players are named as parties. Unfortunately, most arbitration clauses do not allow joinder of any party other than the parties to the contract which contains the arbitration agreement.

Another common disadvantage: Most arbitration procedures do not require arbitrators to follow rules of law. Arbitrators may choose to ignore the strict terms of the contract documents, as well as principles of law and specific legal decisions which may exist addressing the very points being considered by the arbitrators.

This is often a disadvantage for parties who follow the terms of their contract strictly. Parties to an arbitration tend to ask the arbitrators to be fair or to do justice. Most arbitrators are sympathetic to this argument and may choose to ignore the stricter technical requirements of a contract in favor of what they consider to be a just result. Specific obligations contained in a contract can be ignored by arbitrators in their effort to produce a fair result.

If the word *fair* is troubling elsewhere, it can be terrifying in arbitrations.

For example, arbitrators are not required to employ rules of evidence. This results in the introduction of substantial amounts of irrelevant, non-reliable and sometimes bizarre testimony.

The rules of evidence are frequently denigrated in the popular media. They are often portrayed as the technicalities that prevent a bus load of witnesses from testifying that they saw a hardened criminal commit a heinous crime. In reality, however, the rules of evidence exist to ensure that the finder of fact—either the judge or a jury—does not hear evidence until it has been established that the evidence is credible, relevant and subject to cross-examination.

In arbitration, no such safeguards exist. Parties to an arbitration can introduce unfounded testimony, opinion testimony, hearsay, and other evidence devoid of what lawyers call probative value.

It's not unusual for witnesses in an arbitration to try to prove a point by telling the arbitrators that their next door neighbor thinks their argument is a pretty good one. Most arbitrators aren't lawyers and therefore they have little use for the rules of evidence.

When the lawyer, unable to restrain himself, jumps up to object to a ridiculous and unfounded statement, the arbitrators are apt to remind the lawyer that the rules of evidence are not in effect. They allow the statement to be made and then promise to give it "whatever weight it deserves."

Accordingly, you are liable to hear just about anything in an arbitration.

A third disadvantage is something I mentioned as advantage earlier: Most arbitration procedures do not provide for pre-hearing discovery. This shortens the arbitration process and makes it a lot less expensive. This can, however, provide a significant strategic advantage to the party who has possession of pertinent documents and control of key witnesses. Without pre-hearing discovery, the other side cannot accurately determine the evidence which will be presented at the hearing and therefore cannot properly prepare to rebut the testimony or evidence presented there. A return to the days of "trial by ambush" is often the result.

Preparation for an arbitration hearing in the absence of discovery is always difficult and sometimes close to impossible. The absence of discovery usually places one of the parties at a strategic disadvantage.

Another potential disadvantage is the fact that there's no appeal from the decision of the arbitrators. Arbitrators typically do not explain their decisions. Most simply find in favor of one party in a particular dollar amount.

As a result, you cannot determine the basis—if there is any—for the arbitrators' decision. This is particularly troublesome in cases involving non-binding arbitration when you have to decide whether to pursue the dispute in court.

Finally, arbitrators are often inclined to enforce some compromise between the positions of the parties. This results from the conciliatory aspects of human nature—as well as a desire on the part of many arbitrators to avoid alienating either party.

Some arbitrators derive a healthy income from consulting work within the industry of their expertise. These people may view the participants in the arbitration as potential clients and therefore try to rule in favor of both parties in some limited way. This leads the arbitrators to split the baby in many instances.

Knowing this, parties who are involved in arbitration on a regular basis often inflate their claims in the hope of being awarded a portion of the claimed amount. This tendency on the part of arbitrators can work to the detriment of a party in the case where the party is either 100 percent right or 100 percent wrong.

There are few 100 percent decisions in arbitration.

Arbitration can be the most effective way to solve a private commercial dispute, so long as the arbitration agreement is drafted to meet the needs of your individual business.

For example, you may wish to provide for limited discovery prior to the arbitration hearing. By drafting an arbitration agreement which requires the parties to exchange all exhibits to be used at the hearing ten days before the hearing or allows the parties to take a limited number of depositions, you can diminish the possibility that you will encounter unexpected testimony at the hearing.

The arbitration agreement could also contain provisions establishing limits on the number of hearing days, identifying specific individuals who will serve as arbitrators in the event of a dispute, setting the fee to be paid to the arbitrators or any other of a number of specifically drafted provisions.

Mini-Trials and Special Masters

In recent years, some courts have experimented with the use of mini-trials and special masters. These are approaches crafted by the courts in an attempt to reduce the court's case load and facilitate settlement of the case. Although usually non-binding, in some systems the verdict of the mini-trial or the special master's hearing establishes a presumption in favor of the prevailing party.

A mini-trial is, as the name implies, a shortened version of a full-scale trial. In the mini-trial format, each party is given a limited amount of time to present its case. The cases are presented to a jury, a judge, a neutral third party appointed by the judge or even to the senior official of each party (usually aided by a neutral third party adviser).

Each side is given a limited amount of time, allotted a limited number of witnesses and restricted to a limited number of documents. Most mini-trials are completed in one or two days. Upon completion of the mini-trial, the judge or other finder of fact renders a non-binding opinion regarding each of the issues. In many instances, a mini-trial gives the parties a realistic preview of the results of a full scale trial. In this regard, a mini-trial resembles a mediation.

Special masters are employed by courts in complex or lengthy cases. The parties present their respective cases to an individual selected by the court to act as the special master. There is no limitation on the amount of testimony or the length of the presentations. In many instances, trials held before a special master resemble a bench trial before a judge.

At the conclusion of the hearing, the special master drafts a detailed report outlining his findings and submits the report to the court. The special master's findings are often presumed to be correct by the court, although the losing party may be given an opportunity to dispute the report.

The submission of the special master's report often results in a settlement of the case. The settlement dynamics resemble those which occur after a jury returns a verdict. The losing side threatens an appeal—in this case, a challenge to the special master's findings—but then offers to forego any further activity in exchange for a settlement in an amount less than the full amount recommended by the special master.

Each of these procedures has merit. The advantages are similar to the advantages derived from mediation. Mini-trials and special master hearings can often lead to an early settlement of the case, which typically reduces your legal costs. If you determine that it would be to your advantage to use one of these procedures, ask the judge if she will use them in your case.

Alternatives to litigation are gaining favor with businesses, courts, and even lawyers. Businesses have begun entering into agreements providing for alternative dispute resolution methodologies. For example, ten large food companies recently entered into an agreement requiring mediation of trademark, packaging and marketing disputes before resorting to litigation.

Scores of state and local court systems now require civil litigants to engage in mediation or non-binding arbitration as a prerequisite to obtaining a trial date. Even the lawyers are getting into the act. More than 1,500 law firms across the nation have adopted a formal policy requiring their litigators to explore alternative dispute resolution with their clients before plunging into the litigation briar patch. These developments reflect an acknowledgment that litigation is an expensive, time-consuming and inefficient way to resolve private disputes.

You can greatly reduce your legal costs by employing alternatives to litigation.

Chapter Five

How to Hire the Right Lawyer

You may regard the legal system as a cross between a carnival house of horrors and Dante's third circle of hell. This view is exaggerated, but not by much. The numerous pitfalls which await the litigant highlight the importance of selecting an able lawyer to act as your Sherpa guide in this strange land. This leads to another cardinal rule:

THE SELECTION OF YOUR LAWYER IS THE MOST IMPORTANT DECISION YOU WILL MAKE IN THE COURSE OF A LEGAL ACTION.

In one sense, lawyers are analogous to doctors, mechanics or any other individuals who provide expertise in an area which is foreign to the client. A good lawyer is invaluable. A bad lawyer makes a difficult situation worse. All a lawyer has to offer is his counsel, which can be priceless or worthless.

Judge Elbert Tuttle is one of the heroes of the American Bar. As federal appellate judges in the circuit with jurisdiction over a number of southern states in the 1950's and 1960's, Judge Tuttle and a number of his colleagues gave practical meaning to the Brown v. Board of Education decision and other civil rights laws which followed. Even more importantly, they served notice that the rule of law would be obeyed. They did so despite widespread social ostracism, consistent vilification and very real death threats.

In a 1973 speech, Judge Tuttle articulated the role of the lawyer and addressed the issue of the lawyer's worth:

> The professional man is in essence one who provides a service. He has no goods to sell, no land to till. His only asset is himself. It turns out that there is no right price for service, for what is a share of a man worth? If he does not contain the quality of integrity, he is worthless. If he does, he is priceless. The value is either nothing, or it is infinite.

Judge Tuttle's words are valuable words to keep in mind when selecting a lawyer.

The Old Approach

The old system for selecting a lawyer was rather informal. You often hired a lawyer because the lawyer happened to be one of the following people:

- your golf partner,
- your banker's lawyer,
- your neighbor,
- your college roommate,
- your business partner's son, cousin, or friend,
- the lawyer who probated your parents' estate,
- the lawyer your company "has always used,"
- a member of your Moose Lodge,
- your business association's lawyer, or
- your son, cousin or friend.

Although this was a haphazard way to select your lawyer, the system worked fairly well in many cases. Personal recommendations remain perhaps the single best source of information to be used in selecting a good lawyer.

Times change, however, and the conditions which contributed to the success of the old system have changed or disappeared. The old system worked in part due to the smaller size of the business community, the legal community and the volume of the law itself. Informal methods of selecting a lawyer work best when most of the people in the business community know each other, as well as the lawyers.

What's more, years ago a single lawyer could—and often did—represent a company for most of its legal needs. Given the complexity and sheer volume of the law today, it is virtually impossible for a single lawyer to meet all of a company's legal needs.

Finally, there was less need for lawyers years ago. Fewer laws, regulations and lawsuits meant that a business might go for months or even years without needing its lawyer.

New Approaches

Today's legal landscape is quite different. The size of the business and legal communities has increased dramatically, making it all but impossible for you to know all of the local business persons and lawyers. Stricter conflict of interest and ethics guidelines mean that hiring your nephew or the daughter of the mayor may no longer be an option. Most important, however, has been the exponential growth in the body of law itself.

Today it is impossible for a lawyer to remain competent, let alone proficient, in every area of the law. There is too much law to know. No longer can a single lawyer be expected to have expertise in all of the areas of the law. The lawyer who handled your divorce may not be qualified to represent you when a state trooper pulls you over for the fifth time.

In a given month, a business might need legal advice regarding a breach of contract dispute, a discrimination complaint filed with the EEOC by a former employee, a recent IRS ruling, a bond offering, a product liability lawsuit, a worker's compensation claim, a potential merger, an initial public stock offering, a trademark infringement allegation, an ERISA question, an environmental allegation by the EPA, a bankruptcy filing, and a lien filed against the company's property. Like most areas of the law, the foregoing areas have become specialty areas, with certain lawyers restricting their practices to those areas alone. So, it is unlikely that a single lawyer could address all of the foregoing problems.

In light of this, the old approach to selecting a lawyer is not advisable. A more formalized and objective approach is necessary. Unfortunately, some people are hesitant to employ such an approach. The law is often imbued—by lawyers—with great mystery. Non-lawyers are sometimes intimidated or confused by the law, which may cause them to suspend their sound judgment when selecting and dealing with lawyers.

Keep in mind that lawyers are vendors who seek to sell you their wares. In many ways, the selection of a lawyer is no different from the selection of any other vendor who seeks to provide services to your business. You are seeking the same qualities in a lawyer as you seek in selecting other vendors: integrity, a quality service or product and a reasonable price. While much of what follows applies to hiring a lawyer for your business, many of these techniques can and should be utilized when hiring a lawyer to represent you in your individual capacity.

How to Find a Lawyer If You Don't Already Have One

Assume you need to find a lawyer. Where do you begin? The yellow pages are always an option, but you'd probably be better off hiring your golf partner. This is not to denigrate the telephone book or lawyers whose names appear in the telephone book. Most lawyers are listed.

Still, picking a lawyer out of the telephone book is akin to picking stocks by throwing darts at the business page. You may get lucky, but there are smarter ways to make your pick.

There are a number of reasonable ways to select your lawyer. I suggest a three-step approach. You may not, of course, need to employ every step or interview so many lawyers for each matter, but this format can be modified to fit your situation.

Avoid the temptation to use shortcuts. There may come a point when you think, "I'm spending too much valuable time in the selection process. I think I'll just hire my golf partner." Resist this impulse. The time spent in selecting the proper lawyer is a valuable investment.

By thoughtfully selecting your lawyer, you decrease the chances of hiring the wrong lawyer. This is the point in the process where you have the greatest control. Exercise that control.

Step One: References

Ask around. Talk to your banker, your accountant, your customers, your vendors. Ask them who their lawyer is. Ask them how satisfied they are with their lawyer. Ask them whether an adversary's lawyer recently left tire tracks on their lawyer's back. What do they like about their lawyer? What don't they like? Which lawyers do they use for certain types of work?

If you have friends or neighbors who are lawyers, ask them to refer you to lawyers who provide the type of service you need. Lawyers can be other lawyers' toughest critics. While the proliferation of lawyers makes it unlikely that the lawyer next door will know all of the good lawyers, your neighbor can probably provide you with the names of a number of good lawyers. Ask your lawyer friend whom he would use if he needed a lawyer.

A word about lawyer advertising: Lawyer advertising runs the gamut from dignified to embarrassing. White shoe law firms produce understated firm brochures. Smaller firms sometimes purchase advertisements in the telephone book. Personal injury lawyers rent billboards and run television ads featuring maimed plaintiffs waxing ecstatic over the bountiful jury awards or settlements procured by their lawyers.

One memorable billboard depicted a poodle and a German Shepherd with the caption "Who would you rather have representing you in court?"

The purpose of all lawyer advertising is, of course, to bring the lawyer or firm to your attention. While lawyer advertisements present imperfect and sometimes inaccurate portrayals of a lawyer or firm, the advertisement itself may offer insights into the culture of the lawyer or firm. If the lawyer stars in his own television commercials dressed in a clown suit or brandishing a firearm, you may have learned all you need to know.

Local bar associations often provide referral services. Many such services categorize lawyers on the basis of practice areas and specialties. These services can be a valuable asset if you are unable to obtain enough names from your friends and business associates. Keep in mind, however, that few bar associations monitor the quality of the services provided by the individual lawyers included in the referral lists.

This process should produce a list of ten to fifteen lawyers or law firms from which you can select your lawyer.

Step Two: Proposals

After you have a pool of names from which you hope to select your lawyer, contact each lawyer or law firm and ask them to submit either their general credentials or a specific proposal.

If you request general credentials, develop a form letter to be sent to each candidate. In the letter, explain—briefly—who you are, a little about your business and what sort of legal services you are seeking. At this juncture, don't get into any of the details of your specific problem. For example, don't reveal who has sued you or the basis of the lawsuit.

Ask the lawyer or firm to provide certain information to you in writing within a specific period of time. A week to ten days is a reasonable time frame. You may specify the information you wish to receive—hourly fees, experience, and billing policies—or you may leave it up to the lawyer or firm. Leaving it to the lawyer's discretion can in some cases be even more revealing.

Be sure to specify that at this point you want written materials. You don't want phone calls, lunch invitations, cocktail invitations, dinner invitations, tours of the firm's office, invitations to firm parties or complementary tumblers emblazoned with the firm logo. If you don't make this clear, you will be besieged with some or all of these things.

Some prospective clients prefer to receive specific proposals rather than general credentials at this stage. It is difficult for a lawyer or law firm to provide a meaningful proposal in the absence of detailed information regarding the lawsuit or other tasks at hand. If you want a specific proposal, you will need to provide each of the candidates with a good deal of information. I do not advise providing specific details regarding your legal needs to ten or fifteen lawyers, only one of which you will hire. Without such detailed information, however, it will be difficult for the candidates to provide you with meaningful proposals.

Obtaining specific proposals at so early a stage works only when you can describe the needed legal services in generic terms which do not disclose confidential information regarding the specific task at hand. This, obviously, is tricky. It can work when the task involved is the drafting of contracts or other transactional tasks. Litigation-specific tasks—such as picking a lawyer to defend a specific lawsuit which has been filed against you—do not lend themselves to requesting detailed proposals at this stage.

After you've sorted through the responses from the lawyers (which may include resumes, pictures of the firm's office, testimonials and copies of papers written by members of the firm), select a much smaller number of lawyers or firms to interview personally.

Step Three: Interviews

Schedule an interview with each of the remaining candidates. Conduct the interview in the lawyer's office. Much can be learned from viewing the way a lawyer runs his office. While you should guard against drawing superficial conclusions based on the location or decor of the lawyer's office, use your instincts regarding what you see. Is the office neat and clean? (The common areas, anyway—a lawyer's desk usually resembles a New Jersey landfill.) Does the support staff appear and act professionally? Are the office furnishings ostentatious?

If the office looks like a wing of Versailles, remember that somebody—usually the client—has to pay for all of this overhead. You take pride in how your customers feel when they enter your place of business. Does the lawyer's office reflect the same attitude? While the look of the lawyer's office won't tell you everything you need to know about the lawyer, it's a starting point.

Ten Questions to Ask Your Prospective Lawyer

After you've toured the office, obtained a bad cup of coffee and made the obligatory small talk, you're ready for the interview itself.

Let me suggest some specific questions which you should ask your prospective lawyer.

"Describe Your Current Practice."

Find out how the candidate spends her professional life. Is she a full-time litigator or does she practice in other areas as well? How much of her time over the course of the year is spent litigating? Do most of her cases settle or go to trial? How many cases has the lawyer taken to trial? Was she the lead counsel in those cases or was her role as a second or third chair assistant?

Be prepared to find that many of the candidates will not have taken a large number of cases to trial. This is not necessarily the lawyer's fault and doesn't mean that you should not consider hiring that lawyer. As I've mentioned before, 94.6 percent of civil lawsuits are settled prior to trial. This means that there are lots of top-notch lawyers out there who simply have not had an opportunity to try very many cases.

In most instances your objective is to conclude the litigation as quickly as possible, so long as the resolution is acceptable to you. So, you don't care whether the case goes to trial or not—you just want it to be over. In fact, you may prefer that no trial ever be held. You might interview a lawyer who has never tried a case in her life, but for all the right reasons. She may do such a good job in discovery—or may be so brilliant or so feared—that her opponents don't want to take the case to trial against her and settle the case prior to trial on terms which are favorable to her client. It is possible that the best lawyer for your case might be a lawyer who has never tried a case in her life.

On the other hand, it is always possible that your case will be one of the small number of cases that goes to trial. In light of that possibility, you want a lawyer who has lots of actual trial experience. This is logical. Nevertheless, keep in mind that a wealth of trial experience doesn't mean that the lawyer is an effective lawyer. Many civil lawsuits are won or lost in the discovery phase. Look for a lawyer who can demonstrate effective pre-trial skills as well as effective trial skills.

Ask the lawyer whether she generally represents plaintiffs or defendants. Lots of lawyers represent both plaintiffs and defendants, but you will also find a significant number of lawyers who spend most of their time representing one side or the other. Plaintiffs' lawyers and defendants' lawyers often approach cases very differently.

If you are the defendant in a lawsuit, the conventional wisdom is that you want to hire a lawyer who has plenty of experience defending such lawsuits. There is a good degree of truth to the conventional wisdom on this point. Experienced defense lawyers develop effective techniques which can be employed to make life miserable for the plaintiff. All things considered, if your business has been named as a defendant, selecting a lawyer who specializes or spends the majority of her time defending cases is probably a good decision.

The contrarian view is that it makes sense to employ a lawyer who generally represents plaintiffs to defend your case. This view states that by hiring a lawyer who represents plaintiffs, you will be hiring a lawyer who will be familiar with the approaches which will be employed by the plaintiff's lawyer in your case and will be able to thwart them. There is some validity to this view. Having employed many of the approaches herself, the plaintiff's lawyer may be more familiar with some of the tactics employed by your adversary.

How you view this debate is a matter of personal philosophy. On balance, I would hire a lawyer with significant defense experience to defend a lawsuit filed against my company. It should be noted, however, that the ability of the lawyer is much more important than whether the lawyer generally represents plaintiffs or defendants. The outstanding plaintiff's lawyer will always be a better choice to defend you than the mediocre defendant's lawyer.

"Are You a Generalist or a Specialist?"

If the lawyer has a general practice, find out how much time she spends on cases like yours over the course of a year. By definition, a lawyer with a general practice spends her professional life focusing on a number of different areas of practice. While there is nothing wrong with this, you need to know how much experience the general practice lawyer has with your type of case. If the lawyer is a specialist, ask her how she will handle issues which may arise in the course of the case which involve areas of practice beyond her specialty. Some firms which practice in a very narrow specialty area have informal arrangements with other specialty firms pursuant to which the firms consult one another on issues outside their respective specialty areas.

Do you need a specialist? It depends on your particular problem, but in most cases the answer is *yes*. I hasten to add that by specialist I don't mean a lawyer who handles nothing but securities litigation involving the tax-exempt status of certain government securities issued after 1985. Rather, I refer to a lawyer who spends a majority of her professional life handling cases like yours.

Like many businesses and professions, the law has in recent years experienced a consistent reduction in the number of general practitioners. There is too much law for most humans to be able to achieve proficiency on a broad scale. So, whether or not they think of themselves as specialists, most lawyers find themselves practicing in a somewhat narrow range of practice areas after a few years. In most instances, you will be in a better position if you hire someone who spends most of her time handling your type of case.

"What Experience Have You Had with My Legal Problem?"

You want a lawyer who has been down this road before, preferably a number of times. Although many good lawyers can perform magnificently the very first time they handle a particular type of case, it almost always takes them longer—and costs you more—the first time through. Given a choice, why pay for this aspect of the lawyer's professional education? Why not hire a lawyer who has already gotten those mistakes out of her system?

Let your lawyer get her first taste of combat on somebody else's nickel.

In addition to the subject matter of your case, you want to know if the lawyer has experience in the court where a case is pending. Does the lawyer usually practice in state court or federal court? There are important differences between the way a case is handled in federal and state court. Find out how much experience the lawyer has in the court where your case will be adjudicated.

If the lawsuit has already been filed, you will know the judge to whom the case has been assigned. What is the lawyer's track record with that particular judge? Has she ever appeared before that judge? How did it go? If the judge threw the lawyer in jail last month for contempt of court, you want another lawyer to handle your case.

After you have established that the candidate has a wealth of experience handling this type of case, inquire as to the results of each of her previous forays into this thicket. Did her client win or lose? Did the case go to trial or was it settled prior to trial? Was an appeal taken? How long did the litigation last, start to finish?

Asking a lawyer how a case turned out can be a tricky proposition. Few lawyers will tell you that they lost their last case so badly that their client went bankrupt and the lawyer had to start a new practice under an assumed name.

Instead, the response is usually a model of obfuscation like, "Given the difficult factual circumstances and the unsettled state of the law, we were not completely displeased with the outcome." Translated into English, this may mean "We got waxed like a new set of skis."

In defense of lawyers, the attorney-client privilege and the Canons of Ethics prohibit a lawyer from talking too freely about the cases of other clients. Moreover, you don't want a lawyer who is going to be sharing the confidential details of your case with every prospective new client. Avoid blabby lawyers.

It is often difficult to determine whether a client won a lawsuit without knowing all of the details of the case. What appears to be a win to the casual observer may be a disastrous defeat.

For example, assume that your company is sued for $1 million. You know that your employee committed the transgression in question, but the other side won't settle for a penny less than the million dollars, so you have to take the case to trial.

At trial, your lawyer does a masterful job of creating sympathy for your wayward employee and although it's clear your employee erred and the plaintiff was damaged significantly, the jury only awards the plaintiff $50,000. You're jubilant. But, to the outside observer, you lost the case because you had to pay the plaintiff $50,000.

You have to go beyond simple questions of winning and losing when asking about a lawyer's track record. Most good lawyers will not respond by saying that they won or lost particular cases. They realize that in civil litigation, short answers can be misleading. The good lawyers will be willing to amplify their responses (again, assuming that in doing so they are not breaching any attorney-client confidences). Give the lawyer an opportunity to explain her track record fully. The manner in which the lawyer does so may be as revealing as the substance of the answer.

Ask the lawyer if she has any objection to your contacting other clients for whom she has handled this sort of case. Assuming that the former client has given the lawyer permission to tell others of the representation, most lawyers will have no objection to this. While there may be valid reasons why the lawyer does not feel comfortable with this (chief among them being the desire of the former client to be left alone), a lawyer's reluctance to allow you to speak with other clients may indicate a potential problem. If the lawyer agrees to provide you with the names of other clients, contact those clients and get their impressions of the lawyer.

Ask the lawyer whether she likes litigating this type of case. Although the response will often be "You bet! This is my favorite type of case in the whole wide world," the manner in which the response is offered—as well as the length of the pause preceding the response—may give you some insight into whether your case will be attractive to the lawyer for reasons other than the fee.

Despite some evidence to the contrary, lawyers are human beings. They have likes and dislikes just like anybody else. Every lawyer has cases on which she enjoys working and other cases which are less attractive. This may be a function of the subject matter of the case, the client, the area of the law involved, the personal qualities of the people in the industry or some other factor. Look for a lawyer who, for whatever reason, appears to enjoy construction litigation—or whatever subject applies to your situation.

This, of course, calls for a very subjective analysis, but raising the subject may give you some insight into whether your file will be the one the lawyer has to force herself to pick up.

"What is Your General Approach to a Problem Like This One?"

Ask the lawyer about her litigation philosophy. Whether they articulate it or not, most lawyers develop a *de facto* philosophy regarding the best way to handle litigation. Although the varying circumstances in different cases dictate modifications to a lawyer's general philosophy, most lawyers develop certain patterns and approaches which they employ in every case.

Does your prospective lawyer believe in trying to settle the case early in the proceedings? If so, does that philosophy determine the actions the lawyer will undertake at the outset of the lawsuit? Does the lawyer think that any attempt to settle the case before discovery has been completed is premature? Does she believe in taking the deposition of each and every witness or just the two or three most important witnesses?

Does the lawyer believe that counterclaims should be made in every case to provide settlement leverage or does she like to keep the case as simple as possible? Does the lawyer inundate the opposition with massive discovery requests or forego all but the most basic interrogatories and requests for production of documents?

In response to these questions, a good many lawyers will nod knowingly and say that each case is different and calls for a different strategy, which will reveal itself as the case progresses. If pressed, however, most lawyers will expound on their general views on this—or any—subject. Draw the lawyer out. Let the lawyer do the talking. If you decide this is the lawyer you want to hire, you'll have plenty of time later to tell the lawyer about your philosophy. At this point, you want to determine her philosophy.

One of the things you're trying to determine at this stage is whether you feel personally and professionally comfortable with this lawyer. Society at large and business consultants in particular overuse the term *personal chemistry*. Nevertheless, like most ideas which become cliches due to overuse, some validity lies hidden at the core of the jargon.

Many consultants advise that you should not conduct business with anyone unless you have achieved good personal chemistry. My opinion is that good personal chemistry is important, but only to a point.

As you no doubt have learned without any consultant's help, it's a lot easier to work with people who share your general business philosophy and personal style. If a business associate's personal and professional approach varies greatly from yours, it is often difficult to work effectively with that individual.

Difficult, but not impossible. No doubt you have observed numerous situations where the personal chemistry of two business associates could not have been more different, but they nevertheless were able to achieve their goal. I have observed—and have been a participant in—a number of those situations. Some were daily struggles which ended badly. Others produced outstanding results which left both individuals pleased.

You are hiring a lawyer, not asking somebody to join your bridge club. You are hiring a vendor to perform a specific task—to defend you in the lawsuit or sue the other side. The salient point is not whether this person is someone you would like to have as a neighbor or golf partner. What's important to you is whether this person can perform the task for which you are hiring her.

There are, of course, some limits. You should not hire someone with whom you are personally uncomfortable, for whatever reason. You will be spending a lot of time with this person. She is going to be your representative in the legal and business communities. Don't hire a lawyer whom you would be ashamed to have represent you.

For example, if the lawyer can't form a single sentence without using language which would make a sailor blush, you probably don't want this person representing you in your lawsuit or anywhere else. If other aspects of the lawyer's style are personally offensive to you in some way, there is no reason to subject yourself to the presence of such an individual.

One of the few good things about needing a lawyer is that you get to choose your lawyer. Being involved in a lawsuit is unpleasant enough without compounding the problem by hiring a lawyer who irritates you in some way. The realities of life require you to deal with enough unpleasant people—why add to the list when you don't have to? In the late 1970's, Northwestern University's Kellogg School of Management was recognized by some publications as the best business school in the country.

One of Kellogg's professors began his management course each year by telling students that all of the management principles they would learn in the upcoming year could be distilled into a single principle which the professor called MCWJ.

After allowing the students to puzzle over the acronym for a moment, he would write on the blackboard "Minimize Contact With Jerks."

That principle encapsulates many of my thoughts on the issue of personal chemistry and the selection of a lawyer generally.

"Do You Have Any Experience in Our Industry?"

Find out if the lawyer has been involved in cases involving your industry or business. While not as important as the lawyer's legal experience, such experience can be of great value. In any situation, a mastery of the facts is essential to success. If your lawyer is already familiar with your business or industry, you will derive a number of benefits.

First, you won't have to spend time and money educating the lawyer about the rudiments of your business. It can take a fair amount of time to explain the computer business to someone whose knowledge of computers extends no further than how to turn on her dictaphone. If you can hire a lawyer who is already well-grounded in your business or industry, you will be ahead of the game.

Second, your lawyer will be more effective because she won't get sidetracked due to a lack of familiarity with the subject matter. A lawyer who has never been involved in a construction case can spend days talking to a general contractor about certain work without realizing that all of the work in question was performed by a lower-tier subcontractor. If your lawyer has knowledge of the industry, the lawyer can work far more efficiently.

Finally, a working knowledge of the industry will in many cases give your lawyer a significant competitive advantage in your lawsuit. If your opponent's lawyer does not share your lawyer's knowledge of the industry, your lawyer will be in a position to exploit this superior knowledge at a number of points in the course of the lawsuit.

"Describe Your Fee Structures and Billing Procedures."

Most lawyers bill on the basis of fixed fees, contingent fees or hourly fees. Ask the lawyer how she would bill you for the work in question. With regard to each fee arrangement, there are certain specific questions which you should ask.

Fixed Fee: Ask the lawyer how the fixed fee is determined. Ask how the firm avoids setting the fee too high or too low. What happens if the project takes twice as long as anticipated? In such cases, does the firm ask for an additional fee? If so, how would the additional fee be calculated? Conversely, if the matter requires much less time than anticipated, does the firm give the client a rebate of any sort? Finally, is the fixed fee negotiable?

Contingent Fee: How does the lawyer establish the percentage which will represent the lawyer's fee? Are the percentages negotiable? Do the percentages change on the basis of the point in time that a settlement or judgment is achieved? Are litigation expenses deducted before or after the lawyer's fee is calculated? Remember that it is always more profitable for the lawyer to have the expenses deducted from the client's share after the lawyer's fee has been calculated. Is this issue negotiable? Does the firm ever pay for any of the litigation expenses? Is the firm willing to subsidize the litigation by paying the expenses and settling up when the case is concluded?

Hourly Fee: Your first request should be for a schedule of fees reflecting the hourly rates of the lawyers and paralegals in the firm. Review the differences between the hourly fees charged by the different partners and associates. Ask why a first-year associate's rate is $80 per hour and a sixth-year associate's rate is only $110. Given the relative ability of first- and sixth-year associates, such a fee structure may suggest that the first-year associate is overpriced, while the sixth-year associate is, relatively speaking, a bargain. Keep this in mind when you begin to discuss which associate should work on your case.

Beware of broad ranges which appear on the billing schedule. Some billing schedules will state that partners' time is billed at $175 to $325 per hour.

What accounts for the disparity? Is it seniority, clout, ability, reputation or something else? Which partners will be working on your case? What are the specific hourly rates for those partners? Would the firm give you the option of determining which lawyers work on your case? Can you request that all work be performed by the least experienced lawyer possessing the ability to perform that task?

Find out which lawyer will have responsibility for assembling, finalizing and transmitting your bill. Ask that lawyer about the firm's policy concerning the adjustment of bills. Most firms give the billing partner the discretion to adjust a bill if the partner believes that the total hours contained in a draft bill produce a fee that is either too high or too low.

In the majority of instances, a bill will be adjusted downward because the firm's lawyers spent too much time working on a particular task. In some instances, however, a partner may adjust a bill upward to reflect the difficulty of the tasks involved, a good result or some other subjective factor.

Ask the billing lawyer whether she has the authority to adjust bills. Ask the lawyer what happens if a junior associate spends fifty hours on a task which should require only thirty hours. In such a case, would the billing partner write off the last twenty hours? Ask the lawyer if there are any instances in which the firm adjusts bills upward.

Ask specific questions about the hourly rates. How often does the firm raise the hourly rates of its lawyers? If your case is ongoing during a rate increase, will the rates that you are charged rise or are you locked into the rates which were in effect at the beginning of your case?

The hourly billing rates charged by lawyers and law firms are always in flux. Some firms use specialized computer software to increase the rates charged by its lawyers as those lawyers gain additional experience. Ask the lawyer about her firm's policies regarding these matters. Is there any room for negotiation?

Ask the lawyer if the firm has policies in place to discourage and discover bill padding.

While some lawyers may take umbrage at the question—clearing their throat with great drama and stating that "Our lawyers would never do something like that"—this is a legitimate question. Ask the lawyer if her firm has ever discovered one of its lawyers padding a client's bill. If so, what was the firm's response?

Find out how the law firm breaks down its hours. Determine the smallest time increment in the firm's billing system. In some firms, it may be as high as ten minutes. If the smallest time increment is over five minutes, ask the lawyer how much you would be billed for a two-minute phone call. Find out how the firm keeps track of lawyer tasks which consume less time than the smallest time increment. Do they have some method for keeping track of such tasks with an eye toward consolidating such brief encounters with other brief encounters?

This may seem petty, but a firm's policies regarding such issues can reflect its larger philosophy. Some firms have internal policies stating that any phone calls with the client must be recorded as lasting at least as long as the smallest time increment used in the firm's billing system. Other firms have similar policies relating to correspondence.

You need to know if your lawyer has such policies in place. You may or may not believe such policies are reasonable, but you ought to be in a position to make that determination.

Find out if the firm bills the same hourly rates for all services provided by the firm. Some lawyers and firms employ premium billing— that is, higher rates—for specific tasks which are deemed to be more valuable than other tasks. Some litigators, for example, charge one hourly rate for pre-trial work and a higher rate for time spent in court.

Does the lawyer or firm charge for travel time? If so, is the travel rate the same as the rate charged when the lawyer is working on the case? As mentioned above, some lawyers charge for travel time only when the lawyer is working on the case while in transit. Others charge for travel time regardless of whether the lawyer is working on the case. Still others charge a reduced or discounted hourly fee for travel time. Determine the lawyer's policy and whether there are exceptions to the policy.

Alternative Billing Arrangements: Many firms offer alternative fee arrangements which shift part of the risk to the lawyer by giving the lawyer a financial stake in the outcome of the case. Ask the lawyer whether her firm offers such fee arrangements, how long they have offered such arrangements and whether they—and their clients— have been satisfied with the way in which such fee arrangements have worked. If the firm has never used such fee arrangements, ask if they would be willing to use such an arrangement for your case.

Expenses: Obtain a comprehensive list of the expenses you will be expected to pay. Address such issues as whether you will pay for first class air travel, when you will pay for lawyer meals and whether there is any limit on the amount you will pay for such meals. Find out which items are absorbed by the firm as overhead and which items will be specific expense items.

While you're on the subject of money, ask the lawyer about her firm's policy in instances when the client falls behind on payment of the legal fees. Is there a grace period? Does the firm expect payment in advance, by return mail or within thirty days? Whatever the period, does the firm charge interest on bills which are not paid within a specific period of time? If so, what is the interest rate?

The cost of the lawyer should never be the sole—or even the primary—factor in the selection of a lawyer. A lawyer's fee sometimes bears little relation to the quality of representation you will be receiving. Don't assume that the most expensive lawyer is the best lawyer. On the other hand, sometimes you get what you pay for.

Some lawyers who offer bargain basement rates are bargain basement lawyers. Don't be short-sighted. It is almost always a mistake to hire the cheapest lawyer available on the basis of price alone. Take the lawyer's fee into consideration, but don't select your lawyer on the basis of price alone.

"Tell Me About Your Firm."

Unless the prospective lawyer is a sole practitioner, he will be practicing with other lawyers. This means that he—and, by extension, you—will be affected by those other lawyers. Accordingly, you need to know about the lawyer's firm as well as the individual lawyer you are considering hiring.

How large is the firm? Is this by design or accident? There are, of course, advantages and disadvantages associated with size. Generalizations are dangerous, but here are a few generalizations concerning law firm size. The larger firms usually—but not always—have been around longer, are more expensive, have larger bureaucracies, and greater overhead to subsidize.

Large firms traditionally attract a substantial number of lawyers and law students with outstanding paper credentials. Large firms are good at throwing lots of lawyers at a problem, but they are sometimes inefficient.

In many senses, large firms are loose confederations of smaller firms. Trying to describe a large firm may be analogous to the fable of the blind men trying to describe an elephant on the basis of the part of the elephant each man could feel. Your experience with a large firm will depend on whether you are dealing with its trunk or its more southerly components.

Small firms are usually—but not always—less bureaucratized, less expensive and less able to throw large numbers of lawyers at a problem on short notice. Small firms generally offer a narrower range of services than large firms, although you may find a greater percentage of general practitioners working in small firms or as sole practitioners. Small firms are better at avoiding the perils of committees, bureaucracies and massive overhead which can drive up hourly fees.

On the other hand, small firms are vulnerable to overload and can find themselves in dire straits if their key lawyer decides to join a monastery.

Some observers argue that large firms are less likely to make mistakes—not because they have better lawyers, but because in a large firm an assignment is reviewed by more lawyers before it goes out the door.

Having worked in a large firm, a small firm, and as a sole practitioner, I have not found this to be the case. The essential element is the lawyer handling the case rather than the number of lawyers who review an assignment. I saw just as many mistakes per capita at the two hundred-person firm as I did at the ten-person firm.

Discuss the firm's history. Ask how long the firm has been in existence in its current form. Who are the key partners? How long have they practiced together? Are there other lawyers who can step in and handle your case if the lawyer you are interviewing becomes incapacitated or leaves the practice of law?

How many lawyers did the firm have five years ago? Has the firm been growing or shrinking over the past three years? In either case, why? Have any lawyers left the firm in the past three years? If so, why? Did they leave of their own volition or were they asked to leave?

What is the firm's policy concerning lateral hires? Has the firm merged with any other firms or added any new practice areas within the last three years?

Is the firm a general practice firm or does it specialize in a particular type of work? If it is a general practice firm, are there any areas which the firm does not handle? If it is a specialty firm, how do they deal with questions outside their specialty which may arise during the course of a lawsuit or other representation? Do they have arrangements with other firms to handle such questions?

One of the things you are attempting to determine with such questions is whether the firm is a stable business entity. In years past, law firms were generally stable entities. All you had to do was show up, not make any big mistakes, keep the corporate clients happy and start planning that Wednesday afternoon golf date. Lawyers tended to stay with one firm from graduation to retirement.

This is no longer the case. Since the early 1980s, law firms have been thrust into the unpleasant position of being subjected to market forces. This has resulted in substantial turnover in many law firms, as many lawyers in profitable practice areas detached themselves from not-so-profitable firms to start new firms or join other firms. General practice firms jettisoned unprofitable lawyers and practice areas in previously unthinkable numbers.

In light of this, you need to know the firm's track record over the past five years. Identify any trends and try to determine whether those trends will affect your lawyer's ability to represent you.

To the extent possible, you need to know how much the firm itself—as opposed to your individual lawyer—will be involved with your representation. Does your lawyer have the autonomy to make decisions regarding the representation himself, or must all such decisions be made or approved by a committee of some sort?

Many firms have committees which establish firm policies regarding such issues as fees, any discounts to be given, which clients the firm will represent, billing issues, the staffing of cases, publicity, and other matters which may affect your case. The lawyer you are interviewing may be quite confident in quoting particular hourly rates or promising that certain individuals will be assigned to your case, but the final authority regarding such matters may lie with a committee of lawyers you have never met.

While such a situation arises most often in medium to large firms, even small firms may have assigned responsibility for certain business aspects of the firm's practice to a lawyer other than the individual you are interviewing.

Inquire about the firm's malpractice history. This is a sensitive subject for most lawyers and clients, but you deserve to know whether, how often and under what circumstances the lawyer and law firm have been sued for malpractice.

Malpractice allegations against lawyers have increased dramatically in recent years. There are a variety of factors responsible for this increase. Heightened consumer awareness, the rise of the consumer rights' movement, highly publicized awards against other professionals such as doctors, an aggressive plaintiff's bar, society's general unwillingness to accept disappointing results and the ineffectiveness of the organized bar in weeding out dishonest or incompetent lawyers have all contributed to this situation.

Many malpractice allegations made against lawyers are baseless. Malpractice allegations against a lawyer are sometimes nothing more than an attempt by a dishonest client to avoid payment of the lawyer's fee. Accordingly, the fact that a malpractice allegation has been leveled against a lawyer or firm is not, in and of itself, evidence of any errors on the part of that lawyer or firm.

In light of this, be sure to get the complete story when asking about such issues. How many malpractice allegations have been filed against the lawyer or firm over the past five years? How many different clients have made the charges? Sometimes one disgruntled client can account for a host of different lawsuits. Let the lawyer explain his side of the story. What was the outcome of each situation? Did the case go to trial or was some settlement reached? Lawyers are not very popular defendants.

In some instances, a judgment against the lawyer or firm may not be conclusive proof of malpractice. These cases are often settled by the lawyer's malpractice insurer. The insurance company may choose to settle the case because it makes economic sense for the insurance company to do so. This decision is often unrelated to the issue of whether any malpractice occurred.

Trust your business judgment on this issue. While malpractice allegations against a lawyer or firm don't mean that there is a problem, in some cases the nature or quantity of the malpractice claims will suggest that a problem does exist. You must evaluate each situation individually, but in order to do so you must be able to discuss these issues candidly with the lawyer. If the lawyer is evasive or refuses to discuss such matters, chances are you have obtained important information about the candidate.

While you're on the subject, find out how much malpractice insurance the lawyer or firm carries. In a worst case scenario, your lawyer may make a mistake that costs you a great deal of money. Accordingly, it's important to know whether the firm or its insurance company would have adequate assets to compensate you for any demonstrable malpractice the lawyer might commit. Make sure you ask about the firm's deductible. A $10 million malpractice insurance policy provides the client with little protection if it contains a $2 million deductible which the lawyer or firm would be unable to pay.

Some lawyers may resent such questions, viewing them as intrusive, disrespectful and indicative of a lack of trust. Such lawyers are in a fast-diminishing minority. Most lawyers today realize that such questions are legitimate business questions to be considered by the prospective client. The client who fails to make such inquiries will select his lawyer on the basis of incomplete information.

Finally, don't fall into the trap of allowing yourself to be impressed by the firm rather than the individual lawyer.

It's sometimes easy to be dazzled by the firm's pedigree, reputation, offices, size or whatsoever. Remember that although the firm's resources will be at your disposal, your case will be handled by individual lawyers. If those individual lawyers aren't top notch lawyers, all of the firm's resources won't be of much value. Which leads to the next cardinal rule:

HIRE THE LAWYER, NOT THE LAW FIRM.

"What Are Your Credentials?"

The lawyer's credentials offer some insight into his professional achievements and activities. While they are only a starting point and can sometimes present a distorted picture, paper credentials can be helpful in the lawyer selection process.

I hasten to add, however, that excessive reliance on paper credentials can be dangerous. Plenty of lawyers with impeccable paper credentials couldn't find their way out of a phone booth with a map. On the other hand, some of the best lawyers around have unimpressive paper credentials.

A good place to start is a reference book entitled *The Martindale-Hubbell Law Directory*. This multi-volume directory is published annually and is usually referred to simply as *Martindale-Hubbell*. Martindale-Hubbell is the most widely used listing of lawyers in the United States and around the world. It can be found in most law firms, corporate legal departments and public libraries.

There are separate listings for each lawyer reflecting such things as where the lawyer attended college and law school, scholarly papers published by the lawyer, membership in professional associations, and areas of specialty practice. Lawyers pay Martindale-Hubbell an annual fee to be included in the directory and they are allowed to submit their own biographies. So, some of the listed exploits should be taken with a grain of salt.

In addition to listing the lawyers on the basis of their geographical location, Martindale-Hubbell also employs a rating system. The editors rate lawyers and publish a General Recommendation Rating.

The criteria for each rating is explained in the directory itself. Ratings are developed by soliciting confidential opinions from other lawyers and judges. The system is an imperfect one, but can be of some assistance in selecting a lawyer.

A caveat: Most law firms have determined that inclusion in Martindale-Hubbell justifies the cost. Other firms and many sole practitioners choose not to subscribe. If a lawyer does not appear in Martindale-Hubbell, this may simply mean that the lawyer has decided to spend his money elsewhere.

In addition to reviewing the lawyer's Martindale-Hubbell listing, conduct your own inquiry regarding the lawyer's paper credentials. Where did the lawyer attend law school? Various publications publish annual rankings of law schools.

Another caveat: Law school reputations are subjective. The most highly regarded law schools can sometimes produce lawyers who are better suited to academia than the real world.

Regardless of the law school, how did the lawyer perform? Did the lawyer graduate with honors? Look for a listing of *Order of the Coif*, which denotes outstanding academic achievement. Did the lawyer work on the school's *Law Review* or other publication? Did the lawyer participate in clinical programs, write a senior thesis or serve as a teaching assistant?

After law school, did the lawyer serve as a law clerk to a judge? Did the lawyer obtain a master of laws degree or proceed with some other formal course of study? Has the lawyer written any articles or published any papers regarding his specialty? Has the lawyer written or contributed to any books? Does the lawyer or the firm publish a regular newsletter?

Review the lawyer's employment history. How many jobs has he held since graduating from law school? If he has held a number of jobs, ask him to describe each job. Be sure to ask the lawyer why he left each position. Did the lawyer ever work as a government lawyer? Was he ever employed by a corporation, academia or a private or public foundation? Such experiences can provide the lawyer with valuable perspectives.

In short, find out how the lawyer has spent his career to this point in time and, if possible, why.

Ask whether the lawyer is a member of any legal organizations or associations. In this regard, keep in mind that membership in certain national, state and local bar associations is nothing more than a matter of paying the annual dues. Membership in some associations is mandatory. In order to practice law, a lawyer must be admitted to the bar of the state in which he plans to practice.

This is not to criticize membership in such associations—although some of them deserve criticism on other grounds. It is only to say that you should distinguish between those associations whose membership requirements involve nothing more than payment of the annual dues and those which reflect some degree of achievement or merit. In the latter group are such organizations as the American College of Trial Lawyers and the American Board of Trial Advocates.

Ask the lawyer how he stays abreast of new developments in the law. Good lawyers spend a certain amount of time every week reading what are referred to in the profession as advance sheets.

Advance sheets are compilations of new decisions issued by appellate courts and certain trial courts. Once a court issues a written decision, that decision becomes part of the body of the common law. There is a gap between the time a decision is first issued and the time it appears in published form. Some decisions are never actually "published," while others are published in a limited fashion. Good lawyers realize that they must be aware of those decisions long before the decisions appear in a hard bound book. Accordingly, good lawyers use advance sheets—or computerized research services—to ensure that they are aware of the latest rulings.

Most states require lawyers to attend a certain number of continuing legal education seminars each year. Ask your candidate if he does so. Better yet, ask the lawyer if he teaches any of the seminars. Does the lawyer engage in any teaching activity related to the law?

Paper credentials should be scrutinized, but with caution. While help-ful, credentials alone should not determine your selection of a law-yer.

"How Would You Handle This Case?"

Ask the lawyer to give you an idea of how he proposes to handle your case. By this point, you will have given the lawyer certain basic facts about your case. While it is unreasonable to expect the lawyer to provide a comprehensive litigation plan on the basis of piecemeal information, the lawyer should be able to describe a broad strategy.

How many lawyers and paralegals will be used on the case? Who will perform most of the work? What tasks will the lawyer delegate to younger lawyers or paralegals? Does a counterclaim or cross claim appear to be warranted? Are there legal defenses which might allow you to dispose of the case with an appropriate motion? Does the case appear to be pending in the proper court?

You are looking for a lawyer with a plan of action. Litigants whose plan consists of reacting to their adversary's actions are at a signifi-cant disadvantage. Look for a lawyer who has specific ideas about the way litigation should be handled in general, as well as some prelimi-nary goals regarding your case and strategies to achieve those goals.

"Why Should I Hire You?"

Ask each candidate to articulate why you should hire that particular lawyer or firm. You may be surprised at some of the responses. Even if the response is predictable—"I think we can provide you with qual-ity service at a fair price"—the manner in which the response is de-livered may give you additional information on which to base your decision.

Many lawyers are uncomfortable or clumsy when it comes to selling themselves. The lawyer who can talk a dog off a gut rag when arguing on behalf of his client may be incapable of articulating why you should hire him as your lawyer. Nevertheless, a lawyer ought to know and be able to articulate why he deserves to be hired. While you should not place inordinate emphasis on the response to this question, it is a question which may reveal a good deal about the lawyer.

Closing the Deal

Upon completion of the interviews, evaluate each of the prospective lawyers on the basis of all of the foregoing points. Like all business decisions, your selection of a lawyer is deserving of your full attention and careful consideration. If there is no clear choice, conduct additional interviews with the most promising candidates. You may also wish to provide the remaining candidates with additional information about your case and request a more detailed proposal regarding their proposed plan of action.

When larger projects or cases are involved, some clients require the candidates to make competing presentations, sometimes in the presence of the other prospective lawyers. You may decide to require the remaining candidates to submit written proposals, complete with specific financial parameters. Some municipalities now require lawyers to submit proposals containing a guaranteed maximum price. Employ whatever methodology you believe will provide you with the information you need to make an informed decision.

In making your selection, keep in mind those qualities which you value above all others. Each business person will have a different list of most valued qualities. For my money, those qualities are honesty, industry and professional excellence.

> **Honesty:** If your lawyer is honest, many of the situations discussed in this book will never materialize. You want a lawyer who will be honest in all respects. You want a lawyer who will tell you the truth, even when the truth may be painful, embarrassing or expensive. Avoid sycophants and grovelers. Although they may be pleasing to your ego in the short run, they will ultimately lead you to ruin.

Industry: Choose a lawyer who is willing and able to devote long hours to your case. In most lawsuits, the lawyer who is better prepared will prevail. Select a lawyer who will give each facet of your case the time and attention it deserves.

Professional Excellence: Select a lawyer who has demonstrated the ability to achieve favorable results for her clients. Plenty of honest, hard working lawyers regularly lose cases because they do not possess the skills necessary to succeed in today's civil litigation system. Hire a lawyer who has demonstrated that she knows what needs to be done and how to do it in the most efficient manner possible.

Instincts Can Carry the Day

Trust your instincts. When all of the information has been distilled, you may be left with two candidates who are equally qualified on paper. Despite this, you feel more comfortable with Lawyer Smith than with Lawyer Jones. In such instances, your instincts should carry the day. Assuming both lawyers meet all of the objective criteria, you will seldom err by following your instincts. Hire Lawyer Smith instead of Lawyer Jones.

Demand excellence. Never hire a lawyer about whom you have nagging doubts. If the initial round of interviews doesn't produce at least one lawyer in whom you feel complete confidence, keep looking. There are close to 900,000 lawyers in the United States. One of them has an invoice with your name on it.

When you have made your decision, write each of the lawyers who are not selected to thank them for their interest and to confirm that they will not be representing you on this matter. Next, enter into a written agreement with the lawyer you selected. The written agreement may be nothing more than a one-page letter. In other cases, a more formal agreement is appropriate. In either event, the central terms of the agreement should be set out in writing to avoid future disputes regarding fees, the lawyer's duties or any other matter.

The engagement letter is not a superfluous instrument devised by lawyers to limit their liability. There are a host of issues associated with the hiring of a lawyer. When does the lawyer's employment begin? What will the lawyer charge you for his services? Under what circumstances may you discharge the lawyer? By addressing these issues at the outset of the relationship, you protect yourself and your business against the faulty memories that the passage of time can produce.

I am sometimes asked to identify the most common mistakes made by business persons in hiring a new lawyer. Over the years, certain mistakes reappear with metronomic regularity:

- hiring a lawyer without a personal interview,

- hiring a lawyer on the basis of price alone,

- waiting until the last minute to hire a lawyer,

- failing to investigate the lawyer's background sufficiently before hiring the lawyer,

- failing to consider or interview a sufficiently broad pool of potential lawyers,

- allowing yourself to be unduly influenced by the lawyer's paper credentials or the reputation of the law firm,

- hiring neighbors, relatives, or friends,

- hiring a lawyer who has no experience with your type of case,

- hiring a lawyer on the basis of convenience, and

- hiring a lawyer about whom you have doubts.

Chapter Six

What You Should Know About Law Firms

Law firms are the places where many lawyers ply their trade. As such, they merit some scrutiny by clients. Law firms can have a substantial effect upon the conduct of your lawyer. In order to manage your lawyer effectively, you need an understanding of the law firm in which the lawyer practices.

In Their Lair

Law firms are alliances of lawyers. They develop from, among other things, the desire of lawyers to band with other lawyers to increase their resources, their revenues and their ability to provide services to their shared clients.

The desire for collegiality and for plain old-fashioned help with legal problems have always been motivating factors in the formation of law firms. Nevertheless, today's law firms—regardless of size—are the result of economic imperatives. The law firm is an economic unit whose goal is to sell legal services and produce a profit.

Lawyers spend a good deal of time these days talking about the business aspects of the practice of law. Many tout their adoption of time-honored business strategies (such as quality control, long-term planning and target marketing) as evidence that lawyers have moved grudgingly into the twentieth century.

On the other hand, some commentators have deplored the business ethic which has taken hold among lawyers—especially younger ones.

While it is likely that today's lawyer spends more time on business issues than lawyers fifty years ago, it is also true that the vast majority of lawyers consider themselves to be lawyers first and business people in their spare time.

This is not necessarily a bad thing for clients. A lawyer's first duty is to tend to and protect the client's interests, even at the cost of neglecting the law firm's business affairs. Most lawyers take this ethical obligation seriously and deal with their firm's business affairs only after the client's affairs have been addressed.

Still, most lawyers are not particularly good business people. That's one reason why they became lawyers. This will come as no surprise to most business people who have had occasion to work with lawyers. This shortcoming is sometimes evident in the way many law firms are structured and managed.

Law firms are structured in a variety of ways. Some firms are hierarchical and are run by a small number of lawyers. Other firms are democratic to a fault, discussing and voting upon every decision including how much wine to order for the Christmas party. Some firms are centralized, while others are excessively decentralized. Some firms have two lawyers, others have two thousand.

All law firms share one element—they are comprised of a number of lawyers, each of which has a particular function. A working knowledge of those functions is essential to taming your lawyer. What follows is a review of the people you are likely to find in most law firms and the services they provide.

The Junior Associate

Generally, this is a lawyer who has been practicing less than two or three years. In the pantheon of lawyers, junior associates are the lowest of the low. Inexperienced, ill-equipped by law school to do anything other than legal research, this is the lawyer to whom the most basic, mind-numbing, tedious assignments are given. The junior associate typically has no management responsibilities, although in some firms the junior associate is responsible for supervising the work of a paralegal assistant.

The junior associate's job is to do whatever work is placed in front of him without question and in large quantities. It is not unusual for junior associates in both large and small law firms to be required to bill two thousand hours per year. Assuming two weeks of vacation (for such frivolities as Christmas, Hanukkah and national holidays), this translates into *billing* forty hours each week, which can require fifty to seventy hours at work. Every week. Without fail.

The junior associate is often expected to learn his trade by osmosis— that is, by practicing law and by observing senior attorneys at work. While many law firms have structured training programs and local bar associations provide introductory seminars for new lawyers, the junior associate receives most of his training while performing the tasks which have been assigned to him.

The tasks assigned to a junior associate include legal research, the drafting of legal memoranda, the preliminary drafting of certain pleadings and briefs, investigatory work, document review, initial interviewing of witnesses and assisting the more senior lawyers in whatever way those senior lawyers deem appropriate. In many firms, there is little or no distinction between a junior associate and a mid-level associate. In short, the junior associate's role is to do the work, do lots of it, avoid making any mistakes, and try to learn how to be a good lawyer in the process.

Associates are salaried employees of the law firm. Their level of compensation depends on market conditions, the amount of business a firm has, and the profitability of the firm. At least initially, associates are paid on the basis of their experience (or lack thereof).

All of the first-year associates at a law firm are likely to be paid the same salary. Some firms continue the lock step compensation of associates based upon their level of experience for a number of years. Other firms begin to make distinctions among lawyers of equal seniority at an early juncture.

Starting salaries for first-year associates are widely publicized within the legal profession. As a result, it is this salary that is most subject to market forces. While starting salaries vary from firm to firm and city to city, these are representative starting salaries at certain large firms in 1995:

City	Starting salary
Atlanta	$60,000
Boston	68,000
Chicago	70,000
Houston	62,000
Los Angeles	72,000
Miami	64,000
New York	87,000
San Francisco	67,000
Washington, D.C.	74,000

Despite these lucrative salaries, the associate is a profit center for the law firm. Most associates produce revenue for the firm by selling their time (i.e., billing) at an hourly rate. Law firms typically require associates to bill between 1,800 and 2,200 hours each year.

In most medium and large cities, first-year associates bill their time at anywhere from $80 to $105 per hour. An associate's billing rate is generally increased as the lawyer acquires more experience. In an typical model, a firm's first-year lawyers might bill their time at $80 per hour, while second-year lawyers would bill their time at $90 per hour, third-year lawyers at $100 per hour and so forth.

These hourly billing rates ensure that an associate who fulfills his quota of billable hours will produce a profit for the law firm. Assume that an associate is paid $70,000 per year. The associate bills two thousand hours per year at $90 per hour. On paper, the associate has produced $180,000 of revenue. Assume that 15 percent of the billings are uncollectible or can't be billed to the client ($27,000) and that the associate's health insurance, social security and other incidentals raise the true annual cost of the associate by 20 percent to $84,000 per year. The associate has still produced a $69,000 profit for the law firm. The tacit understanding is that in exchange for the associate's production of this profit, the law firm will provide the associate with a salary, work to perform, training and an introduction to clients.

The Mid-Level Associate

The mid-level associate is a junior associate with more experience. A mid-level associate has been practicing for three to five years. She is given increased responsibility over cases, sometimes handling smaller cases on her own. She begins to have some supervisory responsibility over junior associates. She may perform less legal research herself and begins to argue motions and take depositions.

The mid-level associate is often the second in command in the trial of small to medium cases and in some firms is allowed to try cases on her own—often with a more senior lawyer in attendance to provide assistance if needed.

The primary responsibility of the mid-level associate remains the billing of hours, but she is also expected to begin to demonstrate an ability to take on more complicated and demanding tasks. The mid-level associate often edits the work of the junior associate before presenting it to the senior associate or partner for final approval.

The Senior Associate

The senior associate has been practicing between five and eight years. Senior associates are often a firm's work horses. They have enough experience to be efficient, yet retain high levels of energy. They are some of a firm's most valuable lawyers.

Senior associates retain their billable hour quotas. In addition to doing their own work, however, senior associates are given the responsibility of managing one or more mid-level or junior associates, as well as one or more paralegal assistants.

In many firms, the senior associates edit the work produced by junior and mid-level associates before presenting it to the partner for final approval. Senior associates are often given the responsibility for the day-to-day training of younger associates. Senior associates are the lawyers from whom many young associates acquire the greatest amount of knowledge and training.

Senior associates are most concerned with being elevated to partnership. Law firm associates are much like medieval apprentices. They work under the tutelage of the master tradesman, hoping to gain sufficient skill and knowledge—not to mention clients—to be admitted to the charmed circle of partnership. To that end, a senior associate is expected to:

- bill at least her quota of billable hours (more is always better),
- supervise and train younger lawyers and paralegals,
- have significant contact with the clients with an eye toward making the clients comfortable with the senior associate performing tasks in lieu of the partner,
- acquire new clients of her own, and
- develop expertise in one or more specific areas of law.

Senior associates are very busy people.

Of Counsel

Lawyers designated as *Of Counsel* are too old to be considered associates but are not partners either. Neither fish nor fowl, Of Counsel attorneys arrive at this station in a number of ways.

Some Of Counsel lawyers are senior lawyers who have been hired laterally from another firm, a corporation, academia or government. The firm doesn't have enough experience with this lawyer to make her a partner, but partnership may be in the offing if the lawyer's practice and personality mesh well with the firm's practice.

Other Of Counsel lawyers are senior associates whom the firm does not want to elevate to partnership for one reason or another (such as, for example, the inability to generate her own clients). Despite this, the lawyer is a talented lawyer who remains an asset to the firm and the firm wishes to continue to employ the lawyer as a high-salaried employee.

Lawyers who are designated Of Counsel often represent a good value to the careful client. They can often provide the same level of advice as a full-fledged partner at an hourly rate which is less than the partner's rate.

The Non-Equity Partner

Until recent years, there were only two classifications of lawyers in many law firms—partners and associates. The partners were the owners of the firm. They hired the employees, paid the expenses and kept whatever was left as a profit.

Associates aspired to partnership in part—in large part—because they wanted the opportunity to share in the firm's profits. Partnership also meant liability for the firm's debts and some uncertainty as to the level of compensation, but most law firms were profitable and lawyers were more than willing to accept the small risk of failure in exchange for the anticipated profits associated with partnership.

One facet of the old system was that a so-called "up-or-out" decision had to be made regarding an associate after the associate reached a certain level of experience—usually six to nine years of practice, depending on the firm. At the end of the designated period of apprenticeship, the associate was either made a full equity partner in the firm or was told that she was not going to be made a partner and should therefore pursue opportunities elsewhere.

While efficient in one sense (few disgruntled lawyers stuck around to foment dissent), the up-or-out system was wasteful in another sense. Firms often spent six to nine years training the lawyer, familiarizing her with the firm's clients, and trying to instill those clients with confidence in her, only to dismiss the lawyer when she had achieved what may be her highest levels of efficiency and productivity.

If it could avoid the up-or-out decision, the firm could continue to sell the services of the lawyer for a healthy profit if it chose to do so. Nevertheless, if the firm decided not to offer partnership to the lawyer, the up-or-out system meant that the firm would no longer employ the lawyer.

Law firms began to realize the inherent inefficiency of this system in the early 1980s. In response, many law firms created the position of non-equity partner. This position was and is known by different names in different firms: non-voting partner, non-participating partner, permanent associate, and even Of Counsel in some firms.

Whatever the name, the position is usually defined by the absence of the right to participate on a percentage basis in the profits of the firm. Non-equity partners are not owners of the firm in the sense that full or participating partners are. They are assigned a specific—and often quite comfortable—salary and may be eligible for performance bonuses, but they are not entitled to a share of the firm's profits. Nor are they liable for the firm's debts.

In some instances, non-equity partners do not have the right to vote on partnership issues and are not consulted regarding the selection of new partners. In some firms, non-equity partners can become equity partners at some point in the future.

In most other respects, though, non-equity partners resemble equity partners and provide the same services as equity partners. Many firms will not reveal which of their partners are non-equity partners, fearing that the non-equity designation might undermine the client's confidence in that lawyer.

Keep in mind that the decision to award a full equity partnership to a lawyer is often related to the lawyer's ability (or *perceived* ability) to develop business. This, of course, may have very little to do with that lawyer's legal skills. In light of this, you should not attach a stigma to the non-equity partner designation.

Non-equity partners often provide a good value to the client. In some firms, the billing rates of non-equity partners are less than the billing rates of equity partners. Non-equity partners are usually free from the business development concerns and pressures experienced by equity partners. So, in many cases, a non-equity partner may be able to devote greater attention and energy to your problem than an equity partner might.

The Junior Equity Partner

Junior equity partners are senior associates who have been elected to the partnership recently. Junior partners have usually been practicing law less than fifteen years—but the designation junior partner sometimes follows them until they retire.

Some firms refer to only the name partners (those partners whose names appear in the name of the firm) as senior partners. Everyone else is considered a junior partner. Other firms award the designation senior partner to the lawyers who founded the firm, semi-retired partners or partners who have achieved a certain chronological age.

For our purposes, we will define junior partners as those lawyers who have been partners for ten years or less.

Junior partners are the junior executives of law firms. They supervise the work, taking primary responsibility for bringing matters to a successful conclusion. They train younger lawyers, with the help of senior associates. Although in many firms partners do not have a specific quota of billable hours, many junior partners bill close to the number of hours they billed as senior associates.

Junior partners are expected to maintain existing client relationships and to attract new clients. Junior partners are usually given responsibility for numerous matters associated with firm administration such as hiring the staff, employee relations, dealing with the landlord, insurance, health benefits, firm parties and the like.

The ability to manage existing business and attract new business is the most valued attribute of a junior partner. Partnership shares—sometimes called *points*—are determined in a variety of ways, but the ability to attract and keep clients is often the most important factor.

The junior partner is an experienced lawyer who sometimes finds himself spending more time supervising associates, attempting to develop business and handling administrative chores than practicing law.

The Senior Equity Partner

Senior equity partners are the lawyers who founded the firm, run the firm or control the greatest amount of business. In most firms, senior partners are the most experienced lawyers in the firm. They are the lawyers who, by dint of election, client base, or moral authority, run the law firm and establish its policies.

In some law firms, senior partners function as *rainmakers*, with the responsibility for generating business for the firm. In other firms, senior partners are the most prolific billers of hours and spend all of their time providing legal services to clients.

Senior partners are usually the most highly compensated lawyers in the firm. Their hourly rates are usually the highest. In most firms, senior partners are the lawyers who bear the ultimate responsibility for the success or failure of the law firm.

Clients sometimes assume that their interests would be best served by insisting that their case be handled by one of the firm's senior partners. They reason that the senior partner possesses the most experience and therefore can provide the highest level of service. This is only true in certain cases.

While the senior partner may have practiced law longer than other lawyers in the firm, his experience in a particular type of lawsuit may be less than the experience of other lawyers in the firm. Moreover, the senior partner's duties in the firm may involve the generation of new business rather than the actual handling of specific cases. If so, the senior partner's last foray into court may have occurred during the Eisenhower administration.

The hazards of using a senior partner for your case are illustrated by a remark made by the senior litigator in the 180-lawyer firm where I went to work after law school. When asked by a new client how far his office was from the library, the senior partner replied "About twenty years."

In such instances, your interests may be better served by using one of the firm's younger and less expensive lawyers.

Paralegal Assistants

In addition to the lawyers, law firms employ non-lawyer staff members to assist them in providing legal services. Most of these positions are analogous to positions found in the business world—secretaries, bookkeepers, office managers, receptionists, messengers and the like. There is one position, however, that warrants a closer look.

Paralegal assistants have been a part of the practice of law, in some form, for many years. In recent years, however, the position has become more specialized and has produced confusion in some quarters.

A paralegal assistant—often referred to simply as a *paralegal*—is an administrative assistant whose duties entail assisting the lawyer in providing services to the client. A paralegal is not a lawyer, although many paralegals become lawyers. Most, but not all, paralegals are college graduates.

Many paralegals have graduated from paralegal schools which provide technical training. Although paralegal schools have been established in every major city, there is no standard course of study, nor are there universally accepted standards regarding the training a person must receive in order to become a paralegal.

The course of study at most paralegal schools involves an introduction to various substantive areas of law, as well as practical skills such as document-control techniques. The full-time student can typically complete paralegal school in three to four months.

Paralegals perform a host of functions. Simply put, paralegals do just about anything a lawyer might need in the representation of a client. Paralegals review documents, write factual memoranda, interview witnesses, assemble exhibits, prepare charts and graphs, and summarize depositions. Some lawyers use paralegals to prepare preliminary drafts of pleadings or to perform quasi-legal tasks such as summarizing legal opinions.

While some lawyers use paralegals to perform legal research, in my view this practice is ill-advised and dangerous for the client.

It is important to understand the paralegal's functions because law firms bill their clients for the paralegal's services on an hourly basis. Paralegal time is billed to the client in the same fashion as lawyer time, albeit at a lower rate.

Paralegals are healthy profit centers for law firms. Assume that a firm pays a paralegal $28,000 per year and requires the paralegal to bill 1,500 hours per year at the rate of $55 per hour. Again, let's assume that (1) medical insurance, social security and other incidentals increase the true cost of the paralegal 20 percent to $33,600 and (2) 15 percent of the time billed by the paralegal is uncollectible or can't be billed to the client (i.e., $12,375). The paralegal still produces an annual profit of $36,525. Not a bad return on an investment of $33,600.

Law Firm Dynamics

Because a substantial amount of commercial litigation is undertaken by lawyers working in law firms rather than sole practitioners, it is instructive to review some of the dynamics at work in most law firms. An awareness of these factors can assist the business person in managing her lawyer and developing a smooth working relationship with the law firm.

While the described dynamics do not exist in every firm, they are present in some form in the majority of firms, both large and small.

Legal Services for Profit

Law firms exist in order to provide legal services for profit. While it is true that there is a public service aspect to the practice of law, firms are established and operated to produce revenue and provide a livelihood for the lawyers and their employees. In this regard, law firms resemble the vast majority of businesses.

Many lawyers pay little attention to this central tenet. A large number of lawyers regard the business aspects of law practice as a secondary concern and, in some cases, an intrusion into their mission of dispensing justice. Even the more pragmatic lawyers tend to focus on the substance of legal representation, often at the expense of the fiscal well-being of their law firm.

In successful law firms, one or more partners pay substantial attention to the business affairs of the firm. This responsibility is often assigned to a small number of lawyers, with the intention of allowing the remaining lawyers to focus on the practice of law. This dichotomy can in some instances pose a risk for the client.

Law firms are managed in a variety of ways. Whatever the management structure, the real power in any law firm lies with the lawyers who control the most business. This is not necessarily the best lawyer in the law firm. The best technical lawyer is sometimes unable or unwilling to develop a broad client base.

The most powerful lawyer in the firm is the one who has the most clients. These clients may have been developed by providing outstanding legal services, by displaying superior social skills, through effective promotion and marketing or as a result of marrying the daughter or son of the president of the local bank. Regardless of the fashion in which the clients were acquired, the lawyer who controls the business is the most powerful lawyer in the firm.

Relatively few law firms are well-managed and operated in a conventional business sense. While the management techniques and business practices employed by many law firms are adequate, an equal or larger number are managed haphazardly. Lawyers perceive themselves—correctly—as lawyers first and business people second.

Accordingly, the business aspects of a law practice suffer. This situation can affect the client. Inaccurate bills, unreturned phone calls, unpredictable scheduling, missed meetings, and consistent employee turnover are a number of the problems which may exist as a result of a law firm's inefficient business practices.

How Lawyers Advance

There are three ways in which a lawyer can bring value to a law firm. The first (and most important) is to generate business for the law firm. This task is typically undertaken by the partners of the firm.

Second, a lawyer may supervise the work which is being performed by other lawyers in the law firm. This work is often performed by partners and in some cases by senior associates.

Third, a lawyer may perform the work. While all of the lawyers in a firm perform the work, the majority of the work is actually performed by the associates and the junior partners.

Identification of these tasks becomes relevant to the client because the client needs to know what services he is purchasing with his legal fees. You may think that you are hiring a partner to represent you in the lawsuit, only to discover that most of the work is being performed by a junior associate whom you've never met. While there are many instances in which such an arrangement is both appropriate and cost effective, it is imperative that the client discuss such matters with the law firm in advance. You need to know which lawyers will be providing which services.

Many law firms are built on the principle of leverage. The lawyers at the top of the firm pyramid seek to generate enough business to employ a number of broad levels of less experienced lawyers. Each associate represents a potential profit for the firm. If one associate generates $69,000 in profit, ten associates could generate $690,000 in profit.

Even a lawyer can grasp the significance of this arithmetic. As a general proposition, so long as there is enough work for the associates to meet their hourly quotas, more associates mean larger profits—especially for the lawyers at the top of the pyramid.

Consequently, many law firms strive to develop enough new business to justify the hiring of additional associates.

As a general proposition, there is nothing wrong with this approach. It is a fundamental goal of business to seek to increase revenues. There is, however, a danger associated with this tenet as it applies to law firms. The knowledge that additional associates can produce greater profits can create a subconscious—but very real—temptation to create work in order to justify the hiring of additional associates.

In this context, *creating work* does not refer to the generation of new clients. It refers to the creation of additional tasks to be undertaken in the course of the representation of current clients.

In most instances, the creation of additional tasks in a lawsuit is a function of the desire to leave no stone unturned and to avoid malpractice. Nevertheless, economic factors (such as the pressure to bill additional hours, to be responsible for more associates, to produce greater revenue, and to expand the law firm itself) can create an atmosphere in which lawyers find themselves searching for—and creating—additional tasks.

In my experience, very few lawyers perform tasks which are of no value to the client. However, when a lawyer must decide whether to perform a particular task, the lawyer is likely to err on the side of prudence and more billable hours by deciding to perform the task.

You need to be aware that these forces are at work. Throughout your business relationship, you should discuss with your lawyer exactly why she is undertaking certain tasks.

Chapter Seven

Fee Arrangements

Lawyers bill for their services in a variety of ways. Different cases may call for varying types of fee arrangements. Unfortunately, lawyers who seem ready to talk about any subject under the sun become downright laconic when it comes to discussing their fees.

Whether due to embarrassment, oversight, arrogance or more venal motives, many lawyers fail to spend much time discussing fee arrangements with their clients in advance of rendering services. This is not a good thing for the client.

In order to make an informed decision regarding the fee arrangement which best serves your interests in a particular situation, you need a clear understanding of the types of fee arrangements available to you. While your lawyer may not offer all of the following fee arrangements, here's a look at the most prevalent fee arrangements, as well as some alternatives you may wish to suggest to your lawyer.

Fixed Fee

As the name implies, in a fixed fee billing arrangement the lawyer agrees to perform a service or services for a fee which is agreed upon in advance by the client and the lawyer. The fee is typically payable in a lump sum upon completion of the work, although in some instances the lawyer may require payment of a portion of the fee before work commences.

Fixed fees can be utilized for all or a portion of a case or other matter. For instance, the client and lawyer may agree that the lawyer will charge a fixed fee for a certain phase of the case, a certain type of activity—such as depositions—or even a certain period of time—say, $5,000 per month. By using this approach, clients can often predict and budget their legal costs with a greater degree of accuracy. This approach may also foster greater efficiency on the part of the lawyer.

Fixed fee billing arrangements are often used for services which do not vary a great deal from project to project. The incorporation of a business, the drafting of a will and the recording of a deed are examples of the types of tasks for which lawyers often charge a fixed fee.

Lawyers do not usually offer fixed fee billing arrangements for complicated or lengthy matters because it is too difficult to estimate the amount of time which will be required to complete the task.

While the lawyer can always make an educated estimate regarding the amount of time necessary to complete the task, the actual amount of time required will seldom match the estimate. Accordingly, either the client or the lawyer is likely to be short-changed.

If the lawyer underestimates the amount of time needed to complete the task, the lawyer is not compensated for all of the services provided. If, on the other hand, the lawyer overestimates the amount of time needed, the client will overpay the lawyer for the services provided.

arrangement. If the number is lower, he has made less money. In many cases, this computation is academic because the client does not have enough money to pay the lawyer's hourly fee and therefore a contingent fee arrangement is the only arrangement which is feasible for the client.

In contingent fee cases, the plaintiff's lawyer has a vested interest in any settlement. The larger the settlement, the larger the lawyer's fee. Unfortunately, some lawyers allow their personal economic interest to interfere with their judgment when advising a client whether to settle a case for a particular amount.

This dynamic is present to some extent even when the lawyer is being paid an hourly fee. If the case doesn't settle, the lawyer will have an opportunity to continue billing the client during the trial. But the financial pressures are much greater when the lawyer is being paid a contingent fee.

The majority of lawyers do not allow their personal financial interest to color their advice to their clients. Nevertheless, you should be aware of this possibility. If you have been sued and your reasonable settlement overtures have been rebuffed, it is possible that your opponent's lawyer may be part of the problem.

In the 1992 case of *Lewis v. Uselton*, the lawyer appears to have been part of the problem. The lawyer represented his clients in a personal injury case pursuant to a contingent fee agreement, which provided for a 40 percent fee. The agreement also provided:

> [Clients agree] that the said [attorney] shall have full power and authority to settle, compromise or take such action as he might deem proper....

The lawyer settled the case without the approval, and contrary to the wishes, of his clients. The attorney then sued his clients for his fees and his clients counterclaimed, alleging professional malpractice.

The attorney argued that the contract language gave him "full power and authority to settle, compromise or take such action as he might deem proper." He also stated that he had never told his clients that they had any authority over settlement of their case. Finally he argued that the 40 percent contingent fee arrangement made him a "40 percent partner" with his clients.

In affirming the trial court's denial of the lawyer's Motion for Summary Judgment, the Georgia Court of Appeals ruled that:

> [T]his...contract...gives the attorney no "right" to do anything the clients did not authorize him to do; it gives full "power and authority" to settle, compromise or take such action as he might deem proper," which is no more than the common authority attorneys have to implement settlements determined by the client....

> This "full power and authority" to settle accrued only after the amount of the settlement had been approved by the client....

The court emphatically declared "[a]n attorney's right to receive a contingent fee does not make the attorney a partner with his client for any purpose."

Contingent Fee Mechanics

The specifics of contingent fee arrangements are established by the client and the lawyer on a case-by-case basis. While certain percentages are charged more frequently than others, there are no guidelines or limits regarding the percentage fee a lawyer can charge so long as (1) the client agrees to the arrangement and (2) the arrangement does not favor the lawyer so blatantly that it violates the Canons of Ethics or attracts the attention of the local bar association or news media.

As a general matter, lawyers charge anywhere from 25 percent to 45 percent of a recovery as a contingent fee.

The percentage charged by the lawyer can vary depending on the stage of the case at which recovery is obtained. It is not uncommon, for example, for a lawyer to charge a contingent fee of 35 percent if the case is settled prior to trial, 40 percent if the case goes to trial and 45 percent if an appeal is necessary. Such staggered percentages reflect the additional amount of time which the lawyer can anticipate spending on the case.

A second type of staggered contingent fee ties the lawyer's percentage to the amount recovered. The lawyer and client may agree that the lawyer will receive 40 percent of any amount recovered up to $100,000, 20 percent of any amount recovered from $100,000 to $500,000 and 10 percent of any amount recovered in excess of $500,000. This approach allows the client to keep a greater percentage of the amount recovered as the amount of the recovery increases.

If, for example, the recovery is $750,000, under this arrangement the lawyer's fee would be $145,000 and the client would retain $605,000. Compared with the traditional one-third share for the lawyer—which would make the lawyer's fee $250,000 and the client's share $500,000—this represents a more desirable arrangement for the client.

Some lawyers prefer a staggered contingent fee arrangement which places a higher premium on the large recovery in exchange for a smaller percentage of a lesser recovery. In such an arrangement, a lawyer might agree to take 10 percent of any amount up to $250,000 in exchange for 40 percent of any amount in excess of $250,000. Again assuming a $750,000 recovery, this arrangement would produce a lawyer's fee of $225,000 and a client's share of $525,000.

One aspect of contingent fee billing arrangements which causes confusion involves how the expenses of the litigation are calculated and when they are deducted. Although the treatment of expenses is an issue which can be resolved in any way which is acceptable to both the client and the lawyer, the most prevalent arrangement is for the expenses to be deducted from the client's portion of the recovery.

Assume, for example, that the client and the lawyer agree that the lawyer's fee will be 30 percent of any recovery and that expenses will be deducted from the client's share of the recovery. If the lawsuit results in a settlement of $100,000 and the expenses total $9,000, the lawyer's fee will be $30,000 (30 percent of $100,000). The client's share of the recovery is $70,000, less the $9,000 in expenses, which produces a net recovery of $61,000.

An alternative—but less widely used—arrangement would be for the client and the lawyer to share the cost of the expenses. To accomplish this, the expenses are deducted from the settlement amount before the lawyer's fee is calculated. Using the above figures, the $9,000 in legal expenses would be subtracted from the $100,000 recovery before the lawyer's fee is calculated. Accordingly, the lawyer's fee would be $27,300 (30 percent of $91,000) and the client's net recovery would be $63,700.

It should also be noted that the expenses of litigation can mount very quickly. When lawyers refer to litigation expenses, they are referring to the out-of-pocket costs associated with the lawsuit. Litigation expenses include such items as court costs, copying costs, postage, travel expenses and court reporter fees. These expenses can become a major portion of the total cost of a lawsuit. In most instances, clients are expected to pay these expenses as they arise. In some instances, the lawyer may advance the cost of the expenses to his client, subject to a final accounting at the end of the case.

Hourly Fee

The most widely used method of compensating lawyers is to pay the lawyer for the time the lawyer works on a matter on the basis of an hourly fee. The lawyer records the time spent and bills the client— usually on a monthly basis—for that time. The lawyer presents to the client an itemized statement summarizing the time spent by each lawyer or paralegal on the case, a description of the services provided, a summary of the expenses incurred and a total invoice amount. Hours are usually divided into increments of five, six or ten minutes.

In this fashion, the firm keeps track of all of the time spent by its lawyers and paralegals on a particular matter.

The hourly fee charged by lawyers for their time varies from firm to firm and city to city. As a general proposition, the rates charged by lawyers increase on the basis of the size of the city, the specialized nature of the services provided and the experience of the lawyer. In larger cities, many firms charge anywhere from $80 to $200 per hour for an associate and from $125 to $450 per hour for a partner. Paralegal time is often billed at $40 to $80 per hour.

Lawyers can be called a lot of things, but inexpensive isn't one of them.

How, exactly, do lawyers keep track of the time they spend on a particular matter? The methods employed are almost as varied as lawyers themselves. Most law firms have standardized time-keeping systems which are utilized by the lawyers in the firm.

A record-keeping system used by many lawyers involves a time sheet which divides the work day into five- or six-minute blocks of time. As the lawyer begins to work on one case, she draws a line across the page and fills in the name of the case on which she is working. When she stops working on that matter, the lawyer draws another line across the page to reflect that she has stopped working on that case. At that time, the lawyer enters a brief narrative reflecting the services which were provided during the preceding time period. This time keeping method is reflected in Figure 7-1.

Figure 7-1

Date: 3/24/95   Lawyer: Green

```
7:00 ——————————————
:06 Jones—Draft interrogatories
:12
:18 ——————————————
:24 X——————————————
:30 Smith—Telephone call with
:36         Attorney Stevens. Correspondence
:42         to Attorney Stevens. Preparation
:48          for meeting with J. Brown.
:54
8:00
:06
:12
:18
:24
:30 ——————————————————
:36 Jones—Meeting with P. Poindexter
:42
:48
:54
9:00
:06
:12
:18 ————————————————————
:24 Brown—Legal research re: waiver
:30
:36
```

You may be thinking that this system is a lot like the system used by taxi cab drivers. You are right.

In Figure 7-1, Lawyer Green worked on the Jones case drafting interrogatories from 7:00 a.m. to 7:18 a.m. (eighteen minutes or three tenths of an hour). She took a break between 7:18 and 7:24. She began working on the Smith case at 7:24 and worked on that case until 8:30. In that time period, she spoke to opposing counsel about the case, wrote a letter to opposing counsel and prepared for a meeting with a witness. At 8:30 she had a meeting with a potential witness in the Jones case for 48 minutes.

If Lawyer Green doesn't spend any more time working on the Jones case on that day—and if no other lawyers or paralegals worked on the case on that day—at the end of the month the Jones Company's bill will reflect that on March 24, 1995, Lawyer Green spent 1.1 hours working on its case. Assuming Lawyer Green's hourly rate is $125 per hour, the fee for the work on that day would be $137.50.

An alternative time-keeping system employed by many firms is to use a separate daily time sheet for each file. The lawyer records the tasks performed and the amount of time expended on each task as the day progresses.

Each time a lawyer works on a particular file during the course of the day, she records what service she provided and how much time was expended providing that service. At the end of each day, the amount of time spent on each case is totaled. The narrative, amount of time and fee are then transferred to the monthly bill in the fashion described above. This time-keeping system is reflected in Figure 7-2.

Figure 7-2

Lawyer: Green   File: Jones   Date: 3/24/95

Draft Interrogatories .3
Meeting with P. Poindexter .8

DAILY TOTAL 1.1

Some lawyers may tell you that they can mentally track the time they spend on your case and will only record the time at the end of the day (or, in some cases, at the end of a number of days or a week). This is a dangerous practice which produces errors regarding the time spent on a file. Trying to recreate how you spent every minute of your day is difficult enough if you record each activity as it occurs.

To reconstruct a day in detail after several days have passed is beyond the ability of most human beings. A lawyer who doesn't record tasks as they are performed inevitably begins to estimate the time spent on a matter. That estimate will be wrong a fair number of times and either the lawyer—sometimes—or the client—usually—will suffer.

When you employ a lawyer on an hourly basis, be sure to ask the lawyer what method she uses to record her time.

Even when a lawyer records tasks as they are performed, gray areas exist. If a lawyer spends an entire morning working on a single matter, does he subtract from his total the trip down the hall to get a cup of coffee and the two bathroom breaks? How about that two-minute phone call from his wife—during which he continued to edit a set of interrogatories? Such questions underscore the fact that hourly fee arrangements are based in large part upon the honor system.

As a practical matter, there is no way for you to know whether your lawyer spent two hours or three hours drafting a set of interrogatories. You must rely on the lawyer to record the time spent on your case honestly and accurately. This is just one of the reasons why you should take great care in selecting a lawyer.

This said, you should still review each bill to determine whether your lawyer has been spending his time and your money in a sensible fashion. A close review of the monthly bills is an essential element in controlling your legal costs.

There are other time-related issues which you should consider. Assume, for example, that a case requires a lawyer to take a deposition out of town. It will take the lawyer three hours to reach the site of the deposition. Does the lawyer charge the client the travel time? What if lawyer is on an airplane during the three hours watching the in-flight movie? Should the client be charged for the travel time? What if the lawyer is preparing for the deposition during the flight?

What if the lawyer decides to drive to the site of the deposition and prepare for the deposition during the drive by having someone else drive the car or having someone read deposition testimony to him during the drive?

These questions can only be resolved by specific agreement between the lawyer and the client. Some agreements call for all travel time to be billable, regardless of whether the lawyer is working on the case while in transit. Such an agreement is based on the premise that the lawyer is required to travel as part of the representation and that the lawyer is usually unable to work on other matters while in transit.

Other agreements state that travel time is billable only when the lawyer is working on the case while in transit. Under such an agreement, the lawyer could bill the client for the time on the airplane if he is working on the case during the flight, but not if he decides to watch the in-flight movie or spend the flight regaling his seat mate with tales of his legal victories. Still other agreements state that travel time is not billable under any circumstances.

These issues should be discussed by you and your lawyer at the outset of the representation. You should establish certain ground rules concerning the activities for which the lawyer will bill you. Invariably, situations will arise during the course of the representation which are not covered by the initial agreement. You and your lawyer should address those issues as they arise—preferably before the lawyer performs the task in question.

The Risk of Bill Padding

No discussion of hourly billing arrangements would be complete without a discussion of the problem of bill padding by lawyers. Bill padding is the practice of (1) charging clients for more time than was actually spent completing a particular task or (2) charging the client for work that did not take place at all.

I believe that only a small fraction of lawyers engage in bill padding. The vast majority of lawyers are honest and meticulous regarding their timekeeping and billing procedures. When questions arise concerning how much time was expended on a particular task, most lawyers err on the side of the client and charge the client for the shortest possible period of time.

Most lawyers regularly write off time expended on behalf of the client when the time spent was, for one reason or another, not appropriate. For example, if a young associate spends eight hours drafting interrogatories which could have been drafted in four hours (even by a young associate), the senior lawyer in charge of billing the client will often charge the client for four hours.

Nevertheless, the risk of bill padding does exist. Hourly billing arrangements create great pressure to produce billable hours. The lawyer whose livelihood depends on hourly fees may be tempted to increase his monthly revenues by reporting to the client that he spent eight hours writing a brief instead of the five hours actually expended. The associate laboring to meet his annual quota of billable hours may be tempted to report that he spent ten hours in the library researching a legal question rather than the four hours he spent there.

The not-so-meticulous lawyer who failed to record how much time he spent working on a particular file last week may be tempted to report the largest possible amount of time, just to be sure he doesn't short-change himself due to his failure to recall all of the time he spent on a task.

Once a lawyer rationalizes padding a bill—by telling himself "I should be charging this client a higher hourly rate anyway" or "I finished that quickly. The average lawyer would have taken twice as long. I'll charge the client a few extra hours"—a pattern is established and bill padding can become a regular part of that lawyer's practice.

Bill padding is difficult to detect and often impossible to prove. Many activities for which a lawyer bills a client are solitary activities. A lawyer sits at his desk and drafts a brief. There is no one standing at the lawyer's side to ensure that the lawyer is spending the time drafting the brief in question. A lawyer leaves his office at noon and doesn't return until the next day, at which point his time sheet shows ten hours of legal research. Did the lawyer stay at the library until it closed or did he spend the afternoon on the golf course?

The client cannot know how much legal research was necessary to prepare for a hearing or how long it took the lawyer to draft interrogatories or to prepare for a deposition. Certain extreme examples of bill padding would be apparent even to non-lawyers—such as, for example, a twenty-two hour telephone call with the judge. However, in the vast majority of situations, the client can not verify that the time for which the lawyer has billed was actually expended.

How, then, does a client insure that his lawyer is not padding the bills? The single best protection is, of course, to take great care in selecting your lawyer so that you are represented by an honest person. While this is the most important protection, this advice does not offer a great deal of help. This is reminiscent of the comedian who told his audience that he had a sure-fire way to become a millionaire: "First, you get a million dollars...."

Assuming that all clients strive to hire honest lawyers, the best way to prevent bill padding is to monitor your lawyer's activities closely. One way to do this is to scrutinize his bills.

In addition, let your lawyer know you are paying close attention to his work. At the outset of the representation, identify the tasks for which you are willing to pay and the tasks for which you are *not* willing to pay. Discuss both fee and expense items. Stay in close contact with your lawyer at each juncture of the representation. Establish clear procedures regarding which tasks the lawyer may undertake without prior consultation with you and which tasks require specific prior authorization. Require the lawyer to be able to explain why specific tasks required the amount of time reflected on the monthly bill.

Finally, review each entry on the monthly bill and discuss any entries which you do not understand or which do not appear to be reasonable. Even if you are unfortunate enough to have hired a dishonest lawyer, the knowledge that you are paying close attention to the bills may convince the lawyer to pad the bills of other, less watchful, clients.

Retainers

The term *retainer* is widely misunderstood by both clients and lawyers. A retainer is a sum of money paid by a client to a lawyer to guarantee that the lawyer will represent that client with regard to one or more current or future matters.

Years ago, when there were fewer lawyers around, clients would place a lawyer on retainer to ensure that the lawyer would be available in the event the client needed the lawyer and to prevent potential adversaries from hiring that lawyer.

A bank in a small town, for example, might pay a local lawyer $1,000 per year in exchange for the lawyer's promise to (1) represent the bank with regard to any legal problems which arose during the course of the year—at the lawyer's regular hourly fee, of course—and (2) forego representing clients involved in disputes with the bank.

In this manner, the bank could place the three best lawyers in town on retainer and never have to worry about being sued by those three lawyers. This would be a good investment even if the bank never called upon the lawyers to represent the bank.

In its original form, a retainer was a sum of money which did not constitute payment for specific legal services rendered by the lawyer. Rather, it was the consideration paid by the client in exchange for the lawyer's advance promise to represent the client if the need arose and to forego representing any of the client's adversaries. When and if the need for such representation arose, the client would pay the lawyer for the specific services provided.

An advance payment or fee, on the other hand, is payment in advance for specific legal services to be provided by the lawyer.

Especially when dealing with new clients, a lawyer may require that the client make an advance payment against future fees to ensure the client's solvency or seriousness about the case. In such instances, the lawyer might require the client to make a $5,000 advance payment to the lawyer with the understanding that the $5,000 will be credited against future legal fees. The lawyer then deposits the $5,000 into his escrow account and draws money out of the escrow account in payment for his services as they're rendered.

This procedure is sometimes followed throughout the course of the representation. If so, the client may be required to make additional advance payments. In other cases, the client and lawyer become comfortable with each other and the lawyer no longer requires advance payment. The lawyer then begins to bill the client for services on a monthly basis after the services have been rendered.

Confusion developed over the years as the concept of a retainer evolved. Clients began paying lawyers an advance fee and referring to it as a retainer. The retainer would be paid to the lawyer in exchange for the right to use as much—or, the lawyer hoped, as little— of the lawyer's time as needed by the client over the period of time covered by the retainer. The time period was usually a year.

In the standard arrangement, the local bank would pay the lawyer an annual fee or retainer (let's say $50,000—this was a long time ago) in exchange for the right to call upon the lawyer to provide whatever legal services the bank might need over the course of the year. The lawyer could count on $50,000 in revenue and, depending on the amount of work requested by the bank during the year, might not have to perform $50,000 worth of work. The bank capped its annual legal expenses and had a lawyer "on call" to handle any and all problems and projects which arose during the year.

Today, many companies use this sort of retainer for specific types of legal services. A company might have a lawyer or law firm on retainer to perform all of the company's regulatory work or to represent the company in all of its dealings with a particular government agency.

Lawyers and non-lawyers alike confuse retainers with advance payments. Lawyers often refer to advance payments as retainers, thus confusing the client as well. The distinguishing feature is that a retainer may not be tied directly to specific services provided by the lawyer, while an advance payment is. Retainers are typically non-refundable, even where few actual services are provided.

If, on the other hand, a client pays a lawyer an advance payment and the lawyer does not provide any services, the lawyer should—and usually does—refund the advance payment.

Alternative Fee Arrangements

Each of the traditional fee arrangements possesses certain shortcomings.

When a lawyer is working on an hourly fee arrangement, the lawyer has little incentive to work efficiently or to bring the matter to a quick conclusion. Indeed, the hourly fee arrangement often gives the lawyer an incentive to expend as much time as possible on a matter. Conversely, contingent fee and fixed fee arrangements may encourage a lawyer to spend as little time on a case as possible.

In response to these problems, and in an attempt to eliminate any financial conflicts of interest between lawyer and client, the business and legal communities have begun to develop a number of alternatives to the traditional fee arrangements. Widely referred to as *alternative billing methods* or *value billing*, these arrangements seek to provide lawyers with an incentive to perform efficiently by shifting a portion of the risk of the lawsuit or project from the client to the lawyer.

Variations on Hourly Fee Arrangements

Many alternative billing methods are nothing more than variations on traditional hourly fee arrangements. Nevertheless, these variations can reduce your company's legal fees and allow you to more accurately predict your legal expenses from year to year.

Blended Hourly Rates

A blended rate is a single rate charged for the work of all of the lawyers in the firm, regardless of their level of experience. In the traditional hourly rate fee arrangement, a firm might charge $175 per hour for work performed by a junior partner, $135 per hour for work performed by a senior associate and $95 per hour for work performed by a junior associate.

Under a blended hourly rate arrangement, the firm would charge an agreed-upon amount—let's say $125 per hour—for work performed by each of these lawyers.

The blended rate was developed by law firms in response to the reluctance of some clients to pay ever-escalating hourly rates for lawyers as those lawyers gained experience and seniority. By using a blended rate, the law firm could represent to its client that its highest hourly rate was $125 per hour.

But does a blended rate produce savings? Only in certain instances. Let's see how the math works. If each lawyer works 200 hours on the case, a blended rate would reduce your bill from $81,000 to $75,000 (a 7.4 percent savings). If the two senior lawyers each work 250 hours and the junior associate works only 100 hours, the savings is even greater—a reduction from $87,000 to $75,000 (a 13.8 percent savings).

On the other hand, if the majority of the work is performed by the junior member of the team, the blended rate works in favor of the law firm. If the junior associate works 300 hours and the two senior lawyers each work 100 hours on the case, your bill increases from $59,500 to $62,500 (an increase of 4.8 percent).

A blended rate favors the client only where the bulk of the work will be performed by the higher priced lawyers. If the least expensive lawyer will be doing most of the work, there is no financial incentive for the client to adopt the blended rate approach.

Some law firms that lobby for a blended rate assign the majority of the work to the youngest lawyer—with the lowest hourly rate. If you are considering a blended hourly rate fee arrangement, give careful consideration to which lawyers will be doing most of the work on your case.

Discounted Hourly Fee

Many law firms offer a discounted hourly fee in exchange for the promise of a certain volume of work. Some firms will discount their hourly fees in order to obtain a desirable case or to have the opportunity to perform work for a company the firm would like to develop as a continuing client.

The most prevalent discounting occurs in exchange for the promise of a certain volume of work. For example, if your company is required to deal with a governmental agency, a firm might agree to discount all of its regular hourly rates by 15 percent in exchange for your promise to use the firm for all of your dealings with the EPA.

These discounts can also be tied to a specific dollar value of work. In exchange for your promise of $500,000 in legal work over the course of a year, a firm might agree to a substantial discount in its standard hourly rates. This arrangement can benefit both the client and the law firm. The client, which will have to pay a lawyer to do the work anyway, obtains a discount. The law firm is assured of a certain amount of business.

Hourly Fee Caps

Some companies reduce their exposure to unexpected legal fees by establishing a cap on the fee they agree to pay for individual cases or projects. In this model, a client agrees to pay a lawyer or firm on the basis of an hourly rate for all work performed, with the caveat that the total amount which the client will pay for the project will not exceed a predetermined amount.

Assume that your company hires a lawyer to defend a lawsuit on the basis of an hourly rate of $150 per hour with a total fee cap of $100,000. The lawyer bills you for work performed at the rate of $150 per hour until the total billings reach $100,000. At that point, the lawyer stops billing you and pursues the case to completion without additional cost—unless you have agreed to pay all legal expenses, in which case you would continue to receive bills for expenses.

While this approach contains certain pitfalls, most of the problems can be overcome. If the guaranteed maximum amount is set too low, the lawyer will end up working for free in the later—and, arguably, most important—stages of the case. While in a perfect world this wouldn't affect the lawyer's performance, human nature suggests that the lawyer's performance might not be as vigorous once the fees stop flowing. To avoid this, take great care in establishing the amount of the cap. Invest the necessary time and money to develop a feasible and effective fee cap.

Not surprisingly, lawyers are not fond of this approach because it exposes them to the possibility of working for free—and because it establishes a ceiling on the fees which can be generated by a particular case. A lawyer has no real financial incentive to adopt such a fee arrangement other than the desire to land your business. Nevertheless, that desire may be powerful enough to persuade the lawyer to agree to a fee cap.

Some lawyers may accept guaranteed maximum price in exchange for the right to charge higher than normal hourly fees. If so, the lawyer is betting that the case can be resolved in a shorter amount of time. In one sense, the hourly rate is less important to the client in such an arrangement because the client may be most interested in establishing a ceiling on total legal fees.

Critics of this kind of arrangement argue that a guaranteed maximum fee may give the lawyer an incentive to run his fees up to the maximum amount regardless of whether the work is required by the case. While there may be some truth in this reasoning, there are several reasons it would be difficult for the lawyer to do this.

First, a lawyer has little control over when the case will end. Second, even if the lawyer knew when the case would end, it would be difficult for the lawyer to calibrate his work so that he could work the maximum allowable number of hours. Third, the lawyer still has to submit monthly bills outlining the work performed.

The client can monitor the lawyer's work on a monthly basis to ensure that the lawyer is not performing unnecessary tasks in an attempt to reach the guaranteed maximum fee level.

A more realistic concern is that the lawyer may forego essential tasks in an effort to avoid reaching the fee ceiling before the work is completed. Faced with a limited number of hours he can invest in the case, the lawyer might try to stockpile the available hours for use later in the litigation. In this scenario, important tasks might be left undone by a lawyer seeking to ensure that he retains sufficient hours under the cap to accomplish required tasks later on.

One way to address these concerns is to adopt a shared savings provision. Under this approach, a lawyer is allowed to retain a percentage of the difference between the guaranteed maximum price and the actual fees charged. This gives the lawyer an incentive to keep the legal fees down.

Assume that your lawyer is charging you an hourly fee and that you have agreed that the maximum you will pay the lawyer for the case is $100,000. It's a small case. A shared savings provision might state that for every dollar less than $100,000 that you are required to pay upon completion of the case, you will give the lawyer 25 percent of the savings. Accordingly, if the total fee is $70,000, the savings is $30,000 and you would pay the lawyer an additional $7,500. This gives the lawyer an incentive to work more efficiently.

Perhaps the single most effective tool available to a client seeking to reduce legal costs is the prospect of additional work for the lawyer. Despite periodic evidence to the contrary, most lawyers are not fools. They realize that a satisfied client is often a long-term client. Reinforce this notion by telling your lawyer that her efficiency and ability to keep legal fees to a minimum will figure into your decision regarding which firm you will hire for your next case or project.

Blended Hourly/Contingent Fee

In some instances, your interests may best be served by a blended hourly/contingent fee arrangement. In this arrangement, the lawyer agrees to charge a reduced hourly rate in exchange for a percentage of any recovery.

Assume the lawyer's normal hourly rate is $175 per hour. Under this approach, the lawyer might reduce his hourly rate to $100 per hour in exchange for the right to 10 percent of any recovery. This approach is less risky for the lawyer than a traditional contingent fee arrangement because he is assured of being paid—albeit at a reduced rate—for time spent working on the case.

The client benefits because this arrangement produces a lower hourly rate in exchange for a percentage of a recovery which may or may not materialize. This approach is often used when the client wants a reduced hourly rate and the lawyer believes that there is a good chance of a sizable recovery.

This approach can also be used in defensive or reverse contingency fee cases (more on which later). In exchange for the reduced hourly rate, the client agrees that the lawyer will take a percentage of whatever savings the lawyer can produce below a predetermined exposure level.

Incentive Based Fee Arrangements

The term *value billing* refers to fee arrangements which seek to produce more effective work by the lawyer by giving the lawyer a financial stake in the outcome of the case or project. Many forms of value billing require the client and the lawyer to agree upon a benchmark level of exposure which the client faces.

Once established, that benchmark serves as the basis for a variety of financial arrangements between the lawyer and the client. For purposes of the following discussion, we will call this benchmark the Exposure Level.

In order to utilize many value billing approaches, the client and the lawyer must agree upon the client's Exposure Level (EL). The EL is the dollar value of your potential liability. The EL becomes part of the fee agreement between you and your lawyer. Because the EL will in large measure determine the lawyer's fee, great care must be taken to develop and agree upon an EL which is satisfactory to both you and your lawyer.

You establish the EL by analyzing all of the factors which might affect the outcome of the case.

Assume that your company has been sued for a workplace injury. In addition to the workers' compensation claim, the plaintiff claims that you engaged in fraud, opening the possibility of punitive damages. Displaying the thoroughness and diabolical nature for which lawyers are often reviled, the plaintiff's lawyers have also notified OSHA, which now threatens Orwellian sanctions.

You inform your lawyer that you would like to set up a value billing fee arrangement. Your lawyer agrees and you meet with your lawyer and the appropriate members of your staff to establish the EL.

In order to do so, the group must analyze such issues as:

- whether the accident was your fault,
- the strength of your factual and legal defenses,
- whether the trial will be a jury trial,
- how much juries in this area typically award for this type of injury,
- whether your company has been involved in cases like this in the past and, if so, how much money it cost to resolve the matter,

- the caliber of the opposing lawyers, and
- the likelihood that OSHA will impose a large fine.

In addition to all of this, your lawyer has to estimate how much time she will have to devote to this matter so that she can decide whether the specific alternative fee arrangement you propose makes economic sense to her.

After reviewing and analyzing all of these factors, you and your lawyer must assign a specific dollar value to your company's potential liability. The number should be the amount of money your company stands to lose as a result of the lawsuit or other matter. The EL should not include your company's attorney's fees.

Establishing the EL is the single most important—and most difficult—aspect of employing this type of value based fee arrangement. The process requires a high degree of trust and good faith between lawyer and client.

In light of this, it's not surprising that these arrangements work best when undertaken by clients and lawyers with a previous business relationship. Using this approach the first time you work with a lawyer would add to the difficulty of agreeing on an EL.

An experienced company staff or in-house counsel which has encountered similar problems in the past is also helpful. One of the best indicators of the cost of resolving a matter is the cost of resolving similar matters in the recent past.

In most instances, you and your lawyer will need a certain amount of time to develop the facts necessary to produce a meaningful and accurate EL. In light of this, you may agree to pay your lawyer on the basis of a traditional hourly fee for the first few weeks or months, until such time as you have obtained the information necessary to develop an accurate EL.

Hourly Fee Incentive

After you have agreed upon an EL, there are a number of alternative fee arrangements which can be utilized. In the hourly fee incentive approach, the lawyer's hourly rate is determined by the outcome of the case. If the lawyer succeeds in disposing of the case for a cost below the EL, the lawyer's hourly rate increases. Conversely, if the case costs more than the EL to resolve, the lawyer's hourly rate is reduced.

Using our previous hypothetical example, assume that you and your lawyer agree that the EL for this case is $500,000. Your lawyer's standard hourly fee is $150 per hour. You agree with your lawyer that if it costs $500,000 to resolve the case, the lawyer will receive her standard hourly fee. If the case is resolved for less than $500,000, you will pay your lawyer a premium fee—based on a sliding scale—but if the case costs more than $500,000 to resolve, you will receive a discount. This gives the lawyer a direct financial interest in the outcome of the case. More significantly, it ties the lawyer's compensation to her performance.

The fee schedule might look something like this:

Resolution Cost	Lawyer's Hourly Rate
$800,000 or higher	$100
$700,000—799,999	$110
$600,000—699,999	$120
$500,001—599,999	$130
$500,000	$150
$400,000—499,999	$160
$300,000—399,999	$170
$200,000—299,999	$180
$100,000—199,999	$190
Under $100,000	$200

Like many value billing arrangements, this approach rewards the lawyer for a favorable result and penalizes the lawyer for an unfavorable result. In this way, the lawyer shares a portion of the risk that is borne solely by the client when traditional fee arrangements are employed.

Defensive or Reverse Contingency Fee

Value billing approaches can also be used to facilitate the use of contingent fees by defendants.

Again using our previous example, assume that the EL remains $500,000 and you want your lawyer to represent you on the basis of a contingent fee—rather than an hourly fee—arrangement. By using the EL, a contingency fee schedule can easily be developed. You and your lawyer might agree that if it costs your company $500,000 or more to resolve this case, you will consider the result a "loss" and the lawyer will receive no fee. For every dollar less than $500,000 that it costs your company to resolve the case, you agree to pay one-third of the savings to your lawyer as her fee.

Accordingly, if it costs you $250,000 to resolve the case, your lawyer's fee will be $82,500 (one-third times the savings of $250,000). If the case is resolved for $100,000, the lawyer's fee will be $132,000. If all of the charges are spurious and you are not forced to pay either the government or the plaintiff to resolve the case, the lawyer's fee will be $165,000.

Clearly, this approach places greater risk on the lawyer than the hourly fee incentive approach.

Reverse contingent fee arrangements are often used when the defendant concedes liability for a portion of the claimed amount. They are seldom used in all-or-nothing cases in which the defendant is likely to either win the case outright or be hit with a judgment for everything claimed by his opponent.

Budget Based Fee

In this arrangement, the lawyer and client agree upon a budget for the case—the amount the lawyer believes the case will cost—as well as a tolerance range of a certain percentage (let's say 15 percent). If at the end of the case the total cost of the case is within 15 percent of the budget, the agreed upon fee—whether fixed or hourly—remains in effect. If the total cost is beyond the 15 percent tolerance, either high or low, the client and the lawyer split the extra cost or savings.

Merit-Based Bonuses

Finally, there is the use of merit-based bonuses. These are used infrequently, because legal fees are so exorbitant that most clients recoil in horror at the thought of paying bonuses to their lawyers. Nevertheless, businesses have used merit-based bonuses to motivate their employees for years, often with outstanding results.

There is no logical reason why dangling this particular carrot in front of your lawyer would not have a similar effect. Bonuses can be awarded for keeping legal bills down, early settlement of the case, successful jury trials, avoidance of lawsuits altogether or whatever. Just make sure the lawyer knows that the bonuses are discretionary and that you are under no obligation to award them.

Selecting a Fee Arrangement

Some clients view a lawyer's fee as sacrosanct and non-negotiable. Either because they feel uncomfortable discussing a professional's fee— "I wouldn't negotiate with my doctor," they think—or because they perceive that they have no leverage, clients seldom negotiate with their lawyers about the lawyer's fee.

This is unwarranted and unwise. Lawyers are vendors of services—high-priced services, sometimes complex services, but services nevertheless. As the purchaser of those services, you have every right to attempt to negotiate the best available price.

Approach the establishment of the price of your lawyer's services the way you would approach the pricing of other services. Compare prices. Ask for discounts. Explore alternative billing approaches. Remember that you and your case represent revenue to the lawyer. If the lawyer's fee convinces you to purchase your legal services elsewhere, that lawyer is left with no revenue from you. Faced with that prospect, many lawyers will be willing to negotiate their fees.

Begin by determining whether you wish to be billed on the basis of an hourly fee, contingent fee, fixed fee or some alternative billing arrangement. Consider this question in the context of such factors as whether you are the plaintiff or the defendant, the anticipated length of the lawsuit, the financial status of your opponent and the likelihood of an early settlement of the case.

Remember that fee arrangements are in a sense nothing more than an allocation of risk between the lawyer and the client. Keep this in mind as you select and modify your fee arrangement.

Contingent fee arrangements allocate less risk to the client. The client's financial exposure is limited to the expenses incurred in the course of the lawsuit. The lawyer, on the other hand, is betting that he will be able to recover a sufficient amount of money to cover his usual hourly fee. Lawyers generally don't agree to contingent fee arrangements unless they believe that there is a good chance of a sizable recovery.

Fixed fee arrangements carry equal amounts of risk for the client and the lawyer. The lawyer is betting that he can estimate with some degree of accuracy the total amount of time which will be needed to complete the case. Having made that computation, the lawyer sets the fixed fee accordingly, usually at a level higher than the total hourly fee which would be charged. The client is betting that the case will not require as much time as was calculated by the lawyer in exchange for the certainty that the total legal fees will not exceed a set amount.

A fixed fee arrangement is a gamble for both the lawyer and the client. If the case requires much more time than estimated by the lawyer, he will lose money. If, on the other hand, the case requires much less time than anticipated, the client will pay a premium rate for the services received. In either event, one of the parties to the agreement will be short-changed in some sense. For this reason, lawyers will seldom agree to charge a fixed fee for litigation.

Hourly fee arrangements place almost all of the risk on the client. The lawyer knows that he will be paid for all of the time he spends working on the case. The client, on the other hand, faces an open-ended commitment to pay for however many hours are required to complete the case. While the client does not risk paying for services which he may never receive (as is the case in fixed fee arrangements), there is no limit on the total amount of money the client may be required to pay.

Negotiating Tactics

Once you have decided which fee arrangement you will use, there are a number of ways in which you can reduce your legal fees.

Contingent Fees: The percentage of your recovery which will go to your lawyer is limited only by your lawyer's conscience and your pliability. Although many lay persons assume that a lawyer's standard contingency fee is one-third of any recovery, the percentages charged by a lawyer are a matter of agreement—and negotiation—between the client and the lawyer.

Rather than agreeing to pay a certain percentage regardless of when the case is concluded, consider establishing a sliding scale contingency fee agreement with your lawyer. As discussed above, in such an arrangement your lawyer's fee increases in accordance with the stage of the case at which the lawsuit is concluded. A sample sliding scale might call for the lawyer's fee to be:

30 percent if the case settles prior to trial

35 percent if the case goes to trial

40 percent if an appeal is necessary

This scale can, of course, be modified or refined even further. Some sliding scale contingent fee arrangements assign percentages which govern in the event the case is settled prior to discovery, at a certain stage of the trial or based on the number of appeals required. A sliding scale seeks to calibrate the lawyer's fee based on the amount of time spent by the lawyer on the case. Most lawyers are amenable to such a fee arrangement and you should explore this option if you have a contingent fee case.

Fixed Fee: You should, of course, try to negotiate the lowest fixed fee possible. One way to determine whether a fixed fee is reasonable is to take your lawyer's hourly rate and divide it into the fixed fee to determine how many hours of work you are purchasing. If the hours seem too high, the fixed fee may be too high and you may wish to renegotiate the fixed fee.

Hourly Fees: Don't assume that your lawyer charges the same hourly fee to all of his clients. He doesn't. Some clients pay a higher hourly fee than others for the same lawyer's services. While in some instances the difference is attributable to different types of services provided by the lawyer, in the majority of instances the difference is a function of nothing more than the client's ability and willingness to pay the higher rate. For example, insurance companies often pay lower hourly fees in exchange for the promise—or the mere prospect—of volume work.

Begin your hourly fee negotiations by confirming that you are receiving your lawyer's lowest hourly rate. If the lowest hourly rate is higher than you are willing to pay, suggest a lower rate. You'll be surprised how often the lawyer will agree to the lower rate.

TAMING THE LAWYERS

Chapter Eight

Taming Your Lawyer

Once you've selected and hired your lawyer, your next task is to manage effectively—that is, tame—the lawyer. As you consider the suggestions in this chapter, keep in mind the following cardinal rule:

LIKE MOST RAMBUNCTIOUS CREATURES, LAWYERS
SHOULD BE KEPT ON A SHORT LEASH.

Clients who don't control their lawyers often find themselves overwhelmed by escalating legal fees charged for services which the client neither wants nor needs. Such a situation develops incrementally and often without venal intentions on the part of either the lawyer or the client.

Most non-lawyers view a lawsuit as a negative experience. If you or your company is at fault, the lawsuit is an expensive and discomfiting reminder of the error in judgment which spawned the lawsuit. Even in instances where you and your company are blameless and the lawsuit spurious, the lawsuit represents an expensive distraction which diverts you from your primary task.

Most non-lawyers are unfamiliar with the intricacies of the litigation process and are uncomfortable dealing with and making litigation decisions. As a result, many clients are only too glad to delegate responsibility for the lawsuit to their lawyer.

To some degree, this feeling is both proper and justified. One of the things you purchase when you hire a lawyer is the relative peace of mind which results from knowing that a trained professional will be looking out for your interests in matters related to the lawsuit. Unfortunately, many clients go overboard in the area of delegation of responsibility to the lawyer.

They believe that once the lawyer is hired, their duties have ended. They think they are free to stop thinking about the lawsuit, at least until the lawyer's next letter, phone call or bill. This attitude is both erroneous and dangerous. The client who adopts this attitude will lose control of the case and the lawyer at some point in the lawsuit.

A Matter of Perspective

The client views the lawsuit as a nuisance—if not a downright threat. If you or your business has been sued, you want the lawsuit to go away. If you or your business filed the lawsuit, you want the lawsuit to force the dishonest defendant to pay you as soon as possible. In either case, the client views the lawsuit as a means with which to produce a desired result. The quicker and cheaper the lawsuit can produce that result, the better.

The lawyer, on the other hand, has a multi-faceted view of the lawsuit. Like the client, the lawyer sees the lawsuit as a vehicle for vindicating the client's position. But the lawyer also sees the lawsuit as a crucible of sorts. It is a test—a test whose results will be evaluated not only by the client, but also by the lawyer's partners, employer, peers and even the local judge. This perspective produces a number of results unforeseen by most clients.

First, there is the pressure to perform. The lawyer knows that he must do everything allowable under the rules to put his client in the best position to win. If he fails to do so, he is not fulfilling his legal and ethical obligation to the client and might even be committing malpractice. The lawyer responds to this pressure by racking his brain to identify every single thing that can be done to increase the chances of victory.

There are plenty of things which can be done—more witnesses to depose, more questions to ask, more documents to review, more motions to file, more experts to consult. The rules of procedure allow lawyers to engage in a virtually endless series of tasks in preparation for the trial of the case. Completion of each of the tasks theoretically increases the lawyer's chances of victory.

The lawyer also knows that the failure to undertake any one of these tasks might decrease the client's chances to win. This knowledge influences and affects the lawyer's attitude toward the lawsuit. It produces an inclination in favor of action—to do everything allowed by the rules to ensure a greater chance of victory.

Second, a lawyer can get caught up in the gamesmanship of the lawsuit. It's not uncommon for lawsuits to become vehicles for competition between the lawyers. Your lawsuit is an opportunity for your lawyer to prove to the opposing lawyer something of which your lawyer has long been convinced—that he is a great lawyer. Unfortunately, your opponent's lawyer views the case the same way.

This clash of egos can lead to brinkmanship by both lawyers. Opposing counsel wants to take the deposition of your client's president? Well, then we'll take the deposition of *his* client's president. It's of little concern that neither president knows anything about the subject of the lawsuit. We can't allow the other side to take a shot at us without returning fire.

This tit-for-tat mentality can produce mountains of unnecessary legal work. Opposing counsel sends out supplemental interrogatories, so you draft and file supplemental interrogatories of your own. Your opponent hires three expert witnesses, so you hire four expert witnesses. The escalation sometimes progresses throughout the entire lawsuit. Somewhere along the way, the lawyers can lose sight of their initial goals.

Third, the lawyer can fall into the trap of focusing on winning every battle instead of the war. A lawsuit is in some senses analogous to a military campaign. There are a series of pitched battles, separated by periods of inactivity, culminating in one side winning the war or agreeing to a truce. The field general—your lawyer—should always focus on the overall campaign, but he can often become overly concerned with individual battles.

Skirmishes with the other side such as discovery disputes, evidentiary disputes, jurisdictional disputes and the like can drain your resources. Although such disputes often have little bearing on the case, in the heat of battle your lawyer may lose his perspective regarding the amount of time and money which ought to be expended on such disputes. Not every battle in a lawsuit has to be won or even fought.

Fourth, the lawyer may get caught up in the legal issues involved in the case. Sometimes your lawsuit involves novel questions of law. Good lawyers are curious about the answers to such questions. They are almost always interested in being involved in making new law by getting an appellate court to rule on the novel question. In addition to advancing the client's interests, such forays into uncharted legal territory can be a boon to a lawyer's reputation in the legal community.

Unfortunately, making new law is expensive and time consuming. It almost always requires a trip to an appellate court, which extends the life—and the cost—of the lawsuit. Most importantly, the effect of the appellate court's ruling on your case may be negligible at best. Unless the novel question has a direct bearing on the outcome or a major portion of your case, pursuit of the question may not be economically justified.

For all of these reasons, a lawyer's perspective of a case is often quite different than a non-lawyer's perspective. This difference in perspective can lead the lawyer to make choices in the course of the lawsuit which are not the choices the client would make. This is why the client must manage and control the lawyer as the first step in controlling the lawsuit and the accompanying legal costs.

What, then, are the practical steps which you can take to control your lawyer?

Establish Ground Rules

Well begun is truly half done. Begin by having a comprehensive initial meeting with your lawyer to discuss your expectations and requirements. This is not a meeting to discuss the lawsuit itself, the events which led to the lawsuit or even the lawyer's strategy for the lawsuit. While important, those topics typically involve the lawyer telling you what you must do to give yourself a chance to win the lawsuit.

In such a meeting, the lawyer will set the agenda and explain what must be done. This is not the purpose of the initial meeting. The purpose of the initial meeting is for the employer—you—to tell your independent contractor—the lawyer—what you want and expect him to do. Unlike most meetings with lawyers, in this meeting you will do most of the talking.

Discuss every aspect of the case which is important to you. Begin by telling your lawyer your dream outcome. If you could produce any result imaginable regarding the lawsuit—other than inflicting physical harm upon your opponent—what would it be? In most cases your dream outcome will be unattainable, but so what? Give your lawyer something to shoot for.

Most importantly, let your lawyer know your goal. Your goal may be to get out of the lawsuit as quickly and cheaply as possible. It may be to take the case to trial to expose your opponent as the duplicitous weasel he is. It may be to achieve the potent, if momentary, gratification of denouncing your opponent in open court (where you're usually insulated from the defamation laws). Your goal may be to dispose of the case pursuant to a confidential settlement agreement or to delay resolution of the suit until you finish that big project.

Whatever your goal, communicate it to your lawyer at the outset of the litigation. It's best to discuss five or six goals and to rank them according to preference. Your first goal may be to boil your opponent in oil. Failing that, your next preference may be to settle the case for less than $10,000. If such a settlement is not possible, your next goal may be to keep your legal fees under a certain amount. Good luck.

Your next goal may be to conclude the litigation before your company's next board meeting. Review your goals in order of preference and communicate them to your lawyer. The lawyer may be pursuing your first goal when an opportunity arises to achieve your second or third goal. If the lawyer doesn't know what your second and third goals are, he may allow the opportunity to pass.

After discussing the way in which you would like the lawsuit to be resolved, discuss with your lawyer your nightmare outcome. What is the worst possible thing which could happen as a result of the lawsuit? Your nightmare outcome may be losing the trial and being required to pay a mammoth verdict—in addition to paying your lawyer an equally mammoth fee for having achieved that result.

Unfavorable publicity may be your worst nightmare. Being required to spend millions of dollars in legal fees may be the thing that sets your hair on edge. Allowing your opponent's lawyer to ferret through your personal life or your company's files may be the thing which is not acceptable to you.

Whatever your nightmare may be, communicate it to your lawyer.

There are certain matters which transcend a lawsuit. I once had a client tell me that he would rather surrender unconditionally to his opponent than be forced to give his deposition. If he had not communicated this to me, it is likely that I would have agreed to schedule his deposition the first time our opponent asked us to do so. It is vitally important to let your lawyer know things which you want the lawyer to avoid at all costs, although it's always dangerous to use the phrase "at all costs" around a lawyer.

Next, address the administrative procedures which you wish to employ during the lawsuit. Establish procedures which cause the least disruption to your business or your personal life. Inform the lawyer what he should do when he wants access to your employees, documents or physical space. If you don't establish such procedures, you won't be able to monitor and control the lawyer's activities.

Let the lawyer know that certain professional conduct and courtesies must be maintained. The lawyer should give you as much warning as possible when the lawyer needs to meet with you or your employees or to review documents or whatever.

Lawyers are forever putting off tasks until the last moment. Some lawyers call their clients at the eleventh hour to say that interrogatory answers are due tomorrow and therefore the client needs to review twenty pages of responses and call the lawyer that afternoon. Inform your lawyer that you don't conduct your business in such a fashion and you don't expect your lawyer to either. Leaving aside emergencies and situations created by power-crazed judges, tell the lawyer that you expect him to give you and your employees adequate time to respond thoughtfully to requests for information or decisions.

Little things can sour your relationship with your lawyer. Like all humans, you have idiosyncrasies. Let your lawyer know what is important to you at the outset of the representation. Maybe you like to schedule meetings regarding the lawsuit first thing in the morning. Perhaps your pet peeve is people who don't return your phone calls the same day. Possibly the best way for your lawyer to reach you is by telecopier. Let your lawyer know the way you like to conduct business. The lawsuit is a distraction from your business activities. Establish procedures which will minimize the distraction.

Address billing issues in your initial conference with your lawyer. As discussed earlier, let your lawyer know what you consider to be valid billable activities. Discuss which expenses you are willing to pay. If you have a legal budget which cannot be exceeded, apprise your lawyer of this figure. Make sure that you and your lawyer agree regarding these issues.

With regard to settlement, let your lawyer know if there is an amount for which you would be willing to settle. Discuss with the lawyer how much the company is willing to invest in the lawsuit, taking into account both a settlement amount and the legal fees which the company will have to incur in order to achieve the settlement.

Some companies formalize this process by adopting standard guidelines for outside counsel. While each case is different and may require modifications to the general approach, certain standards are applicable in each case. Codifying those guidelines in a standard document can ensure a certain level of consistency in a company's dealings with a variety of lawyers and firms.

Your lawyer may be unable or unwilling to meet some of your requirements. You may, for example, wish to restrict your deposition to a maximum of two hours. While your lawyer can sympathize with this sentiment, the rules of procedure in most jurisdictions allow the opposing party at least six hours for most depositions.

In the absence of special circumstances such as health considerations, your lawyer has no control over this requirement. Nevertheless, it is preferable for you to learn of this requirement at the outset of the case rather than on the eve of your deposition.

In other instances, the lawyer may be unwilling to agree to certain of your requests. If, for example, you tell the lawyer that you would like to pay your fee in a lump sum at the end of the litigation, the lawyer is unlikely to accept such an arrangement. If the lawyer is unwilling to agree to such a point, you will either have to agree to the lawyer's terms or find another lawyer. If the issue is sufficiently important to you, hire another lawyer.

Keep in mind that situations will develop during the course of a lawsuit or transaction over which neither you nor your lawyer will have any control. Judges make rulings, the law changes, witnesses leave town or die. There are, however, plenty of situations which you can control. Use the initial meeting to identify those situations and establish the ground rules.

Give the lawyer an opportunity to voice her opinion regarding your expectations. In some cases, your expectations may be unreasonable or even ludicrous. If so, an honest lawyer will tell you so. Let the lawyer make suggestions for additional ground rules. The lawyer may have employed certain approaches which have proven effective in other cases. If such approaches make sense to you, incorporate them into the ground rules for your case.

At the end of your initial meeting with your lawyer, write a brief letter or memorandum outlining the ground rules established at the meeting. This need not be a formal document. Nevertheless, it is important to memorialize the meeting in writing in order to avoid any future disagreements about the ground rules.

List the ground rules established in the meeting. At the end of the letter, state that unless the lawyer notifies you in writing, you will assume that everything in your letter is accurate and acceptable to your lawyer. Instruct the lawyer to write you if the letter is inaccurate in any respect.

Your first reaction may be that such a letter is superfluous, a typical lawyer idea and potentially harmful in that it might imply that you don't trust your lawyer. While the letter may be a typical lawyer idea, it is not superfluous, nor does it imply a lack of trust. When you are in the sixth year of the lawsuit and neither you nor your lawyer can remember if you agreed to pay the lawyer's full hourly fee for travel time to Australia, where that last witness now resides, you will be glad you have the letter.

As for hurting your lawyer's feelings, I would respond that (1) lawyers are accustomed to being distrusted, (2) lawyers are accustomed to everything being memorialized in a letter, and (3) lawyers love detailed written instructions.

One last thing—write the letter yourself. Don't ask the lawyer to write the letter. By writing it yourself, you retain control over its contents and you avoid paying the lawyer to write the letter.

Require a Strategic Plan

Upon completion of your initial meeting with your lawyer, request that the lawyer prepare and submit to you a strategic plan outlining the way in which the lawyer plans to conduct the lawsuit. As discussed above, in some ways lawsuits resemble military campaigns. The side which has the better plan and executes its plan more adroitly usually wins. Your lawyer should be able to tell you how he plans to win your case for you.

The strategic plan should explain what your lawyer's plan is, why the lawyer believes the plan represents the best possible strategy, how the plan will be implemented, how much it will probably cost to implement the plan, the results the plan should produce, when the lawyer believes those results will occur and how long the entire affair should last. Give your lawyer the latitude to include whatever he thinks may be pertinent in the plan, but set a page, time or dollar limit on the crafting of the plan to avoid paying for a rewrite of *The Art of War*.

There may be specific issues which you would like the lawyer to address in the strategic plan. Such issues will, of course, differ from case to case. In most cases, however, the following questions will be pertinent:

- Do you need to bring any other parties into the lawsuit?

- Do you have any legal defenses which might be complete defenses to the claims which have been brought against you?

- How many depositions do you anticipate taking in the course of the lawsuit?

- What litigation expenses do you anticipate?

- Who will be your primary witnesses?

- What are the key legal and factual issues in the case?

- What are your chances of prevailing on each of the legal and factual issues?

- If the case doesn't settle, how long will it take to get to trial?

- What is your strategy for dealing with an adversary intent on delaying the case?

- How do you plan to hold down my legal costs?

- How do you plan to staff this case?

- Will you need any expert witnesses? If so, how much do you anticipate they will cost?

- If a judgment is entered against you in the case, would any of your current insurance policies cover all or part of the judgment?

- Is any form of alternative dispute resolution available in this case? If so, should you use it?

An Analysis of Your Case

The strategic plan will allow—or, in some cases, force—your lawyer to give concerted thought to how he will achieve your goals in this case. This may sound obvious, but in many instances lawyers just crank up the litigation machine and hang on for the ride. Often called into a case at a time when an answer is due in a few days, it is not uncommon for lawyers to adopt a reactive stance and remain in that stance for the remainder of the lawsuit. The strategic plan encourages creative thinking about proactive measures which can be taken to achieve your company's goals.

The plan should include a section in which the lawyer outlines what he believes to be the strong and weak points of your case. The lawyer will often need to conduct a preliminary investigation in order to address this topic in detail. A more comprehensive analysis should be completed upon the close of discovery.

Still, the lawyer should be able to give you a preliminary idea of the relative strength of each party's case at this point. This section should include assessments of the likelihood of victory and, in cases where you are the plaintiff, of your opponent's ability to pay a judgment.

The strategic plan should contain an assessment of what your lawyer thinks the opposition's strategy will be. Based on the initial pleadings, his knowledge of the issues involved and, possibly, his knowledge of your opponent's lawyer, ask your lawyer to anticipate the opposition's strategy and to develop your strategic plan accordingly.

Make sure the plan includes a discussion of settlement prospects. What does the lawyer think the settlement prospects are? Have there been any initial settlement overtures from your opponent? What are the junctures in the course of the case when conditions are most favorable for a settlement? Settlements are most likely to occur at the following points in the life of the lawsuit:

- immediately before or after the lawsuit is filed,
- immediately before or after a major motion,
- immediately before or after the deposition of an important witness,
- at the close of discovery,
- at the pretrial conference stage,
- immediately prior to trial, and
- after the verdict but prior to an appeal.

Clients often ask the lawyer to estimate the total legal costs which will be incurred by the client. In hourly fee cases, it is difficult to develop an accurate fee estimate at the outset of the case. Numerous factors which will affect the fees (such as the amount of discovery in which your opponent plans to engage, the motions which your opponent may file, the judge, and the judge's docket) are beyond the control—or even the estimation—of the lawyer. Nevertheless, have your lawyer prepare a proposed budget based upon reasonable assumptions concerning the case. Ask your lawyer to assume a reasonable number of depositions, motions and the like in producing an estimate of total legal costs.

You should also ask your lawyer to estimate the periods of time when your legal costs will be the greatest. A lawsuit does not progress steadily. The lawyer should be able to identify the points at which your legal costs promise to be the greatest. This will allow you to develop a workable litigation budget.

Some cost-conscious managers may view the drafting of such a plan as an expensive and unnecessary option. There are few guarantees in life, but here's one: The drafting of a strategic plan is not superfluous. It will provide you and your lawyer with a road map for the often lengthy journey which lies ahead. It will prove valuable—and some-times invaluable—to both client and lawyer as the lawsuit proceeds.

As for the cost, you can control the cost of the plan by instructing your lawyer to spend no more than a certain amount of time on the plan. This will be some of the best money you will ever spend on legal fees. Properly crafted and executed, a strategic plan can save you thousands of dollars over the life of the litigation.

After your lawyer submits the plan to you, review it in detail outside the presence of your lawyer. Discuss the plan with any business asso-ciates whom you feel ought to review it. Make notes during your review. Note items with which you disagree or agree, items you be-lieve should be in the plan and items which you simply do not under-stand.

After you have conducted your review, meet with your lawyer to discuss your reaction to the plan. Give the lawyer an opportunity to explain any items about which you have a question. If you disagree with the plan, let the lawyer know it. Give him an opportunity to explain why he believes a certain approach is advisable. In many in-stances, the lawyer's explanation may convince you. If not, adopt an alternative approach which is acceptable to both you and your law-yer.

Don't hesitate to modify the plan where necessary. If the modifica-tions are significant, ask the lawyer to revise the plan and resubmit it to you. At the end of this meeting, you and your lawyer should be in agreement regarding the strategy which the lawyer will employ in the litigation.

Determine what level of deviation from the strategic plan would require the lawyer to contact you in advance. You don't want or need your lawyer calling you every time he thinks he ought to speak to opposing counsel or perform an hour's worth of legal research. This is inefficient and results in unnecessary legal expense.

On the other hand, if the lawyer decides he needs to bring a new party into the lawsuit or depose twenty previously unknown witnesses—all of whom live in Paris—you want to discuss these issues at some point before he starts brushing up on his French.

The strategic plan should be used as a compass to keep the lawsuit and the lawyer headed in a consistent direction throughout the life of the lawsuit.

Designate a Corporate Representative

Businesses should select a corporate representative who will act as the company's liaison with your lawyer or law firm. Lawyers can waste inordinate amounts of their time and your money dealing with different company employees. Throughout the course of the lawsuit, your lawyer will need assistance in answering questions about your business, identifying potential witnesses, locating documents, inspecting your facility and other related tasks.

If the lawyer has to make five phone calls in each instance to locate the employee who can provide him with the information he is seeking, the lawyer will disrupt your business and run up your bill. Avoid this problem by designating one individual through whom the lawyer should communicate with the company. Instruct the lawyer that all inquiries should be directed to that liaison person.

Similarly, all instructions to the lawyer should be channeled through the liaison person. It is frustrating, inefficient and sometimes downright dangerous for a lawyer to be unsure of the company employee from whom he should obtain instructions and decisions. Like automobile accidents, lawsuits tend to attract crowds.

It is not uncommon for employees who are on the periphery of a lawsuit to become interested in the lawsuit and to begin to inject themselves into the case. It is imperative that you identify and designate the individual to whom the lawyer should look for company decisions and instructions.

The liaison person and the decision maker may not be the same individual. Some businesses choose to assign liaison duties to one individual and invest decision-making authority in a different, more senior, individual. If you divide these two jobs, make sure that the liaison person has sufficient authority to facilitate the lawyer's requests. If the liaison person does not have sufficient authority, he may not be able to produce the necessary results for the lawyer.

Neither the decision maker nor the liaison person should be the individual who is involved in the situation which led to the lawsuit. Although he will have the greatest amount of information regarding the facts of the case, that individual will not be the most effective decision maker. That individual's personal involvement will make it very difficult for him to make objective decisions regarding the litigation. For the same reason, the individual involved in the dispute should not be the liaison person either. The involved individual should be available for consultation, but should not have the ability to influence the flow of information to the lawyer.

Monitor Your Case Closely

Effective control and management of your lawyer requires that you monitor your lawsuit. Some clients believe that they can stop worrying about—or at least stop paying attention to—a lawsuit once the lawyer has been hired. While this is possible, it is ill-advised.

Your lawsuit is of central importance to you. With luck, it is the only lawsuit in which you and your company are currently involved. Even if you are involved in a number of lawsuits simultaneously, each of those lawsuits is important to you. The lawyer, on the other hand, is in all likelihood handling dozens of lawsuits on behalf of numerous clients. Depending on the lawyer's practice, she may have an active caseload of anywhere from five to fifty cases at any given time. The lawyer must allocate her time and energy among all of those cases—a task which sometimes results in certain cases receiving an inordinate amount of attention at the expense of other cases. When a crisis erupts in one case, the lawyer must attend to that case. Inevitably, the lawyer's other cases suffer until the crisis is resolved.

This is not to say that your lawyer will ignore your case just because she is also handling other cases. In most instances, lawyers seek and receive assistance from other lawyers in their firm to ensure that all deadlines are met in all of the cases they are handling. This is only to say that there is no one—not even your lawyer—to whom your case is more important than it is to you. It is your business, your reputation and your money which are at risk.

You can be an important asset in the effort to bring your case to a favorable conclusion.

You and your business associates know more about the case than anyone. You know the facts of the dispute, the people involved and the business context in which the problem arose better than anyone. Accordingly, you can provide a great deal of assistance to your lawyer during the lawsuit. You are a valuable resource. It would be foolish for you to remove yourself from the proceedings once the lawyer has been hired. By doing so, you deprive your lawyer of an important asset.

Your perspective is broader and deeper than your lawyer's perspective, at least as it relates to the lawsuit and its effect on you or your business. The lawyer is—properly—concerned with legalities, the strategy of the lawsuit and achieving the best possible result in the case. While you are also concerned with those matters, you must also take into consideration the broader implications associated with the lawsuit.

If you are involved as an individual, what effect is the lawsuit having on your personal life and your family? If your business is involved, how is the lawsuit affecting the company's financial posture? Is the lawsuit causing concern among customers and potential customers? What effect would a trial have on your employees, investors, customers and potential customers? Is the lawsuit producing morale problems? If you settle the lawsuit, will your company be seen in the industry as an easy mark and become a target for similar lawsuits in the future?

You are in a much better position to assess such issues than your lawyer. Your role—your responsibility—is to analyze the lawsuit in the context of the larger business issues which are in most cases beyond the lawyer's zone of competence. If you cede all decision-making authority to the lawyer, it is unlikely that these vital non-litigation issues will be given appropriate consideration.

Your perspective also adds a needed balance to the lawyer's perspective and can act as a check on the lawyer. The exercise of explaining a prospective decision to you forces your lawyer to crystallize his thinking. Lawyers sometimes embark upon courses of action for no better reason than habit. A lawyer might, for example, always depose the opposing party's chief financial officer. In your particular case, however, such a course of action may not be advisable. By requiring the lawyer to obtain your approval before scheduling the deposition, you force the lawyer to consider whether the deposition is needed. By engaging in this exercise, the lawyer may come to the conclusion that, in this particular case, the deposition of the chief financial officer is unnecessary.

On the other hand, there are instances in which a client can become too involved in the day-to-day progress of the lawsuit. If you speak with your lawyer on a daily basis over the course of the litigation and find yourself editing the lawyer's correspondence, you've probably crossed the line from prudent monitoring to micromanagement.

Although there will be periods of high activity in which you are in contact with your lawyer on a daily—or even hourly—basis, as a general proposition such a level of activity suggests that you are spending too much time conversing with your lawyer about the case. In addition to increasing your legal bill, such micromanagement makes it difficult for your lawyer to do her job.

This level of input also decreases your ability to maintain a broader perspective regarding the lawsuit. If you become involved in the day-to-day minutiae of the lawsuit, you will reduce your effectiveness as the member of the team responsible for the so-called big picture.

What steps should you take to monitor the case as it progresses? There are dozens of ways to accomplish this. The system you employ is less important than the fact that you have some sort of system in place. Whatever system works best for you and your lawyer is the best system to employ.

Many clients require a monthly status report as the primary feature of their monitoring system. The advantage of this system is that it requires the lawyer and the client to think strategically about the lawsuit at least once each month.

It is important to remember that in lawsuits which span a number of years, lawyers often set cases aside for months at a time. Moreover, lawyers can spend long periods of time focusing on nothing more than the short-term tasks which confront them in the lawsuit. The monthly status report can be used to prevent your case from developing large quantities of mold.

What's in the Status Report

An effective monthly status report should include the following elements:

- **Background**

   A brief narrative of the facts and issues involved in the case. This section is especially important if the status report will be reviewed by a number of people in your organization, some of whom may not be familiar with the case. It is also helpful to remind everyone what the case is about as the litigation drags into its fifth year. This section should be brief—no more than three or four paragraphs. Your lawyer can use the same or a slightly modified narrative for this section in each month's status report by leaving the narrative on his word processor. In this fashion, the lawyer doesn't have to recreate the background portion of the status report each month.

- **Current Status**

As the title implies, this is a summary of the posture of the case on the date of the status report. This section should be brief.

- **Recent Activity**

This section outlines the activity which has occurred in the case since the last status report. The lawyer can include a detailed analysis of those events in this section or the analysis can be placed in a later section.

- **Anticipated Activity**

This section tells the client what the lawyer believes will occur in the lawsuit in the near future. This section gives the client an opportunity to discuss the lawyer's plans with the lawyer before the lawyer puts those plans into effect. The client may learn that the lawyer is planning to do something which, for some reason, the client doesn't want the lawyer to do. If so, the client can confer with the lawyer before the lawyer proceeds with the activity in question. This section also forces the lawyer to review the file and to schedule matters which he may have been intending to schedule for a number of weeks.

- **Long-Term Strategy**

This section requires reference to the original strategic plan. Litigation regularly veers in unanticipated directions. As unexpected battles materialize, it is not difficult for both lawyer and client to lose sight of their original goal and strategy. Monthly reference to the original strategic plan forces the client and the lawyer to either return to the original plan, modify the original plan in light of recent developments or at the very least acknowledge that they are deviating from the original plan.

The lawyer should also update estimates made in the original strategic plan. Does the lawyer still believe that the case will go to trial at the end of the year? Is the strategy contained in the original plan still valid? The status report can reveal flaws in the original plan and give the lawyer and client an opportunity to make necessary modifications.

This section should also identify the lawyer's progress in carrying out the strategy outlined in the original strategic plan. If, for example, the original plan calls for your lawyer to take fifteen depositions, how many of those depositions have been taken to date? Have events led your lawyer to add new activities to the list of anticipated activities? This section should tell the client what the lawyer plans to do between the date of the report and the conclusion of the lawsuit.

- **Cost Summary**

   The proverbial bottom line. The status report should reflect the client's legal costs—both fees and expenses—for the past thirty days, as well as the total costs incurred by the client to date. The cost summary should also reflect the original budgeted cost for the litigation (another reference to the original strategic plan) and the lawyer's estimate regarding the anticipated cost to complete the litigation.

   This section allows the client to gauge how much the case has cost to date and how much it appears it will cost to complete the case. The cost-to-date item is important. Over the course of a protracted lawsuit, it's easy for a business person to lose track of the total amount of money the business has invested in the lawsuit. This line item reminds the client on a monthly basis of his company's ever-increasing investment in the lawsuit.

- **Settlement Prospects**

   This section apprises the client of the status of any settlement discussions. Lawyers are ethically obligated to report immediately to the client any settlement offers made by the opposing side. Accordingly, this section should never be the first place a client hears about a settlement offer.

   The lawyer should summarize all settlement offers made to date, including which party made the offer, at what point in the litigation and for what amount. The lawyer should then report whether any recent events in the case might alter the settlement postures of the respective parties and, if so, in what way. As stated above, a crucial deposition, ruling or document may alter a litigant's chances for ultimate success. Such factors can alter a party's settlement posture. This section should identify and analyze any such developments.

In the absence of any specific developments, this section should review the client's settlement strategy to determine whether the strategy remains valid in light of recent events. A litigant may have begun a case refusing to consider settlement, but as the case wears on, the legal bills increase and the issues become less clear, the business person may conclude that settlement would be in the best interest of the business. The lawyer should offer advice regarding whether a new settlement strategy should be pursued. This advice includes whether any settlement offer should be made and, if so, in what amount. The settlement issue should be visited on a regular basis. The monthly status report can trigger such regular reviews of a litigant's settlement strategy.

- **Recommendations and Analysis**

  This is perhaps the most important section of the status report. In this section, the lawyer distills all that has occurred in the case to date, assesses the client's current prospects for success and recommends what activities should be undertaken.

  Assume, for example, that last month your opponent took the deposition of your company's chief executive officer and, unfortunately, your chief executive officer performed poorly. As your company's key witness, the CEO will play a large role at trial and will have a major impact on your company's prospects for success. The lawyer must assess the effect of the CEO's poor performance on the case and report it to the client so that a revised strategy can be adopted if necessary.

  The lawyer must also analyze whether the company's chances for success have been sufficiently damaged that the company should consider settling the case for more money than was previously deemed reasonable. If this is not an option, perhaps the lawyer and client can embark on a program to help the CEO perform better at trial. Whatever the decision, the client and lawyer need to begin discussing the impact of the deposition in order to determine what action is necessary. The status report can assist in ensuring that such discussions take place in a timely fashion.

Fulfilling Potential

Monthly status reports can be of great value. The only way to ensure that they *will* be of value is for you and your lawyer to act upon the information contained in the report.

The best monitoring system in the world is useless if the client and lawyer don't take timely and thoughtful action based upon the information contained in the report. If the status report languishes untouched on the client's desk for weeks or months, there is little point in paying the lawyer to prepare the report. Monthly status reports are a tool. If they aren't used by the client and the lawyer to generate dialogue and action, they are of little or no value.

Compare status reports over a period of time to determine whether the lawyer is providing consistent information and advice. For example, the April status report may state that the lawyer is planning to depose a particular witness in May. Upon review of the May status report, however, you may discover that the deposition didn't take place. If so, the May status report should state why the deposition wasn't taken. If it doesn't, ask the lawyer the question. While there is probably a good explanation, the status report allows you to track such activities.

Successive status reports may also signal a shift in the lawyer's outlook. The April status report may be optimistic in its assessment of your company's chances for success in the litigation. By the time you read the August status report, however, the prognosis has become downright bleak. What happened? Have intervening events dimmed the prospects for success? Is your lawyer trying to hedge his bets? Comparison of a series of status reports can alert you to such discrepancies and changes in tune.

The monthly status report should not be viewed as a panacea which will relieve you of your responsibility to think about the case for the other thirty days of each month. The client who relies solely on a monthly status report to monitor a case is making a large mistake. A client's primary monitoring tool should be frequent meetings or conversations with her lawyer. The activity in a lawsuit does not, of course, correspond with the status report schedule. In many instances, decisions must be considered and made long before the next status report is due. The status report is one of a number of tools which a client can utilize to monitor the progress of the lawsuit.

Questioning All This Reporting

Some clients may question the necessity of such reports and whether their usefulness justifies the cost of having the lawyer produce a status report each month. I am a firm believer in monthly status reports. While there are other ways to monitor a case effectively, in my experience the use of a monthly status report is the most practical and effective means by which a client can keep abreast of a case.

Most good lawyers can produce a comprehensive monthly status report in less than two hours. Assuming an hourly rate of $150 per hour, that's only $300 per month. When viewed in the context of the amount of money at stake in the lawsuit—not to mention your overall legal bill—$300 per month is a small amount to pay for the benefits provided by a monthly status report.

In addition to regular written status reports, many business people rely on periodic meetings or conversations with their lawyers to keep them apprised of the progress of the lawsuit. Some clients like to speak with their lawyers on a regular weekly basis. I once had a client who insisted upon calling me every Friday morning to discuss his company's lawsuit. The call would come every Friday without fail. Often I would have little or nothing new to report, but this was of little concern to the client. He paid for whatever time the call consumed. It was clear that this was his preferred system of keeping track of the case and that it gave him peace of mind to be able to discuss the case with me for ten or fifteen minutes each Friday.

Some clients like to keep track of the case by monitoring the pleadings, correspondence and other documents produced in the course of the lawsuit. If you prefer this method, instruct your lawyer to send you copies of all pleadings filed in the case by any party, all correspondence sent or received by your lawyer pertaining to the case and transcripts of all depositions and hearings. This will produce a regular flow of paper for you to review, but if you have the time or inclination to do so, it is an excellent way to monitor your case.

You should also instruct your lawyer to apprise you immediately of all significant developments in the case. The trick here is to agree upon a definition of *significant*.

Although you are certain to want to know if your adversary has offered to settle the case, you don't want your lawyer to call you each time he speaks with opposing counsel. Determine the level of reporting you wish to receive. Make clear to the lawyer how you wish to be notified of the events in question. Some clients prefer an immediate telephone call, while others prefer written notification. If you request written notification, specify whether the lawyer is to transmit the letter via modem, telecopier, regular mail, overnight delivery or courier.

These monitoring methods may be used individually or in concert with one another. The goal is for you to remain fully apprised of both the general progress of the case and important specific developments. Information is power. The more you know about your case, the greater your ability to control both the case and your lawyer.

Attend Key Events

You or your company's designated representative should attend certain important events in the course of the litigation. Attendance of the client is not required at most of these events, but by attending them you can observe how your side is faring—not to mention the added advantage of keeping your lawyer on his toes.

Depositions are a prime example. The rules of procedure allow named parties or a designated company representative to attend any deposition in the case. While you won't want to attend every deposition, make a point of attending the depositions of key witnesses for both sides. By attending the deposition of one of your adversary's witnesses, you will have an opportunity to observe and evaluate the performance of the witness, your lawyer, and your adversary's lawyer. In many instances, you will be able to assist your lawyer during the deposition by alerting your lawyer to factual inconsistencies—or outright lies—in the witness' testimony.

You will also have the opportunity to hear your adversary's version of the dispute in great detail. This can provide you with fresh insights into your opponent's position and may even demonstrate the validity of some of your opponent's points. The deposition will provide you with additional information which can be used in forming your assessment of the case.

Attending the deposition of your opponent may also provide you with an opportunity to meet your counterpart in your opponent's company. In many instances, the decision makers for the respective parties have never met one another. Opportunities for informal settlement discussions may develop as a result of meeting your counterpart at a deposition. To be sure, such situations must be approached carefully. For example, in the absence of an agreement regarding confidentiality, any statements you make to your counterpart may find their way into evidence. Nevertheless, a deposition may provide an opportunity for settlement discussions which may in turn lead to settlement of the case.

Be aware that there may be certain depositions which you shouldn't attend. One of your key witnesses may be a friend or a business associate who would be quite nervous if you attended the deposition. In such situations, your interests would be better served if you did not attend the deposition. Discuss with your lawyer which depositions she believes might pose a problem. If the lawyer convinces you that it would be better for you to stay away from a particular deposition, you can always read the transcript of the deposition at a later date—assuming that neither the applicable law or the judge prohibit such a review.

Pre-trial hearings also offer the client an opportunity to monitor the lawsuit by personal attendance. The rules of procedure will allow clients to attend all hearings held in open court. Also, the rules in your particular jurisdiction or the judge in your particular case may allow—and in some cases even encourage—the clients to attend status conferences, settlement conferences and pre-trial conferences.

Like depositions, such events allow you to observe and evaluate the witnesses, the lawyers, and, to some extent, the legal issues. In most jurisdictions, the judge who will conduct the trial of your case will also conduct these preliminary hearings. The hearing provides you with an opportunity to evaluate the judge from a business person's point of view. Your long-term strategy and perspective may be affected by the performance of your judge at a pre-trial hearing or conference.

Conduct Performance Reviews

Conduct periodic reviews of the performance of your lawyer. You are subject to such reviews, as are your employees, vendors and other independent contractors. Your lawyer should also be subject to such reviews.

Select a period of time which makes sense in the context of the matter being handled by the lawyer. Six months is generally an effective period of time. Quarterly reviews are fine, but given the glacial pace of litigation, you may find that there is little new activity on which to base a review from one quarter to the next. A year is too long.

The performance review should be used to assess the lawyer's performance in the preceding time period. The review should not focus solely—or even primarily—on the lawsuit itself. The lawsuit and the issues associated with the lawsuit should be discussed in the separate and more frequent case review discussions described above. The performance review, on the other hand, should focus on the relationship between the lawyer and the client.

Has the lawyer been providing the type, quality and frequency of service desired by the client? Has the lawyer's fee been in the range expected by and acceptable to the client? Has the lawyer provided timely and accurate responses to the client's inquiries? Has the lawyer kept the client apprised of the progress of the case? Has the lawyer involved the client in major decisions concerning the progress of the lawsuit? In short, is the client satisfied with the lawyer's performance to date?

The performance review can be structured in whatever form you wish. The secret to its success is adherence to a regular schedule of performance reviews. The prospect of an upcoming performance review has a beneficial effect upon both the client and the lawyer. The client is forced to set aside time to evaluate the lawyer's performance. Regular performance reviews encourage clients to note issues as they arise during the lawsuit and to keep those notes for reference purposes during the performance review.

The lawyer, on the other hand, is often spurred to higher levels of performance and greater attention to the case by the prospect of regular performance reviews.

Remember that you will be just one of many clients competing for a finite amount of your lawyer's time, attention and energy. The knowledge that you will evaluate the lawyer's performance has a galvanizing effect on the lawyer, often causing the lawyer to focus more closely on your case and on you.

Conduct the performance review in much the same way you would conduct the performance review of a business associate. Tell the lawyer whether you are pleased or displeased with his performance. Identify the specific conduct on which you base your evaluation. Tell the lawyer what you like and dislike about his performance.

If you believe the case has cost too much to date (especially in relation to the progress—or lack thereof—of the case), tell him so. If you can never reach the lawyer without making sixteen phone calls and calling the FBI, tell him so. If you feel the lawyer hasn't been aggressive enough in his dealings with the other side or hasn't undertaken enough activity on your behalf, tell him so.

The performance review is your opportunity to let the lawyer know how you evaluate his performance to date. Utilize this opportunity to tell your lawyer what needs to change.

Give the lawyer an opportunity to respond to each issue you raise. In some instances there may be valid reasons for your lawyer's conduct. For example, the lawyer may explain that the bills have been large in the past three months because the judge ordered all of the discovery to be completed during that period.

Alternatively, your lawyer may have deferred significant activity in the case for some strategic reason. Let the lawyer explain his performance. In addition to addressing your specific concerns, the lawyer's response may tell you a great deal about the lawyer.

After the lawyer has responded to your concerns, ask him to identify what he will do to address those concerns. With regard to certain issues, the lawyer may need a few days to crystallize his thinking regarding remedial action. If so, establish specific deadlines for the lawyer's response. Recognize that, in some instances, the lawyer may not be able to address your concern. While instances in which no compromise can be reached should be rare, the performance review is an appropriate place to identify such impasses.

Don't forget to let the lawyer know which aspects of his performance have pleased you. Even lawyers need positive reinforcement from time to time. If you love the fact that your lawyer always returns your phone calls within one hour, let him know. Performance reviews allow you to reiterate the aspects of your business relationship which are important to you.

Upon completion of the performance review, memorialize the review in a letter or memorandum to your lawyer. This will reinforce the seriousness of the performance review in the mind of the lawyer. To some lawyers, an event did not occur unless it is recounted on paper. The letter should summarize the topics discussed and outline the action which the lawyer—or, in some instances, the client—plans to take in the future.

In addition to decreasing the likelihood of future disputes regarding the performance review, the letter establishes a baseline against which future performance reviews can be compared. If three reviews in a row feature your complaints about the lawyer's responsiveness, you have a pretty good idea that drastic action is necessary. When you prepare for a performance review, it is often difficult to remember what was covered in the last performance review six months ago. The letter or memorandum provides you with a record of earlier performance reviews and allows you to identify any recurring problems.

Require Authorization for Certain Courses of Action

Require your lawyer to obtain express prior authorization from you or the designated representative before embarking on certain courses of action. Your lawyer will face hundreds of decisions regarding activities which could be pursued in your lawsuit. With regard to the majority of these decisions, the lawyer should be allowed to exercise her professional judgment without specific consultation with the client in advance. Some decisions, however, should be made by the client after the lawyer has explained the issues to the client. Identify the areas in which you do not wish your lawyer to proceed without first consulting you and obtaining your authorization.

The areas covered by such an arrangement will vary with different cases, clients and lawyers. Some clients want the lawyer to obtain express authorization regarding more matters than other clients. Discuss this issue with your lawyer. Ask her to tell you whether your proposed list is a reasonable one. Ask her to suggest additions to or deletions from the list. Work with your lawyer to develop a list which is sufficiently comprehensive to give you the comfort level you seek, while not preventing your lawyer from doing her job.

Matters for which clients often require the lawyer to obtain prior express authorization include the addition of new parties to the lawsuit, the hiring of consultants or expert witnesses, the scheduling of certain depositions, the ordering of expensive demonstrative evidence—charts, graphs, mock-ups—and fact-finding missions to Tahiti.

This concept applies with particular force to the area of settlement negotiations. Every competent lawyer knows that the client must authorize any formal settlement offer in advance and that the lawyer is required to advise the client of any and all settlement offers made by the other side. In addition to this, however, statements made by your adversary or your adversary's lawyer may provide you with useful insights regarding your ultimate settlement strategy.

Instruct your lawyer to report all substantive statements, comments, correspondence, conversations or communications of any sort with your adversary or your adversary's lawyer regarding settlement. If you are going to be making decisions regarding your settlement strategy, you need complete information—or at least as complete as possible—on which to base your decisions. The only way to obtain such information is to insist that your lawyer report to you in detail any substantive communication from the other side which might affect your settlement strategy.

Diversify

Use a number of different lawyers or law firms to perform your legal work. If you use a single lawyer or law firm for all of your legal work, that lawyer may become complacent. The lawyer may begin to take your business for granted. The lawyer may begin to pay more attention to the new clients he's attempting to woo rather than his established client—that is, you.

On the other hand, if you split your work between two or three lawyers or law firms, each of those lawyers or law firms has an incentive to keep your legal costs down and provide you with first-rate work. The knowledge that you have a relationship with other lawyers in town serves to keep each of your outside lawyers focused. Each lawyer is aware of the quiet—but very real—competition which exists between each of the firms. Many businesses take advantage of this dynamic by splitting their legal work between two or three law firms and by establishing an ongoing competition between those firms for future work from the company.

Questions, Questions, Questions

Ask questions. Lots of questions. One of the best ways to control your lawyer is to ask him every single question which occurs to you. Ask your lawyer why he is taking a particular course of action, why your opponent reacted in a certain way and why a judge made a particular ruling—the latter usually being a question to which there is no reliable answer.

You will have plenty of questions. Ask them all. Don't be afraid of appearing stupid. With luck, lawsuits aren't your area of expertise. It's unreasonable to think that you will understand all or even most of what goes on in a lawsuit. Let your lawyer know that you're paying attention to the case by asking questions whenever they occur to you.

Such questions will occur to you at random times. Keep a pad handy and jot down the questions as they occur. Call your lawyer when you have a question, even if the phone call only lasts two minutes. Don't worry if some of the questions lead to obvious answers. You have every right to ask any question which occurs to you. The lawyer works for you. He is paid to answer your questions. Good lawyers are delighted to answer the client's questions. The fact that you are asking questions demonstrates that you care about the case and are trying to help the lawyer succeed.

Frequent questions from the client often spur lawyers to do better work. If the lawyer knows the client is paying attention to the case and that he will be required to justify his actions, the lawyer is more likely to give thoughtful consideration to all of his recommendations and actions. Moreover, the knowledge that the client may call at any time with a question serves to prevent the lawyer from allowing the case to lie dormant for long periods of time.

Samuel Johnson's observation about the salutary effect of the prospect of being hanged in the morning applies with particular force to lawyers.

Most importantly, your questions may be of great value to the lawyer and to your prospects for success in the lawsuit. Clients regularly ask questions and make suggestions which lead to a successful resolution of the lawsuit. The lawyer can become so consumed with the day-to-day requirements of the lawsuit that he may overlook an important strategy or opportunity. Your questions can cause the lawyer to consider a new strategy or re-think the current course of action.

Don't be surprised or concerned if on some occasions your lawyer doesn't know the answer to your question immediately. There will be plenty of instances in which your lawyer will have to investigate the question before responding. This is normal. If, on the other hand, the lawyer is clueless in response to every question you ask him, you may have a problem on your hands.

Maintaining Control

In summary, you should employ all means at your disposal to manage and control your lawyer effectively. This discussion has been by no means exhaustive. Clients can and do utilize a variety of procedures to assist in the effective management of their lawyers.

Structure your system to fit your particular needs. Whatever the components of your system, it is essential to structure and implement a system to manage your lawyer.

Chapter Nine

Handling Your Lawyer's Bill

In the quest to control your lawyer, few approaches can match the effectiveness of carefully monitoring the bills generated by the lawyer. Unfortunately, many clients devote insufficient time and attention to the review of their lawyer's bills. There are a number of understandable reasons for this.

First, the bill is an unpleasant reminder of an unpleasant situation—the lawsuit and the events which led to the lawsuit. Some clients tend to delay review of the lawyer's bill and then review the bill in a cursory fashion. The goal for such people is not to review the bill or to use it as a tool to assist in the management of the lawyer. Instead, they want to spend as little time as possible dealing with the bill and the unpleasant memories the bill evokes.

Second, lawyer's bills are confusing to many non-lawyers. The bills often contain more jargon and cryptic abbreviations than an OSHA manual. Even when the narrative is comprehensible, the activities described can be esoteric enough that the client has no idea whether they are appropriate activities. Faced with this situation, some clients resort to reviewing nothing more than the total amount of the bill.

Third, the bill represents a drain on the financial resources of the company or the individual. The lawyer's bill is another cost of doing business which you grudgingly incur. Unlike other costs, though, there is no tangible asset received in return for payment of the bill.

Finally, there is the time factor. Most clients are busy with a variety of business and personal matters which don't include dealing with a lawyer. The lawsuit itself has already taken the client away from his or her business and personal life for too long a period of time. The last thing the client wants to do is to spend even more time scrutinizing a bill from the lawyer. Better to review the bill quickly, get it off your desk, and return to the tasks—or the football pool—at hand.

Resist these impulses. If you don't, the results can be awful.

Monthly Scrutiny Beats Chaos

A client who fails to scrutinize his lawyer's bill each month risks paying for unnecessary services and forfeits an important opportunity to control the lawyer. The monthly review of the lawyer's bill can also provide the client with an opportunity to provide the lawyer with valuable input regarding the substantive issues involved in the dispute and the way in which the case is progressing.

This discussion will focus on monthly bills which reflect an hourly billing arrangement. This is the most common type of bill you are likely to receive from a lawyer. However, the principles discussed are also applicable to other billing arrangements.

Progress in Billing Systems

In years past, lawyers didn't even bother to itemize bills. When I began practicing law, it was not uncommon for lawyers to send out bills which contained nothing more than the following notation:

"For Professional Services Rendered....$5,400"

Such bills were inscrutable. The wonder of it all is that clients paid these bills for so many years, often with little or no idea of the services which had been provided in exchange for the fees.

Today, the majority of lawyers provide their clients with more information regarding the services provided by the lawyer in exchange for the fee. Most lawyers' invoices will reflect the specific services provided, the lawyer or paralegal who provided each service, the amount of time expended by the lawyer or paralegal in providing each service, the hourly rate of the individual who provided the service, the legal expenses incurred and, at some point, a total of all of the foregoing items.

Figure 9-1 is a portion of a standard hourly fee bill.

Figure 9-1

DATE	ATTORNEY /PARALEGAL	SERVICES	TIME
2-15-95	JDS	Review Johnson contract. Draft interrogatories. Telephone call from Attorney Jackson. Prepare memorandum to file.	3.4
2-15-95	PKJ	Review and organize Johnson documents. Prepare memorandum to Attorney Smith.	6.4
2-16-95	JDS	Draft interrogatories. Review Johnson documents. Review memorandum. Conference with SLW.	4.7
2-16-95	SLW	Conference with JDS.	.7

This bill shows the date of each service, the lawyer or paralegal who provided the service, a description of the service and the amount of time expended in providing each service. The business person should insist on at least this level of detail from his lawyer. The bill should reflect all of this information, as well as a detailed breakdown of expenses.

Tell your lawyer you expect the narrative to be comprehensive, detailed and—most importantly—understandable. A bill which is replete with terse entries such as "Research—7 hours" or "Lawyer Conference—2 hours" is of little value. If the lawyer has performed legal research, the bill should reflect what issues the lawyer researched. If the lawyer had a conference, the bill should reflect the names of all the participants, as well as the subject matter of the conference. The greater the level of detail, the better.

You might even require your lawyer to provide a greater level of detail than is reflected in Figure 9-1. While the narrative in Figure 9-1 informs the client of each of the activities undertaken by Lawyer JDS on February 15, 1995, it doesn't tell the client how much time Lawyer JDS spent on each individual activity.

This is important because one of the things the bill should allow you to do is to track a particular activity throughout the month and determine how much time was spent by your lawyer on that particular activity. In the absence of specific time entries for each individual activity, you cannot determine how much time was spent on any given activity.

For example, if you want to determine how much time was spent drafting the interrogatories, you can't do so using the narrative in Figure 9-1. That bill shows that Lawyer JDS spent a certain amount of time drafting interrogatories on February 15, 1995 and an additional period of time drafting interrogatories on February 16, 1995. It does not, however, reflect how long Lawyer JDS spent drafting interrogatories on each of those days.

This problem can be addressed by requiring the lawyer to provide you with specific amounts of time spent on each separate task. This approach requires the lawyer to keep more detailed records and may encourage the lawyer to be more efficient and economical with her time.

Figure 9-2 reflects such a bill.

Figure 9-2

DATE	ATTORNEY /PARALEGAL	SERVICES	TIME
2-15-95	JDS	Review Johnson contract (.5). Draft interrogatories (2.3). Telephone call from Attorney Jackson (.2). Prepare memorandum to file (.4).	3.4
2-15-95	PKJ	Review and organize Johnson documents (5.6). Prepare memorandum to JDS (.8).	6.4
2-16-95	JDS	Draft interrogatories (1.9). Review Johnson documents (1.2). Review memorandum (.9). Conference with SLW (.7)	4.7
2-16-95	SLW	Conference with JDS (.7).	.7

This level of detail allows the client to review the amount of time spent by the lawyer or paralegal on individual activities, compute the total amount of time spent on an activity by all of the lawyers or paralegal and compare the entries of various lawyers and paralegals for certain activities.

For example, the client can now determine that Lawyer JDS spent 2.3 hours drafting interrogatories on February 15, 1995 and 1.9 hours drafting interrogatories on February 16, 1995. Assuming there are no additional entries regarding interrogatories, the client can determine that the Lawyer JDS spent 4.2 hours drafting these interrogatories.

The client can also compare the time expended by different lawyers and paralegals with regard to specific tasks.

Figure 9-2 shows that on February 16, 1995, Lawyer JDS and Lawyer SLW met for .7 hours (i.e., 42 minutes). The entries of Lawyer JDS and Lawyer SLW conform to one another. Both lawyers report .7 hours. In some instances, however, the entries might be inconsistent. Without the level of detail reflected on Figure 8-2, it would be impossible for the client to determine how much time Lawyer JDS allocated to the conference with Lawyer SLW on February 16, 1995. Without this level of detail, the client cannot discern any such inconsistencies.

Testing Specific Activities

The greater level of detail also enables the client to review the bill to see whether the time expended by the lawyer on specific activities appears appropriate. You may wonder what Lawyers JDS and SLW discussed for 42 minutes on February 16, 1995. With this level of reporting, you can ask your lawyer that question.

You should track a certain activity throughout the bill to determine the total time allocated to that particular activity. This is a good test of the overall reliability of the reporting system.

A lawyer's bill may reflect that the cumulative total of the notation "Preparation for deposition of witness Smith" is twenty hours. The bill may further reflect that the deposition itself lasted only twenty minutes. While this level of preparation for a twenty-minute deposition may be justified, the client deserves to know how long it took his lawyer to prepare for the deposition of witness Smith.

Review the narrative to see whether it appears that any unnecessary duplication has occurred. In Figure 9-2, it appears that paralegal PKJ spent 5.6 hours reviewing and organizing the Johnson documents on February 15, 1995. On the next day, Lawyer JDS spent 1.2 hours reviewing the Johnson documents. Does this reflect a duplication of activity? It may not, but the client should review the bill and ask the lawyer to explain such instances where the narrative suggests that the lawyer and the paralegal each spent time on the same task.

Select particular tasks which involve multiple days or lawyers. Compute the total amount of time expended on a particular task to determine whether the total cost of the task appears reasonable.

For example, your monthly bill may reflect that Lawyer Smith spent four hours on Monday, three hours on Tuesday, and two hours on Wednesday drafting interrogatories. The bill may also reflect that Lawyer Jones spent two hours on Thursday editing the interrogatories and that Lawyer Smith then spent an additional two hours on Friday revising the interrogatories—no doubt to insert Lawyer Jones' revisions. All told, Lawyer Smith spent eleven hours drafting and revising the interrogatories, while Lawyer Jones spent two hours editing the interrogatories.

In order to determine the true cost of the preparation of the interrogatories, add all of Lawyer Smith's hours, multiply them by his hourly rate, then add all of Lawyer Jones' hours, multiply them by his hourly rate, and add the two figures together. Assuming that Lawyer Smith's rate is $100 per hour and Lawyer Jones' rate is $150 per hour, it cost you $1,400 to have these interrogatories prepared. This may or may not be a reasonable figure, but you will never know the true cost of such items unless the bill provides this level of detail and you go through the foregoing exercise.

Many companies have begun asking their lawyers to break down their bills in this fashion so that the company can see how much individual tasks cost.

Using a Historical Perspective

If the representation has been ongoing for some time, compare the cost of similar tasks on different bills. For example, your April bill may reflect that the preparation of a set of interrogatories by a certain lawyer required fifteen hours at a total cost of $1,500. Your June bill may reflect the preparation of another set of interrogatories, but this set took thirty hours to draft, was drafted by a different lawyer, and resulted in a cost of $3,750.

There may, of course, be a reasonable explanation for the divergence. The preparation of one set of pleadings seldom requires exactly—or even nearly—the amount of time required to prepare an earlier set of pleadings. Nevertheless, a detailed bill enables you to discuss these matters with your lawyer.

If the same or similar tasks show up on successive bills with exactly the same time entry, question your lawyer. If every telephone call is billed as a twelve minute event (a .2 entry on many lawyers' timekeeping systems), your lawyer or his firm may have an internal rule that requires that all telephone calls be billed as no less than .2 hours. If so, you are probably paying for time which was not spent on your behalf. Your lawyer may have been on the phone for thirty seconds, but you are being charged for twelve minutes of his time.

This may seem a small matter, but those twelve-minute entries add up. If you're paying your lawyer $125 per hour, a twelve-minute entry is worth $25. In the foregoing scenario, you pay your lawyer $25 every time he touches the phone, even when he's only on the phone for thirty seconds.

Next, review bills from a number of months to ensure that your lawyer is working efficiently. Assume that your lawyer must prepare for the deposition of the opposing side's expert witness, Mr. Green. If your monthly legal bills reflect that your lawyer spent thirty hours preparing for the deposition in April, thirty hours preparing for the deposition in May and thirty hours preparing for the deposition in June—followed by the deposition itself, which occurred in late June— you should question your lawyer regarding his preparation methods.

While preparation for a major deposition often begins weeks and even months in advance, if the lawyer prepares too far in advance, he may have to duplicate certain facets of his preparation on the eve of the deposition.

The bill in Figure 9-2 could contain additional information. For example, it would be better if the narrative described the issues discussed in the meeting between Lawyers JDS and SLW on February 16, 1995. Similarly, the narrative could be improved by providing greater specificity concerning the "Johnson documents" and specifying whether the interrogatories in question are the first, second or third set of interrogatories.

Anticipating Simple Errors

Also, you shouldn't hesitate to check the lawyer's arithmetic. Most hourly bills contain a summary of the hours expended by each lawyer or paralegal, the hourly rate for that individual, the total cost of the services provided by that individual and the total fee for the month. A representative fee summary appears in Figure 9-3.

Figure 9-3

ATTORNEY /PARALEGAL	HOURS	HOURLY RATE	TOTAL
JDS	34.6	175.00	$6,055.00
SLW	14.2	110.00	1,562.00
PKJ	42.4	55.00	2,332.00
TOTAL FEE			$9,949.00

A large number of lawyers and law firms calculate their bills using hand-held calculators or adding machines. So, the client should verify each figure and rate. Review each daily entry for each lawyer or paralegal to ensure that the time reflected for each separate activity adds up to the total time for that individual on that day. After you have verified this, add the time for each lawyer or paralegal to confirm that the number reflected in the summary is the correct sum of that individual's daily time entries.

Perform the multiplication by the hourly rate of each individual and total the fees of each individual to ensure that the lawyer or the book-keeper hasn't made any mistakes. Don't assume that lawyers don't make math errors. They do.

Checking Expenses

The expense section of a lawyer's bill is often given little attention by the client. Perhaps because the expenses pale in comparison to the fees, clients tend to overlook this portion of the bill. As discussed above, however, legal expenses can represent a significant portion of a company's total legal bill. This section of the bill should be scrutinized.

Legal expenses are generally defined as all of the costs associated with the lawsuit with the exception of the lawyer's fee. The client is usually responsible for the payment of these expenses as they become due.

In some contingent fee arrangements, the lawyer will agree to pay the expenses and bill the client for the expenses upon completion of the lawsuit, but such arrangements are usually limited to instances in which the client cannot afford to pay the expenses as they become due. It should also be noted that some clients negotiate agreements with their lawyer which require the lawyer to absorb routine expenses such as postage, telephone charges and small copying jobs.

Meet with your lawyer at the outset of the litigation to establish your policy concerning expenses. Require the lawyer to develop a list of anticipated expenses, including the cost of each expense and the reason why the expense will have to be incurred. Generate your own list of anticipated expenses and review the list with your lawyer.

Tell your lawyer that you want him to exercise his judgment to keep expenses as low as possible. If two court reporters of identical quality are available for a deposition, you want the lawyer to hire the less expensive reporter. If discount tickets are available for travel, you want the lawyer to use them. If taking a taxi is less expensive than renting a car, you want the lawyer in the back of that cab. Most lawyers realize their clients want them to cut costs in this way, but many lawyers tend to forget this as the case progresses.

Tell your lawyer you expect to be billed for expenses at cost. Amazingly, some law firms engage in the practice—usually undisclosed—of marking up expenses before passing them on to their clients. This is done to cover overhead and to create additional profit.

One large New York law firm raised this practice to an art. This firm added surcharges to a host of expenses—all without informing their clients of the practice. If the lawyer traveling on a client's case spent $10 for breakfast, the expense item on the client's bill would be $14. Surcharges were added to such expenses as telephone calls, telecopier charges, postage charges and computerized legal research—all for no reason other than to increase the firm's profit margin.

While such practices may be the exception, make sure your lawyer or law firm does not engage in such activity. Require your lawyer to give you a schedule of the amount the firm charges for particular expense items such as photocopies and telecopier transmissions. Review each expense item to determine the reasonableness of each item and to ensure that no surcharge has been added.

Next, confirm that you will not be billed for items which constitute generally accepted office overhead or for unnecessary services.

For example, specify that you will not pay for administrative tasks such as preparation of your bill. If your lawyer plans to charge you for each piece of paper consumed while working on your case—or each envelope or for regular secretarial time or for a pro rata portion of the firm's electric bill—you need to know this in advance.

Similarly, identify those expenses which are necessary and refuse to pay for any additional expense items unless approved by you in advance. One law firm, again in New York, billed its clients $.45 per minute—$27 per hour—for a firm employee to stand by a printer to make sure the printer didn't jam while printing a document.

To avoid such chicanery, inform your lawyer which expenses you are willing to pay and insist on detailed, comprehensive explanations for each expense in your monthly bill.

The Etiquette of Expenses

The issue of which expenses will be borne by the client should be determined on a case by case basis between you and your lawyer. As a general proposition, however, the following expenses are often paid by the client:

- copying expenses,
- long distance telephone charges,
- telecopier charges,
- postage,
- overnight delivery service charges,
- filing fees,
- courier charges,
- court reporter charges,
- expert witness fees,
- reasonable travel and lodging expenses, and
- reasonable transportation expenses.

On the other hand, the client should not pay for the following expenses unless there is a particular reason to do so in a specific case:

- office overhead,
- standard secretarial services,

- office staff services (librarians, word processors, proof readers, copy machine operators),

- stationery,

- standard office supplies,

- local telephone calls,

- first class air travel,

- in-town meals,

- unlimited out of town meals, and

- incidental travel expenses (use of the hotel health club, in-room movies).

Items such as secretarial overtime can be addressed on a case by case basis. As a general proposition, however, such costs should be borne by the lawyer or firm.

Legal expenses are a hidden—but often significant—component of the client's total legal costs. You should discuss each expense item with your lawyer to insure that (1) you're not paying for expenses which should be part of the lawyer's overhead and (2) the lawyer is not marking up the expenses in order to create an additional profit center.

The expense portion of a lawyer's bill will usually list each expense with a minimal amount of explanation. A typical expense portion of a bill is found in Figure 9-4.

Figure 9-4

EXPENSES

In-house copying charges .... $ 65.25
Outside copying charges 125.75
Telecopier charges 32.00
Long distance telephone charges 28.32
Postage 33.50
Courier fees 55.00

Court reporter fees	565.00
Witness fees	150.00
Expert witness fees	2,500.00

Travel Expenses:	
Airfare	1,450.00
Mileage	78.00
Hotel	424.00
Meals	124.50
Car rental	178.00
Parking	24.00

TOTAL EXPENSES	$5,833.32

As was the case with the bills relating to services provided by the lawyer or paralegal, a client should require the lawyer to provide the greatest reasonable amount of detail in the expense portion of the bill. Some clients require the lawyer to provide backup documentation for expenses, while others simply require the lawyer to have such documentation available in the event that the client asks for it. In either event, the lawyer should be able to document each expense item.

The expense summary contained in Figure 9-4 is representative of the way expenses are summarized by most lawyers. Categories are listed, followed by specific dollar amounts. Here are some suggestions regarding the expense items listed in Figure 9-4.

Copying

The per sheet rate charged for both in-house and outside copying should be reflected. There will usually be a large difference between the two rates; in-house copying usually costs more. Ask your lawyer why certain copying is performed in-house and other copying is sent to an outside copying service. This will often be a function of the volume of documents to be copied. Ask the lawyer whether he solicits competitive bids from local copying services and, if not, ask the lawyer how he selects his outside copying service.

Telecopier (Fax) Charges

Most lawyers charge clients for telecopier transmittals. Determine the charge per sheet and ask the lawyer how that amount was chosen. Ask the lawyer if the client is charged for both incoming and outgoing telecopier transmittals. If the monthly telecopier charge is high, ask the lawyer why so many telecopier transmissions are necessary. As a group, lawyers have become over-dependent on telecopier machines. In many instances, there may be no real need for a document or letter to be telecopied. For documents over ten pages in length, a courier or overnight mail service is usually less expensive—so long as time considerations do not preclude their use.

Long Distance Telephone Charges

Find out who the lawyer is calling and why. If the monthly charge seems high, ask the lawyer why so many long distance calls are necessary. Determine whether the lawyer or law firm uses direct dial or the more expensive operator-assisted method of making long distance telephone calls. Be sure that you are being billed only for the long distance telephone calls necessitated by your case—as opposed to being allocated a percentage of the firm's overall long distance telephone bill.

Ask the lawyer how his firm keeps track of long distance telephone calls and what system is employed to match specific calls with specific clients.

Postage and Courier Fees

This expense item can include United States mail, private overnight delivery services and couriers. Determine whether your lawyer uses couriers and overnight mail services when regular mail will suffice. While I confess a personal lack of confidence in the United States Postal Service, some lawyers use couriers and overnight delivery services to excess. If these monthly charges seem large, ask your lawyer about his postage policy.

Court Reporter Fees

Court reporter fees are an inevitable consequence of litigation. Court reporters are used to report and transcribe the testimony and lawyer conversations at depositions and many hearings. In the case of a hearing, the parties typically share the cost of the court reporter. In the case of depositions, the party who has scheduled the deposition pays for the takedown and for the original transcript—if they choose to order it.

The other parties pay for their respective copies of the deposition transcript. The cost is much greater if your lawyer scheduled the deposition because the takedown fee and the original transcript fee are much greater than the cost of copies of the transcript.

Due to the fact that court reporter fees can run in the thousands of dollars, many lawyers require their clients to pay court reporter fees directly. This is in contrast to most other expenses, which the lawyer will usually pay on behalf of the client and then bill the client at the end of the month. Most good court reporters charge about the same amount of money for their services. While a lawyer can do some degree of price shopping, the lawyer is much more concerned with the court reporter's accuracy.

There are a number of ways to limit court reporter fees. First, make sure your lawyer does some price shopping for court reporters. Second, advise your lawyer that when possible, the lawyer should allow the lawyers for the other parties to schedule the deposition—thus ensuring that the other parties will incur the larger court reporter fee. Third, instruct your lawyer to order the transcript of the deposition only when the facts warrant ordering a copy.

Some lawyers order copies of every single deposition taken in the case. While it is true that lawyers usually want the transcript of each deposition, there may be some instances in which the testimony of the witness has nothing to do with your portion of the case and therefore you do not need the transcript.

Finally, tell your lawyer to schedule only those depositions which are essential to the case. Some lawyers have gotten into a bad habit of deposing every witness who happened to be breathing at the time of the dispute. This is overkill, pure and simple. Remind your lawyer that he should only take essential depositions.

Witness Fees

These are statutorily imposed fees which a party is required to pay to a fact witness when the party requires the witness to appear at a deposition or trial. Witness fees are typically nominal and intended to cover travel expenses. Require your lawyer to list each witness and fee separately. If the list resembles the local telephone book, ask your lawyer why he needs so many witnesses.

Expert Witness Fees

Now we enter the high-rent district. If you need an expert witness in your case, you will learn that expertise isn't cheap. Expert witnesses run the gamut from invaluable to worthless. Similarly, the fees charged by expert witnesses run the gamut from bargains to highway robbery.

Like court reporter invoices, expert witness invoices are typically sent to the client for direct payment. The amount charged by most expert witnesses is too large for most lawyers to feel comfortable paying the fees on behalf of their client. Ask your lawyer a series of questions about the expert witness he has hired. Does the expert witness charge an hourly rate or at a flat fee? Did the lawyer do any price shopping? Are there other expert witnesses who could provide the same level of expertise for less money?

Be sure to pay particular attention to the invoice submitted by the expert witness. Apply the same principles to the expert witness' invoice as you would to your lawyer's bill. Make sure that the expert witness is not charging you for unnecessary services.

Finally, remind your lawyer that you don't want to hire expert witnesses needlessly. Some lawyers hire two or three expert witnesses in every case. In most instances, this is not necessary. Tell your lawyer that you want to hire the smallest number of expert witnesses possible and that you want to be sure that you need an expert witness before you hire one.

Travel Expenses

Extensive detail is important in the area of travel expenses. As any seasoned business traveler knows, the cost of travel can vary greatly depending on the approach taken by the traveler. Air fare costs can be reduced through advance ticketing. Two hotels located a block apart may charge different nightly rates. Instruct your lawyer to save stays at the Ritz for his vacation.

Establish clear policies regarding travel and require your lawyer to provide documentation reflecting adherence to those policies. Require the lawyer to separate the cost of the hotel room from incidentals such as the in-room movie or health club fees. Require your lawyer to explain why he needs to rent a car on every trip. In many instances, public transportation or shuttle buses will suffice.

Paying the Expenses

Make sure expense items are paid promptly. You can often obtain discounts of ten percent or more by paying legal expense bills within thirty days. Court reporters almost always offer discounts for prompt payment and many copying companies offer similar discounts. Such savings add up over the course of a lawsuit.

As you review the bill, keep a running list of any questions you may have for your lawyer. The list should include entries on the bill which you do not understand, entries with which you do not agree, ex-

penses you do not believe you should have to pay and any other subjects suggested by the bill. Don't be shy. Require your lawyer to explain every item on the bill which you do not understand. Do not pay
the bill until all of your questions have been answered.

When those questions have been answered, pay the bill promptly.
Lawyers are not finance companies. By allowing a bill to remain unpaid for months, the client may be hindering the lawyer's ability—or
inclination—to proceed vigorously with the prosecution of the case.
Unpaid bills can become a source of friction between the client and
the lawyer, jeopardizing the ability of the client and the lawyer to
work effectively in tandem to defeat your opponent.

As the unpaid balance increases, the issue of the lawyer's bill can
become a distraction which diverts the attention of the lawyer and
client from the shared goal of prevailing in the lawsuit. In addition to
being the right thing to do, prompt payment of your lawyer's bills is
smart business.

TAMING THE LAWYERS

Chapter Ten

Taming Your Lawsuit

Sometimes, despite your advance planning and prudent conduct, a lawsuit is inevitable. You may have engaged in every preventive measure available. Your people may have been well trained and may have kept meticulous records. Faced with an incipient dispute, you may have attempted to negotiate and compromise.

Despite all this, your adversary ignores all reason and files a lawsuit against you.

Your focus now shifts to effective management of the lawsuit itself. Your goal should be to minimize the impact of the lawsuit on your business—and your life. One component of this task involves controlling the costs incurred as a result of the lawsuit.

The cost of the lawsuit is, of course, a function of the activities in which the litigants engage during the life of the lawsuit. Effective cost control depends, therefore, on effective management of those activities.

You should rely upon your lawyer's judgment regarding the necessity of certain activities. Different lawsuits require different measures and you should give your lawyer the latitude to suggest the steps which should be taken in your particular lawsuit. Nevertheless, such ad hoc decisions should be made in the context of your strategy for the litigation. In creating that strategy, there are certain principles which apply to almost every lawsuit.

You should identify your goals at the outset of litigation and establish a strategy for achieving those goals. Your goal may be to extricate yourself from the lawsuit as quickly and cheaply as possible. On the other hand, your goal may be the public humiliation of your adversary. You will probably have a number of goals, which you should rank in order of importance. Whatever your goals, identify each of them and communicate the goals to your lawyer.

You should establish a strategy to achieve those goals. Develop the strategy with your lawyer and reduce the strategy to writing for reference throughout the lawsuit.

Regular reference to the original goals and strategy is essential to remaining on track. If you stay on track, you will reduce unnecessary activities and, consequently, your legal costs.

Narrow the Issues

Every lawsuit arrives complete with issues—factual issues, legal issues, strategic issues, tactical issues, financial issues and so forth. Your lawyer can spend enormous amounts of his time and your money addressing all of these.

Left to their own devices, lawyers tend to burrow into every conceivable issue. Why? Because lawyers don't want to miss anything. A good number of lawyers are compulsive and an even larger number of lawyers realize that investigating more issues produces larger fees. Whichever impulse is at work, the best way to avoid missing something is to investigate everything.

It's up to you to help your lawyer combat this tendency. While lawsuits can involve hundreds of issues, the relevant issues are usually small in number. Work with your lawyer in the early stages of the lawsuit to isolate and identify the issues which are germane to the outcome of your case.

Once those issues have been identified, instruct your lawyer to restrict activity to those tasks which are essential to the resolution of the identified issues. If a task does not have a direct relationship to an identified issue, it should not be undertaken.

You will need to give your lawyer some degree of latitude in this regard. Some issues may not be apparent to the non-lawyer. Your lawyer may believe that a particular issue is central to the resolution of the case, while you think it is unrelated to the case. Allow your lawyer to explain his theory to you. If the explanation seems logical, allow the lawyer to pursue the issue for a period of time. This is the sort of legal judgment for which you are paying the lawyer.

Some issues develop as the lawsuit progresses. The original strategic plan will have to be modified as the case progresses to address new issues which may develop. Require your lawyer to advise you when a new issue develops and to explain to you why that issue is central to the resolution of the case.

Narrowing the issues at an early juncture prevents the expenditure of your money on issues which are at best ancillary and at worst irrelevant. Insistence on such narrowing of the issues also has a salutary effect on your lawyer. Faced with the knowledge that his client is fully informed about the issues and is insisting upon a consistent reexamination of the case to eliminate extraneous issues, your lawyer will be encouraged to engage in such issue-narrowing himself.

Shorten the Life of the Lawsuit

Time may be money in most businesses, but when it comes to lawsuits, time is encrusted with gold. On this count, one of my cardinal rules bears repeating:

THE LONGER A LAWSUIT LASTS, THE MORE MONEY IT COSTS.

This is an immutable law of litigation. The four-year lawsuit costs more than the two-year lawsuit. This applies most directly to lawsuits in which the lawyers are being paid on the basis of hourly rates, but it is also true to a lesser extent in contingent and fixed fee cases.

Even if you are paying your lawyer on the basis of a contingent or fixed fee arrangement, the lawyer will incur greater expenses in a four-year lawsuit than in a two-year lawsuit.

The 1994 case *Gary Bogle v. Phillips Petroleum Co.* shows how a complex and lengthy lawsuit can bounce around the court system for years, benefiting no one except lawyers.

In October 1989, an explosion at Phillips' Houston Chemical Complex caused 24 deaths, a number of personal injuries and property damage affecting thousands of people. Gary Bogle and other employees and victims of the explosion filed suit in Harris County, Texas, in November 1989, alleging negligence on the part of Phillips. This lawsuit was eventually consolidated with other legal actions arising out of the explosion.

During the course of the consolidated proceedings, Bogle and the other plaintiffs filed a supplemental petition alleging that Phillips wrongfully denied them medical benefits, terminated part of its medical program and breached its fiduciary duties. Phillips argued that many of the plaintiffs, "who belatedly sought medical or psychiatric treatment, were faking their injuries or malingering."

The employees had filed their lawsuit in Texas state court. Texas courts are known for handing out big judgments against big companies. When the employees filed their supplemental petition regarding the medical benefits, Phillips saw a chance to escape from the state court.

Phillips asked that the case be moved to federal court. The company claimed that the medical benefits issue brought into play provisions of ERISA—a federal employee benefits law.

Not surprizingly, the employees fought the move, arguing that there was no ERISA question. Later, they also tried to drop the medical beenfits claim.

The federal trial court agreed with the employees. It allowed them to drop the medical benefits claim and ordered the case back to state court. Phillips promptly appealed.

The federal appeals court ruled that the order sending the case back to state court wasn't appealable. The lower federal court had ruled that the "case does not contain a federal claim, and three years of important work and preparation occurred in state court." The magic words "this case does not contain a federal claim" rendered the district court's order unreviewable. The case had to go back to state court.

But the federal appeals court added its own twist to the proceeding. It ruled that:

> Having made the critical decision that [the federal employee-benefits law] did not preempt any of the state law claims, the district court lacked jurisdiction to rule on the...plaintiffs' motion [to drop some of their claims]. Therefore, its decision...was in error, and the order implementing it is void and of no effect.

So, five years after the plant explosion that had started the whole dispute, the case was sent back to state court. None of the plaintiffs had received any money. The defendant company hadn't resolved its possible liability. Phillips' lawyers, on the other hand, had five years of legal fees in the bank.

Of course, in some instances time must be invested in order to recover money. You don't want to truncate the case if doing so limits your lawyer's ability to win.

We can stipulate that rushing the case to trial before your lawyer is ready would be a bad thing to do. In reality, though, it is nearly impossible to do this—even if you wanted to. The rules of civil procedure afford your lawyer ample opportunity to prepare just about any case adequately before being rushed to trial.

How, then, can you accelerate your lawsuit? The best way to do so is to tell your lawyer that the fastest possible disposition of the lawsuit is one of your primary goals. Instruct your lawyer to present you with a plan for expediting the resolution of the lawsuit. While certain matters are beyond your lawyer's control—the court's docket, certain statutory time periods—there are a number of tactics he can employ to expedite your case.

Direct your lawyer to complete all necessary tasks within the minimum amount of time allowed by the rules. To the extent possible, tell your lawyer to require your opponent to do so as well. Instruct your lawyer not to request extensions of any time periods. Similarly, tell your lawyer that you will not agree to any extensions which may be requested by your opponent.

Lawyers regularly receive time extensions from each other and from the judge throughout the course of the lawsuit. The extensions usually begin with the time for the filing of an answer, segue into extensions of the time for filing responses to discovery requests and culminate with postponements of the trial itself. Many lawyers have become accustomed to such extensions and are often content to allow a lawsuit to proceed at a leisurely pace.

You can avoid this pitfall by instructing your lawyer not to request or consent to any unneeded extensions. Have your lawyer notify your opponent's lawyer of this policy at the beginning of the case. Instruct your lawyer to tell your opponent's lawyer that you will not agree to any time extensions and will oppose any requests for extensions made by your opponent to the court. While a small number of situations may be beyond your control, the majority of time extensions are granted by lawyers, not judges.

This policy will have a number of ramifications, almost all of which are positive. First, you will become less popular with your lawyer. Second, your lawyer will become much less popular with your opponent's lawyer. Third—and most importantly—you will shorten the life of your lawsuit.

Next, instruct your lawyer to engage only in such discovery as is essential to the thorough preparation of your case for trial. Lawsuits often get bogged down in the discovery phase as lawyers try to address every issue, ask every question, review every document and depose every witness. Require your lawyer to present you with a detailed plan regarding proposed discovery and the reason why each discovery activity is essential.

Once the discovery plan has been submitted, instruct your lawyer to complete each item on the list as soon as possible. Tell your lawyer that you want him to complete discovery well in advance of the end of the applicable discovery period. Tell your lawyer to file the initial interrogatories and requests for production of documents along with your answer, rather than waiting weeks—or even months—to do so.

Have your lawyer interview potential witnesses immediately and schedule depositions sooner rather than later.

Absent any pending motions, lawyers can begin to seek a trial date upon the close of discovery. Most lawyers do not do so. Given the crowded state of the dockets of most judges, a case can remain in legal limbo for extended periods of time after discovery has been completed.

Avoid this pitfall by instructing your lawyer to press for the earliest possible trial date. Notice that I said that the lawyer should press for an early trial date. The trial calendar is controlled by the judge's calendar clerk and is a function of a number of factors beyond the control of you or your lawyer.

Nevertheless, persistent efforts to place a case on a trial calendar will almost always result in the setting of a trial date at an earlier date than would have been obtained in the absence of such efforts.

The Reasons Quick Is Good

There are a number of advantages to be derived from obtaining an early trial date. The prospect of an early trial date may cause your opponent to settle the case. A substantial number of cases settle immediately prior to trial. This occurs regardless of whether the trial is scheduled to begin three or five years after the filing of the lawsuit.

The trial itself—or, more accurately, the prospect of going to trial—acts to foster settlement. Accordingly, an earlier trial date often results in an earlier settlement.

Simply stated, your opponent may not be ready to go to trial. Many lawyers are not ready to try a case when it first appears on a trial calendar. This may be the result of sloth, a heavy case load, conflicting cases, or plain ordinary garden variety negligence. Whatever the reason, your opponent may be unprepared and the prospect of going to trial at that point may be unacceptable.

This is one of the dirty little secrets of civil litigation—cases sometimes settle not because of the merits of the dispute, but because the lawyer is not prepared to try the case. The lawyer rarely reports this fact to the client. Instead, the lawyer begins talking to the client about how much it will cost to try the case, how difficult the case will be to win and how much smarter and safer it would be to settle the case.

In light of this, the earlier you can obtain a trial date, the greater your chances of placing your opponent's lawyer in this uncomfortable position. If your opponent is unprepared, he will have two options, neither of them attractive. The lawyer can either settle the case or go to trial unprepared.

If your opponent proceeds to trial unprepared, you will have a distinct advantage at trial. If your opponent seeks settlement of the case—knowing he can't afford to proceed to trial—the terms of the settlement will almost always be more favorable to you. These results can be achieved by spurring your lawyer to prepare your portion of the case quickly and pressing for an early trial date.

Staff Your Case Properly

An essential component of controlling your legal costs—assuming you're being billed on the basis of hourly rates—is to ensure that tasks are performed by the least expensive qualified individual.

For basic legal research, you want the $90 per hour associate rather than the $275 per hour partner. Instruct your lawyer to reduce your costs by assigning all tasks to the least expensive qualified individual. This approach should also include the use of your employees to perform certain tasks whenever possible.

For example, if your lawyers need to locate and organize thousands of your internal documents, there is usually no reason why such a task cannot be performed by one of your employees—as opposed to a lawyer or paralegal. Why pay a junior associate $100 per hour to wade through a warehouse full of documents when the task can be performed by one of your employees whose salary you have already committed to pay?

The use of paralegals can reduce your legal costs. Identify the tasks which can be performed by a paralegal, as opposed to a lawyer. The initial review of documents produced by your opponent in a lawsuit is a good example. Most commercial litigation involves mountains of documents produced by each party. The conscientious lawyer knows that each piece of paper must be reviewed to determine whether that document contains information which is important to the case. An initial review of all of the documents must, therefore, be conducted.

The documents can be reviewed by a junior associate at the rate of $100 per hour or by a paralegal at the rate of $55 per hour. If both the lawyer and the paralegal require eight hours to review the documents, your cost will be $800 if the lawyer reviews the documents and only $440 if the paralegal reviews the documents.

Even if you assume that the lawyer can review the documents more quickly than the paralegal—a dubious assumption—the savings remain significant. If the lawyer can complete the task in six hours, resulting in a $600 fee, you will still save $160 by using the paralegal. Over the course of a protracted lawsuit, such savings add up.

A caveat: You should monitor the use of paralegals closely. In some situations, a lawyer may duplicate work performed by a paralegal.

For example, if a paralegal reviews a file cabinet full of documents one by one, the lawyer should not subsequently review each document. Instead, the paralegal should prepare a summary of the documents indicating which documents need to be reviewed by the lawyer.

In general, you should watch out for duplication of effort. Don't allow each pleading to be reviewed and edited by three or four lawyers before the pleading is finalized. Tell your lawyer that each deposition does not require the attendance of three lawyers and two paralegals. Insist upon efficient staffing of your case.

Some may regard such instructions as micromanagement which produces measured savings at best. This is not the case. Scrutiny can produce significant savings.

As an illustration, consider deposition attendance. Some lawyers and law firms are in the habit of sending multiple lawyers and paralegals to each deposition. It is not uncommon for some firms to send the following cast of characters to a single deposition: the senior partner who has ultimate responsibility for the case ($250 per hour); the junior partner or senior associate who will do most of the work in the case and who will conduct the examination of the witness ($150 per hour); the junior associate who has performed the preliminary factual investigation of the case, as well as the legal research ($100 per hour); and the paralegal who has reviewed and organized the documents and prepared the deposition exhibits ($55 per hour).

Your combined hourly rate for this cadre of legal talent is $555 per hour. If the deposition lasts five hours—not an unusually long deposition—your cost will be $2,775. And that doesn't include the court reporter's fee.

This cost can be reduced by more efficient staffing of the deposition. In most cases, the senior partner and junior associate are superfluous. Eliminating those two individuals reduces your cost by almost two-thirds to $1,025. Unless the number of exhibits is massive, you can usually eliminate the paralegal as well. This reduces your cost an additional $275, bringing your cost down to $750.

You may not make as large an impression on the other side by sending fewer lawyers, but you have reduced your legal costs by $2,025 on a single deposition. If your case involves ten depositions, you could reduce your costs by $20,250. Not an insignificant amount.

Use Motions Wisely

Pre-trial motions can be of significant utility in the quest to control legal costs. Discuss with your lawyer when such motions are applicable in your case.

Certain motions can end or shorten the lawsuit. Ask your lawyer whether a Motion to Dismiss or a Motion for Judgment on the Pleadings is applicable in your case. Motions for Summary Judgment can, if successful, end a lawsuit—assuming that they are not overturned on appeal. Motions for Partial Summary Judgment can reduce the issues in a case, thus reducing the time your lawyer will have to spend preparing the case for trial.

Motions to Add additional parties to the lawsuit can sometimes facilitate settlement of the case. By adding to the number of parties with exposure to liability, you increase the number of potential contributors to a settlement.

Instruct your lawyer to determine whether there are any unnamed entities which might share responsibility for the events which led to the lawsuit. If so, you may wish to file a Motion to Add certain individual entities or a Motion to Consolidate your lawsuit with another pending lawsuit involving the same or related issues. Although such a consolidation may complicate your lawsuit, it will bring additional potential contributors into your lawsuit and will reduce the likelihood that you will have to endure multiple lawsuits pertaining to the same matter.

Reduce Legal Research

Lawyers spend a substantial amount of time conducting legal research. While comprehensive and accurate legal research is the foundation of all successful legal representation, much legal research is duplicative and inefficient. Legal research tasks are typically assigned to younger lawyers, who may be less efficient in their legal research than more experienced lawyers. Moreover, the younger lawyer is concerned with not missing anything and often engages in overkill.

Perhaps most importantly, when a young lawyer is given a research assignment, the lawyer typically starts from scratch. This is unnecessary. In many instances, a business will pay its lawyers to conduct the same legal research over and again. If your business is involved in legal disputes or situations which recur with some degree of regularity, your lawyers should not conduct the same legal research each time a dispute arises.

For example, if you are in the securities industry and you are faced with frequent lawsuits involving the securities laws, your lawyers should not have to perform the same background research in every case. The memorandum written last year about a particular issue probably needs only to be updated—not written all over again.

Instruct your lawyers that, where appropriate, you want them to utilize legal research which the lawyers have previously performed. This research need not even have been performed for your business. If, for example, your lawyer recently conducted legal research on behalf of another client which is the same research you need for your case, there is no reason for the lawyer to perform the research again for your case. While the lawyer must, of course, take care to avoid any breaches of confidentiality or the attorney-client privilege, this is a way in which you can reduce your legal research fees.

This doesn't take unfair advantage of the other client. If your lawyer represents two clients who have a need for the same legal research, the clients can split the cost of the research.

Keep a file of the legal research performed for you by your lawyers over the years. Those legal memoranda can be used as starting points by your lawyers in the future. They can also be used by different lawyers if you choose to employ a number of different lawyers. While a new lawyer will always want to verify and update another lawyer's research, the memoranda can save the new lawyer substantial time and may even suggest certain approaches or theories to the new lawyer.

Legal research data bases are currently being established which will allow businesses to access legal research without hiring their own lawyers to conduct the research. Assuming the service ensures the quality and accuracy of the legal research—and has the financial resources to pay for any damages you might incur as a result of any mistakes—this approach has the potential to produce significant reductions in the cost of legal research.

A final word about on-line legal research. Properly utilized, these systems are invaluable to both lawyer and client. The two largest providers, LEXIS and WESTLAW, compile and constantly update legal opinions, statutes, regulations and a variety of other legal research resources. Lawyers pay a subscription fee for access to these services and are then charged, in some fashion, for the time they spend on line.

Most lawyers pass the on-line charges on to their clients. There is nothing wrong with this practice, so long as the client has agreed in advance to pay such charges. The problem occurs when lawyers who are unfamiliar with these systems spend exorbitant amounts of time on line due to the inefficiency of their search requests. If your lawyer is going to use one of these services (and she probably should), make sure you instruct the lawyer to hone her on-line research skills before she logs on to the system.

Control the Discovery Process

Discovery can be the black hole of civil litigation. Like its astronomical counterpart, discovery consumes matter of all sorts—especially money—and is virtually insatiable. In order to control your legal costs, it is essential that you control the discovery process.

Controlling the discovery process involves identifying the essential tasks, completing those tasks expeditiously and avoiding unnecessary tasks. Reduce the life of the discovery period by refusing requests for extensions and avoiding any such requests of your own. Reduce the cost of discovery by monitoring your lawyer's activities during the discovery period, with special emphasis on the lawyer's staffing of the case.

In addition to these approaches, avoid discovery disputes with your opponent. Discovery disputes are disagreements between lawyers regarding the information requested by one lawyer from her adversary. The requesting lawyer believes she is entitled to certain information. The responding lawyer disagrees. The dispute involves such matters as the production of certain documents, the scheduling of a deposition or the inspection of a facility. In every instance, discovery disputes involve an escalating clash of wills between the lawyers.

Discovery disputes can be resolved by agreement of the parties or by order of the court. If the parties cannot agree, they file the appropriate motions asking the judge to settle the question. The lawyers troop into court, lower lips protruding, with the air of school children on their way to inform the teacher that a classmate is cheating at kickball.

The judge views the lawyers in much the same way as the teacher views the school children. The judge wonders why these tykes can't settle their petty differences themselves and is more than a little put out at having to referee the quarrel. Many a lawyer has made trouble for himself and his client at trial by bothering the judge with an endless stream of discovery disputes.

In addition to irritating the judge, discovery disputes consume both time and money. Each lawyer must write at least one brief explaining the dispute to the judge. An oral argument is sometimes required. In either case, the parties must await a ruling from the judge before resolving the dispute, thus lengthening the life of the lawsuit.

Certain discovery disputes are beyond your control. If your opponent refuses to produce a piece of evidence to which you are entitled, you have no choice but to file the appropriate motion (the aptly named Motion to Compel Discovery) to force the issue.

Prior to doing so, however, consider how important the requested evidence is. While your opponent's reluctance to produce the evidence may, in and of itself, provide you with sufficient reason to pursue the evidence, in other instances you may determine that the value of the evidence you are seeking does not justify the cost you will incur in attempting to force your opponent to produce it.

The frequency of discovery disputes can also be reduced by producing all discoverable documents and other evidence to your opponent when such evidence is requested. The rules of civil procedure are broad and allow the discovery of all information "reasonably calculated to lead to the discovery of admissible evidence."

Recent amendments to the Federal Rules of Civil Procedure obligate litigants and their lawyers to produce all information which might be relevant to the dispute. When faced with a discovery dispute, judges tend to decide a majority of such disputes in favor of production of the requested evidence.

As a practical matter, this means that your opponent is probably going to be allowed to see just about everything you have which might in some remote way have some bearing on the issues in the lawsuit. Unless the evidence in question is a trade secret, attorney work product or protected by the attorney-client privilege, you will probably be required to produce the evidence if your opponent requests it.

Produce the evidence when it is first requested. Don't be distracted by the fact that you can't see what possible relation the evidence has to the case. Don't be concerned if the evidence is voluminous or if it contains embarrassing—but irrelevant—information. Avoid the discovery dispute and the attendant loss of time and money by producing the evidence when it is first requested.

This is not, of course, to suggest that you should automatically comply with all of your opponent's discovery requests. Lawyers sometimes request things to which they know they are not entitled, just to see if the other side will slip up and produce it.

Discuss each discovery request with your lawyer to ensure that your opponent is entitled to the requested evidence. If he is entitled to it, however, don't become embroiled in a lengthy and expensive discovery dispute which you will probably lose. If your opponent requests information to which he is not entitled, consider filing a Motion for a Protective Order rather than waiting for your opponent to file a Motion to Compel Discovery.

This accelerates the process and allows you to initiate resolution of the issue rather than being in a reactive position and appearing to the court to be a recalcitrant litigant who has to be dragged into court kicking and screaming by his opponent.

Control Expert Witnesses

Expert witnesses are widely used in civil litigation, to explain certain technical issues to the jury and to give an opinion regarding certain issues in the case.

Years ago, the use of expert witnesses was much less widespread. Expert witnesses were used primarily in cases involving professional negligence or complex technical issues which were presumed to be beyond the grasp of a lay jury.

Today, however, expert witnesses are used by litigants in a broad array of disputes. You're being sued because the computer system you sold allegedly doesn't work properly? Hire an expert witness to explain how the system usually works and why your system meets the industry standard. Your customer claims that industry standards allow him to pay your bill at the rate of $20 per month for the next hundred years? Hire an expert in your industry to testify that no such industry standard exists.

There is a fundamental contradiction in the role of an expert witness. The expert witness is allowed to testify because she is an expert in the field who is expected to analyze the issues at hand and offer an unbiased opinion based on her expertise. However, the vast majority of expert witnesses used in civil litigation are hired and paid by one of the parties to the lawsuit. This creates the potential for mischief, primarily when the so-called expert is in reality nothing more than a hired gun who will develop opinions tailored to fit the position of the litigant who is paying her fee.

Expert witnesses are well compensated. Depending on their area of expertise, expert witnesses charge anywhere from $500 to $5,000 per day. Almost all experts are compensated on an hourly or daily basis. Some experts charge a certain amount for pre-trial analysis and a different—higher—amount for testifying, either at a deposition or at a trial.

How do you know if you need an expert witness? Your lawyer can help you answer this question as it pertains to your specific case. In general, however, expert witnesses are helpful when your lawsuit involves issues with which a lay jury is unlikely to be familiar. This is, of course, a very broad definition which could encompass any commercial dispute. For example, insurance may not seem complex, but unless your jury is comprised of people in the insurance industry, you could probably use an expert witness to explain the industry to them.

In some instances, you may need an expert to refute the testimony of your opponent's expert. Juries place great credence in expert witnesses. If your opponent has an expert and you do not have an expert at trial, it is possible that the jury will infer that you could not find an expert who would take your side of the case.

Credible expert witnesses can be of great value to the commercial litigant. A good expert witness can place the issues in context, assist in determining what happened, explain what should have happened and educate the jury regarding all of these issues. Bad expert witnesses, on the other hand, can have a disastrous effect on your lawsuit.

A bad expert witness is an individual who lacks superior knowledge and analytic skills in her area of expertise, lacks forensic skills or is a hired gun willing to craft her opinion to meet the perceived needs of your case. A bad expert witness has the potential to doom your case.

How do you avoid hiring a bad expert witness? Begin by meeting with your lawyer to identify the tasks which you want your expert witness to perform. Are you concerned with explaining to the jury how a complicated computer system works? Is your goal to hire a polished speaker who will be a forceful advocate for your position at trial? Do you want an expert who can create impressive models, graphs or charts for the jury to view? Do you want an academic or a seasoned veteran of the private sector?

After you have determined the skills and services you are seeking, conduct a well-planned search for your expert. Your lawyer may take primary responsibility for locating potential expert witnesses, but make sure that he does so in a rational fashion and that he utilizes all available sources.

There are companies which develop lists of expert witnesses in every discipline imaginable. These companies will provide you with these experts for a fee. In some instances, the fee will include the expert's fee. In other instances, the expert's fee is a separate charge.

These companies run the gamut from useful to dangerous. The credible companies investigate the credentials of their experts and maintain some level of quality control. The less credible companies are more interested in compiling large inventories of experts than in the ability of the listed individuals. Approach these companies with great care.

You and your lawyer should jointly interview a number of potential expert witnesses before hiring one. Focus on the services you want the expert to provide and on each candidate's apparent ability to provide those services. Ask the candidate to provide you with a detailed resume, including references and all materials which she has authored. Make sure that nothing written by the expert conflicts with your position in your case. Analyze the candidate's appearance, demeanor and verbal skills. The expert will be called upon to convince a jury of her expertise and credibility through oral testimony. The leading authority in a particular field may be unable to explain your position to a jury.

Determine how often the candidate works for litigants as an expert witness. While some experience with the litigation process is helpful, you don't want to hire an expert who makes a living by testifying as an expert witness. Rightly or wrongly—and it's usually rightly—juries tend to view such individuals as hired guns. This impression can impair the expert's credibility.

Discuss the expert's fee. Find out if she charges a higher rate for depositions and court testimony. Avoid experts who want to utilize contingent fee payment schemes or who ask for a percentage of any judgment which you may receive. Such fee arrangements can undermine the expert's objectivity and may well indicate that the expert is a hired gun in the worst sense of the term. Your opponent's lawyer will make sure the jury learns of this arrangement.

Determine how much time the expert can devote to your case. The best expert in the world is of little value if she cannot devote significant attention to your case when you need her to do so.

Finally, avoid at all costs the expert who lets you know that she will adopt whatever position you want her to adopt. This leads to the another cardinal rule:

HIRED GUNS OFTEN MISFIRE.

Hired guns are unscrupulous charlatans who will lead you to ruin.

Few things cause a trial lawyer to salivate more than the prospect of cross-examining a so-called expert whose opinions and testimony are unsupported by the facts of the case and the general literature in the field. You want an expert who will tell you the truth. Period.

If your position is unsupported by facts or theory, you want your expert to tell you so and to do so early in the process. Sometimes your position is simply untenable. If so, you want your expert to tell you so. Far better to learn this from your own expert at an early stage in the case than during your opponent's cross examination of your expert at trial.

If you can, have your lawyer hire the expert. In certain jurisdictions, having your lawyer hire the expert can insulate the expert's work product from discovery until your expert is ready to testify.

Have the expert conduct a preliminary analysis of your case. Make sure the expert does not produce a written report at this stage. Such a report is usually discoverable by your opponent. Until you know what the expert's opinion will be, you don't want that opinion reduced to writing.

It is imperative to obtain the expert's preliminary analysis at the earliest possible juncture in the case, especially if expert testimony will play a large role in the case. Remember that one of the reasons you hired the expert was to tell you whether your case is a strong one. If the expert concludes that you have a weak case, you need to know this as soon as possible. If the expert believes you have a strong case, early knowledge of this opinion will help shape your litigation strategy.

The expert's preliminary analysis will also help you decide whether you have selected the proper expert witness. The expert's work product will confirm either the wisdom or the folly of your selection. If the expert's performance in the preliminary analysis stage is awful, you want to know this as soon as possible so that you can start looking for a new expert.

Assuming the preliminary analysis is a quality effort and you decide to stick with this expert, discuss with the expert how much additional time the expert will need in order to make final conclusions concerning your case. While you don't want to prevent your expert from making all necessary preparations, neither do you want to give the expert free rein to undertake the reinvention of the wheel.

Keep in mind that the expert works for you and is subject to the financial parameters you establish. Some experts can run up staggering bills during the life of the lawsuit by engaging in ongoing analysis, research and review.

Avoid this pitfall by monitoring the activity of your expert witness in the same way you monitor the activity of your lawyer.

Avoid unnecessary payments to your expert. For example, if your opponent wishes to depose your expert prior to trial—as he most certainly will—the law in many jurisdictions allows you to require your opponent to pay your expert for that time. If your expert needs to review files—as she most certainly will—have the expert review the files previously prepared for your lawyer.

Lawyers sometimes depend on expert witnesses too heavily. Although expert witnesses can be of great value in assisting your lawyer in the preparation of the case, be sure that your lawyer doesn't begin to use the expert witness in the role of a paralegal assistant. Identify the specific tasks you wish the expert witness to undertake and establish time limitations beyond which the expert should not proceed.

Settle Early

Almost 95 percent of all civil litigation cases end in settlement. There is typically no reason to believe that your case will be in the minority. Accordingly, the next cardinal rule is:

SETTLE EARLY, NOT LATE.

Unfortunately, most cases settle late. It usually takes the very imminent prospect of trial to cause one or both of the parties to begin serious settlement negotiations.

Not until the trial is scheduled do many parties begin to give serious thought to the fact that they may have to risk losing a lot of money in the form of legal fees and a potential adverse verdict. Not until the trial is scheduled do the lawyers have to begin the usually uncomfortable—and often excruciating—trial preparation process. Not until the trial is scheduled does the judge meet with the parties and beat them about the head and shoulders trying to persuade them to settle the case because the last thing the judge wants to do next week is try another case.

The confluence of these forces usually produces a settlement. Unfortunately, the settlement is reached after the clients have spent years paying their lawyers and dealing with the case. A favorable settlement may be a Pyrrhic victory when the time and money invested over the life of the case is calculated.

In light of this, make every effort to settle the case when it is in its early stages. This is, of course, easier said than done. Many lawyers believe that it is foolish to settle a case before engaging in a fair amount of discovery. This belief is often justified. It is sometimes impossible to assess the value of the case without determining—through discovery—what the evidence would show at trial.

However, it is equally true that the parties will have to spend lots of money to discover what the evidence will show at trial. Much of the evidence in question will be known to the parties without engaging in any discovery whatsoever. The central facts of the dispute which led to the lawsuit are well known to the parties long before the lawyers arrive on the scene.

By going through the discovery process, you may be paying a lot of money to obtain that last 25 percent of the facts. In most instances, this is not a good investment. Besides, nobody knows what the last 25 percent of the facts will show. Those facts could buoy or sink your case. In light of this, you may wish to consider negotiating a settlement on the basis of the facts at your disposal prior to discovery.

When you settle early, you also avoid having to continue to pay your attorney. While civil litigants almost always ask the court or jury to award them their attorney's fees, such awards are rare. Even where specific statutes provide for the award of attorney's fees, there is an element of risk involved. A good example is the 1985 U.S. Supreme Court case of *Marek v. Chesney*. *Marek* was a civil rights action which arose out of the shooting of the plaintiff's son by police officers.

The father, on his own behalf and as administrator of his son's estate, filed suit against the police officers in Federal District Court. Prior to trial, the officers made a timely offer of settlement of $100,000, expressly including accrued costs and attorney's fees, but the father did not accept the offer. The case went to trial and the father was awarded $5,000 on the state law claim, $52,000 for the civil rights violation, and $3,000 in punitive damages.

The father then filed a request for his attorney's fees under the federal civil rights law, which provides that a prevailing party in a federal civil rights action may be awarded attorney's fees "as part of the costs." The claimed attorney's fees totalled in excess of $170,000 and included fees for work performed subsequent to the settlement offer.

The District Court declined to award these latter fees pursuant to Rule 68 of the Federal Rules of Civil Procedure, which provides that if a timely pretrial offer of settlement is not accepted and "the judgment finally obtained by the offeree is not more favorable than the offer, the offeree must pay the costs incurred after the making of the offer." Recognizing that the plain purpose of the rule is to encourage settlement and avoid litigation, the District Court held that the term *costs* includes attorney's fees incurred after rejection of the settlement offer.

On appeal, the Court of Appeals reversed and held that the father was entitled to all his attorney's fees. The Court of Appeals reasoned that to hold otherwise would deter plaintiff's attorneys "from bringing good-faith actions because of the prospect of losing the right to attorney's fees if a settlement offer more favorable than the ultimate recovery were rejected."

The issue faced by the Supreme Court on appeal was whether a plaintiff who rejects a pre-trial offer of settlement, and thereafter recovers a judgment and pre-offer costs award that added together are not more favorable than the originally offered amount, is precluded from recovering all post-offer costs, including attorney's fees.

The Supreme Court held in the affirmative and denied recovery of all of the plaintiff's post-offer attorney's fees. The Court pointed to the fact that the original drafters of Rule 68 failed to define the term *costs* in the Rule. The Court assumed the drafters must have been aware of other statutes consistently defining fees as costs when they drafted the Rule. It concluded that attorney's fees were meant to be included in Rule 68—as evidenced by the drafters' failure to expressly exclude them.

Taking a Logical Approach

Assuming that you believe that your interests would be served by negotiating a settlement early in the case, how can you persuade your opponent to do so? For starters, try logic. Tell your opponent everything we've considered in these pages—the case will probably settle at some point anyway...it makes sense to settle now rather than after the lawyers have added to their respective retirement funds...it will mean lots of extra free time for both of you.

If logic fails, try financial incentives. Tell your opponent that you've placed a value on the case which is not subject to negotiation—say, $50,000. Tell your opponent that if the case settles in the next 24 hours, you will add to the settlement kitty a portion of the money you would have to pay your lawyer in the absence of a settlement—say, $10,000. Then tell your opponent that if he does not accept the offer in the next 24 hours, you will begin reducing the base offer by the amount you have to pay your lawyers and by an additional—unknown—amount to compensate you for your time and frustration. Tell your opponent you're serious about this and that you will never agree to pay a larger amount in settlement than you are willing to pay today.

The trick to this approach is convincing your opponent that you mean what you say. Lawyers engage in this sort of bargaining all the time and they seldom stick to their original positions. A final offer is rarely final in the world of lawsuit settlement negotiations. So, you have to find a way to convince your opponent you aren't kidding about this.

One way to do this is to reduce the offer to writing. At the very least, this will get the attention of your opponent's lawyer. A second way is to convene a settlement conference with the principals present. Your opponent's lawyer may not take such an offer seriously, but your opponent might. If you can persuade the judge to attend the settlement conference—in his chambers, if possible—all the better.

Be sure that the lawyers are not impeding a possible settlement. This can occur when your opponent's lawyer is not giving your opponent an accurate view of the case. It can also occur due to a personality conflict between your lawyer and your opponent's lawyer.

Question your lawyer periodically to determine whether either of these situations exists in your case. If so, formulate a strategy regarding how best to overcome this problem. While your lawyer cannot directly contact your opponent, you can. Such contacts should be made carefully and only in certain situations—but they can be effective in circumventing a lawyer who is impeding a potential settlement.

Finally, stick to your guns. Never stake out a position you're not willing to defend. Put another way, never make a threat you're not willing to carry out.

It also helps to convince your opponent that you're just crazy enough to do what you are saying you will do, even when it ceases to make economic sense.

TAMING THE LAWYERS

Chapter Eleven

Preventive Measures

It is axiomatic that the best way to reduce your legal costs is to decrease the occasions on which you need a lawyer. It costs a lot less to establish and implement a system to decrease problems than it does to pay a lawyer to resolve the problems. Your goal is to avoid the need for lawyers to the greatest extent possible.

There are a number of ways in which a person or a business can reduce the chances of becoming embroiled in disputes which will lead to litigation.

Documentation and Record-Keeping Techniques

Legal disputes develop in a variety of ways. One party misunderstands another party. Someone forgets a commitment and fails to meet certain obligations. Somebody else sees an opportunity to pull a fast one and tries to do it. Unexpected developments produce unanticipated changes to a situation or agreement.

All of these matters share a common element: They are triggered by human conduct. As such, they are subject to differing interpretations by the individuals involved in each situation. Human conduct is mercurial, unpredictable and sometimes unfathomable.

One thing, however, is certain—if forced to rely on memory alone, the participants in any transaction will produce differing accounts of the transaction. Any tool which can be used to reduce reliance on human memory and subjective interpretation will also reduce the frequency of disputes.

Moreover, situations often change after an event or transaction. People leave a company. Everyone's memory gets a little weaker. Companies are purchased and sold. Financial conditions alter. In short, life goes on. The only constant is that piece of paper in the old file cabinet that establishes what really happened on a particular day. Those pieces of paper can win, lose or—in some cases—prevent lawsuits.

Effective documentation and record keeping serve a variety of purposes. First, good records can prevent or limit disagreements with customers, business associates and employees. Second, if a disagreement arises, good records can help resolve the dispute. Third, good records will assist you in defending your position in the event that a full-blown dispute or lawsuit materializes.

You should create and implement a system for keeping records and documents generated in the ordinary course of business. Make sure that the system is user-friendly. If the system is too complicated, your employees will probably not use it as often as they should. Make sure that the documents are maintained in a rational, consistent and organized fashion.

The best records in the world are of little value if you can't find them.

Your system should require the creation of a written record of the transactions which comprise your business. This kind of system does not require a great deal of equipment. It can be started by distributing to your employees a humble note pad, along with the direction to create a written record—however brief—of each business transaction.

This is not as onerous or time-consuming as it might sound. How long does it take to write a three-sentence memorandum of a meeting or telephone conversation? The key is to train your people—yourself included—to create a written record of each transaction.

Confirmation

Written records work best when they are co-authored by, sent to or agreed to by the other participants in the transaction. As a practical matter, your business associate, customer, or vendor is probably not going to sit down with your employee after each conversation or meeting and draft a joint memorandum.

The next best thing is to send the other participant that staple of American business, the *confirmation letter*. This is nothing more than a brief letter sent to your counterpart that says something along the lines of "This will confirm our telephone conversation of this morning in which you ordered five hundred widgets for delivery on Monday at the total price of $5,000, payable upon delivery."

That's it. It doesn't have to be any more complicated. Train your people to stick to the facts. Leave the editorial comments to the television pundits.

Of course, a confirmation letter can generate a variety of responses. Your counterpart may respond with a letter stating "I beg to differ. I only ordered one hundred widgets and the total price we agreed on was $500."

This, in turn, produces another letter from you and the battle may be joined. It is far better to resolve the dispute at this point than to wait until after the widgets have been delivered or, heaven forbid, the lawyers have been summoned.

On the other hand, your letter may produce a deafening silence from your counterpart. This is not necessarily bad. As far as the law is concerned, silence implies assent. You can make the situation even clearer by adding this sentence to your confirming letter: "If I don't hear from you, I assume you agree with the contents of this letter and will proceed accordingly."

Record and book club companies have generated a great deal of business using this approach.

Responding on Your End

Failure to respond to an issue raised by a potential adversary can be prejudicial at a later trial—that's something you want to avoid. Make sure your employees respond in writing to all business communications.

Your response should correct any inaccuracies in the correspondence. If this is not done, your silence may be interpreted as agreement with the contents of the letter or telephone conversation.

It's also essential to keep a copy of the confirmation letter for your own file in a place where you can retrieve it if the need arises. Pick a place, put all such documents in that place and make sure the records aren't discarded by an overzealous cleanup crew or a junior vice president intent upon avoiding the purchase of yet another file cabinet.

To accomplish this, establish a company-wide record retention policy. Decide how long you need to keep different types of records and tell everyone in the company about it. Ideally, most records should be kept until the statute of limitation regarding a particular transaction or project expires.

Because some statutes may allow the filing of lawsuits up to ten years after the transaction has been completed, you could be faced with some pretty steep storage costs. Compared to the cost of a lawsuit, though, such storage costs can be a bargain.

You may, of course, choose to establish a shorter retention period. Whatever the period, make sure everyone in the company is aware of the policy and adheres to it.

You may wish to designate a particular employee as your company's records czar. There is something to be said for assigning responsibility for all records to one individual or department. Give that person the responsibility for gathering and organizing all of the records. On the other hand, your company may prefer a less centralized approach. In either event, make sure your employees know that they are required to keep certain records and where those records should be kept.

Prioritizing the Paper

What records should you keep? Generally, any document which evidences a business transaction. These documents include correspondence, letter agreements, formal contracts along with any amendments, working drafts of agreements and contracts, personal notes generated by the participants in each transaction, invoices, receipts, other payment requests, internal memoranda, meeting minutes, financial statements, leases, deeds, promissory notes, photographs, audio or video tapes, checks, and anything else that looks like it might be important.

If this sounds as though I'm suggesting that you keep everything, you're not far from the truth. You never know when you will be called upon to prove that something happened. In such instances, a written record of the transaction in question is invaluable. Space limitations notwithstanding, a file cabinet costs a lot less than a lawyer.

There is one caveat to all of this: Any document which you create can be subject to discovery if a lawsuit develops. This means that your opponent's lawyer will have the right to make you give him copies of all of these documents, including the handwritten notes in which you question your opponent's ancestry.

This is not to say that this possibility should deter you from establishing and implementing a comprehensive documentation and record-keeping policy. Just keep in mind—and remind your employees—that anything and everything you write may well end up in the hands of your adversary's lawyer (or, even worse, shoved under your nose on the witness stand).

Once again, the majority of these problems can be avoided by refraining from including editorial comments and personal attacks in your memoranda. Avoid writing letters in the heat of the moment which contain threats, accusations or other invective.

The establishment of an effective record-keeping and documentation policy will not eliminate business disputes. Even in the face of clear written evidence, some individuals will dispute the facts—or simply lie.

I once deposed a man who swore he had never purchased a piece of equipment despite being shown his check for the purchase price, a receipt for the equipment and a photograph of him using the equipment. In most cases, however, written evidence of a transaction or agreement is the best way to avoid disputes which can grow into full-fledged lawsuits. If a lawsuit results, the written evidence will be a valuable asset in your effort to prevail at trial.

Failure to implement an effective record-keeping and documentation procedure places your company at a significant disadvantage in attempting to resolve a dispute or prevail in a subsequent lawsuit. Without the documents, you are dependent upon people's memories and, to a limited extent, the persuasiveness of your argument or personality. You don't want to have to rely on these things. You want evidence—cold, hard, irrefutable evidence.

Your adversary will probably have his own evidence. In court, documents are more persuasive than people's memories. You should assume that your adversary will have documents and that those documents will support his version of the facts. It's often said that history is written by the winners. When it comes to commercial disputes, those who write the history often emerge victorious.

Training Employees to Reduce Legal Problems

When it comes to legal costs, a company's employees are its greatest asset and greatest vulnerability. Most commercial disputes have their genesis in the acts or omissions of individuals. So, a work force can contribute to the conditions which lead to business disputes.

Properly trained, however, employees can also reduce the incidents and severity of those disputes.

Begin by addressing the conduct of employees in their dealings with customers, vendors and business associates. Assess the way the work force conducts itself in those dealings. Do the employees meet the commitments they make? Is there an established chain of command? Do the people making the decisions and commitments have the authority to do so? Do employees require other business people to honor commitments made to the company? Does the company have standard policies regarding the commitments employees are allowed to make to customers and other business associates?

Although these issues deal with business policies rather than legal policies, they are at the heart of the conduct which often produces disputes and lawsuits.

In the business context, if your employees make fewer mistakes, you will become involved in fewer disputes and lawsuits. In addition to hiring the best employees possible, you can reduce conduct which leads to disputes and lawsuits by establishing certain procedures to be followed by your employees.

Educate your employees about lawsuits. How they develop. How much they cost your business each year. How long they last. Their intangible effect on your business. How the employees should utilize your lawyers.

There is a great amount of misinformation concerning lawyers and lawsuits. Some employees may have a cavalier attitude toward lawsuits, while other employees may be afraid of them. You may have employees who consider lawsuits part of the normal course of business and regularly threaten to file lawsuits. Unbeknownst to you, this employee may be engaging in conduct which leads to disputes as a result of his nonchalant attitude toward lawsuits. Other employees may be so afraid of lawsuits that they concede every disputed point to customers and business associates in order to avoid any chance of a lawsuit.

You want to avoid both of these approaches.

Explain to your employees the proper role of a lawsuit. While you will want to make modifications based on your personal business philosophy, it's usually helpful to explain to employees that lawsuits are serious business and should not be threatened lightly. Every attempt should be made to resolve a dispute informally, so long as the resolution is honorable and economically tolerable.

In certain instances, however, someone may simply be trying to take advantage of you and your business. In such instances, a lawsuit may be warranted. Your employees should not hesitate to let your customers and business associates know that your company is willing to engage in litigation in such instances.

Alert your employees to the warning signs which often indicate that a company is positioning itself for a lawsuit.

For example, if a customer who has never confirmed anything in writing begins writing confirming letters which misstate facts, that customer may be positioning himself for a lawsuit.

Similarly, if the customer begins tape recording meetings, bringing lawyers to meetings, or starts telling you that they have to check with their lawyers before making any commitments, that customer probably is contemplating something other than an amicable business transaction.

Teach your employees how to respond to such activity. Set up reporting procedures and a chain of command to address this kind of positioning. Establish a policy which requires all employees to report such conduct to a designated member of your management team.

Business correspondence is a fertile breeding ground for business disputes. Inform your employees what they should do if they receive threatening or inaccurate letters. If such letters are not answered, they can provide your adversary with damaging evidence in a subsequent lawsuit.

It's a good idea to have a policy which requires that all business correspondence be answered within a specific period of time. Encourage employees to arrange backup assistance from other employees to respond to correspondence when the primary employee is unable to do so. Determine which letters should be reviewed by designated managers before a response is generated.

Make sure your employees know what to do in the event that they are served with a lawsuit or other legal documents. Establish a central repository for all such documents and stress the importance of transmitting such documents to that repository immediately. Your company can forfeit valuable strategic advantages if a lawsuit or other legal document languishes unattended on someone's desk for weeks before it is sent to your lawyer or designated legal administrator.

Impress upon your team the importance of the record-keeping and documentation procedures discussed above. Get your employees in the habit of documenting transactions, sending confirming letters, writing memoranda and creating meeting minutes. Be sure your employees know the purpose of each document and where each document should be sent. Publicize the record retention policy to avoid accidental destruction of important documents. Discuss with your employees the things which should not be reduced to writing. In short, make sure your employees understand and implement your record-keeping and documentation procedures.

In-House Dispute Resolution

An increasingly large portion of corporate legal fees involves the costs associated with the resolution of disputes with the company's own employees. Any company with more than a handful of employees is well aware of the wide array of potential employee disputes. Allegations of discrimination based upon race, sex, age, religion and physical appearance have become a major concern for companies with even a handful of employees. Disputes regarding promotions, demotions, transfers and job assignments are common; disputes over pay, insurance, pension funds and other benefits are even more common.

You can reduce your legal costs by establishing a system to resolve these disputes without resorting to litigation. Most businesses have formal or informal grievance procedures which are available to employees.

In many instances, however, such administrative procedures involve a review of the dispute by a company employee. Employees often perceive that such a system is biased in favor of the company. Dissatisfied with the decision of the company representative, the employee often resorts to litigation.

This shortcoming can be addressed by establishing a dispute resolution procedure pursuant to which the dispute is evaluated by an independent third party who is not employed by the company. The dispute resolution procedure should require the employee and the company to make presentations regarding their respective positions to the independent third party. The independent third party makes a determination regarding the dispute.

The third party's decision can be either binding or non-binding. In either event, the fact that the decision is being made by an individual who is not employed by the company invests the process with greater credibility than a process in which a management representative makes the decision. Such a system can prevent many lawsuits, thus reducing the company's legal costs.

Evaluating Disputes and Lawsuits

Many lawsuits are unnecessary. In most instances, there are a number of opportunities to resolve a dispute informally before a lawsuit is filed. The parties often fail to take advantage of those opportunities because one or more of the parties is not aware that those opportunities exist.

When I was a young lawyer, I received a valuable piece of advice from a senior lawyer who was supervising my work on a particular case. A problem developed with our opponent's lawyer. I wanted to prove to my supervisor—and to myself—that I could solve the problem. I spent weeks trying to solve the problem, but to no avail. Finally, I consulted my supervisor, explaining the problem and my Herculean efforts to solve it.

My supervisor proceeded to solve the problem in a matter of minutes with a single phone call. He then suggested that I should have consulted him when the problem first arose. I had wasted large amounts of my time and the client's money trying to solve the problem alone.

He also gave me some valuable advice: "Don't be the Lone Ranger." He explained that one of the advantages of working with a group of people—whether it be a business or a law firm—is that you have a wealth of resources on which to rely as you try to do your job. It would be foolish not to take advantage of those resources. By failing to do so, you forfeit great potential assistance.

Business disputes tend to snowball with the passage of time. As a problem ages, more levels of management get involved. The reputations—and pride—of a greater number of people are injected. Positions harden. Threats are sometimes made. Someone vows never to concede. Finally, the lawyers are called, at which point any opportunity for a quick or informal resolution of the problem disappears.

Incipient problems are sometimes not addressed because the individual who is involved in the problem is reluctant to reveal the problem to his superiors in the company. Fearful that the mere existence of a potential problem may reflect badly on him, the employee tries to handle the problem himself without involving the very people in the company whose experience could provide valuable assistance in addressing the problem.

While this attitude is understandable, it must be overcome. It is dangerous, inefficient and almost always counterproductive for employees to attempt to resolve potential major problems by themselves.

I hasten to add that I do not mean to imply that you want your employees to be fearful of making decisions on their own. Many companies are paralyzed by a work force which is afraid to order lunch without approval from upper level management. I simply mean that your employees should know when to seek assistance and advice concerning matters which have the potential to develop into major disputes and lawsuits.

Create a business atmosphere in which employees will feel comfortable reporting potential problems at an early stage. Make it clear that you want your employees to report potential problems and that it is the failure to report those situations which may reflect badly on the employee.

One way to promote early detection of problems is to institute a reporting system pursuant to which all employees of a certain level are required to submit a brief report identifying any matter which appears to have the potential to develop into a dispute or a lawsuit. While employees should not, of course, wait until the designated reporting period to report an incipient dispute, this reporting tool forces employees to review potential problems on their respective projects at least once each month.

Designate one or more members of your management team to review these reports. Makes sure your employees know that those individuals are available to discuss potential disputes or lawsuits at any time. Select the individuals for this position carefully. These individuals should have experience with dispute analysis and resolution. Perhaps most importantly, assign these responsibilities to individuals who are unlikely to be involved personally in the disputes you have asked them to evaluate.

This dichotomy of responsibility is essential. If the dispute evaluator is involved in the situation under review, it will be difficult to analyze the situation objectively.

Perhaps the single most prevalent mistake I have observed in corporate efforts to evaluate incipient disputes is the delegation of dispute analysis responsibility to people involved in the dispute in question. These people often have two simultaneous—and often conflicting—objectives. First, they want to resolve the dispute on terms favorable to their employers. No problem so far. Second, they want to resolve the dispute in a fashion which will not reflect badly on them.

This inherent conflict has a tendency to skew the individual's judgment regarding the course of action the company should take. For example, if Fred in purchasing makes a costly mistake, he may determine that it is better to deny the mistake and fight for vindication than to admit he goofed. It may not concern Fred that the company will spend large sums of money en route to a jury deciding—rightly—that Fred made a mistake. The important thing to Fred is that he will not have to admit his mistake and lose face.

To avoid, or at least minimize, this problem, don't allow Fred to make the decision regarding the course of action the company should take. Get Fred's input, to be sure. But in the end, the decision should be made by an individual who is not involved in the matter under review.

Evaluate, Arbitrate and Negotiate

Evaluate each potential dispute thoroughly. The evaluator should begin by gathering all of the facts. Review the written file carefully. Don't rely solely on the oral report of the employee involved in the situation. Determine the current status of the situation.

Is the other side waiting for a response from your company? Have any specific demands been made by either side? Do any deadlines exist which require a response by a particular date? Has the other side injected its lawyers into the situation?

After you have compiled all of the facts, create a hierarchy of desired results. List the things you want from the other side in decreasing order of preference, along with the chances of obtaining each such result. For each desired result, determine the steps which would have to occur in order to attain such a result. Continue the analysis by assessing your chances of achieving each of the steps.

Your first goal should be the amicable resolution of the situation. In order to achieve such a resolution, you may be required to compromise your original position. Decide how far you are willing to go and go no further.

In the course of determining how much of a compromise will be acceptable, examine the ramifications of failing to reach a settlement through compromise.

If you don't settle, is a lawsuit inevitable? Will the passage of time affect your company's position? If a lawsuit results, how much time and money will your company be required to invest in the lawsuit? What are your chances for success? How much of a disruption to your business would a lawsuit cause?

Determine whether there are other parties which might contribute to a settlement. Are there insurance carriers or bonding companies which might bear some of the cost of solving the problem? Are there other individuals or companies which might have some responsibility for the situation? If so, you may wish to contact them to determine if they will acknowledge their potential exposure and contribute—financially or otherwise—to a solution.

Consider whether any type of alternative dispute resolution methodology is available. Is there a written contract which contains an arbitration clause? If not, would your adversary consider arbitrating or mediating the dispute?

Private dispute resolution companies have multiplied in recent years and many of these services provide a cost-effective means of resolving private commercial disputes.

After you've taken all of this into account, develop a list of possible courses of action. Try to anticipate your adversary's response to each such course of action. Assess the cost and the chances of success of each proposed course of action.

Who should be involved in the decision-making process? I'm not a fan of committees, but you should obtain input from a number of sources before deciding on a course of action. In addition to the individual involved in the situation, consider consulting the individual's immediate superior, the highest appropriate company manager, the company's chief financial officer and the company's in-house or outside lawyer. These individuals will provide factual, financial and legal perspectives on the problem, all of which need to be considered before a course of action is selected.

This may sound complicated and bureaucratic. It doesn't have to be. Although the process has been described in some detail, it can be distilled into the following steps:

- Make sure you have all the facts.

- Develop a range of options.

- Consider the ramifications of each option.

- Select and implement one of the options.

There's nothing revolutionary here. Nevertheless, many businesses make important decisions regarding potential disputes without going through these steps.

Time—and timing—are of the essence. As time passes, the available options decrease. Accordingly, the trick is in identifying the potential problems at a point when a variety of options remain viable.

Your challenge is to implement a system which will allow you to identify a potential problem early enough for you to go through this process of analysis. Potential problems are often not addressed early enough for the business person to engage in thoughtful analysis or careful development of a range of options.

Practicality and Principle

After reviewing your options, you may reach the business person's Rubicon: To sue or not to sue?

Faced with an unreasonable adversary who refuses to pay you or stop engaging in a particular type of conduct, it may become apparent that nothing short of litigation offers a reasonable chance of rectifying the situation. How, then, do you decide whether to jump into this particular abyss?

Every business person has to apply her own criteria to this question. You need to decide how important it is in the long run for you to achieve your goal—payment, new terms or whatever else it might be—and how much you are willing to pay in time, money, effort and distraction to achieve that goal. If the cost is acceptable, sue. If not, don't sue.

Put another way, determine as best you can the worst possible result of filing the lawsuit. If you're willing to accept that result in exchange for the opportunity to achieve your goal, file the lawsuit.

What about filing a lawsuit on principle alone—because you believe it is the right thing to do or because you want to demonstrate to your adversary that his conduct will not go unpunished? This is fine, so long as you do so with a clear understanding of the possible ramifications.

The 1977 federal district court decision *Rolls-Royce Motors v. A & A Fiberglass* is a great example of a principled stand that a business felt it had to take.

Rolls-Royce sued A & A Fiberglass, claiming that one of its auto customization kits infringed on the Rolls-Royce's grill and hood ornamentation designs. Rolls-Royce sought to recover for federal, state and common law trademark infringement and unfair competition, injury to business reputation, deceptive trade practices and trademark dilution. A & A countersued for cancellation of the plaintiffs' state and federal trademarks, unfair competition and antitrust violations.

The case concerned a kit A & A designed for the Volkswagen Beetle model. Included in this *Elegant Beetle* kit were parts for radiator grill modification and hood ornamentation which the plaintiffs contended were copies of similar parts installed on Rolls-Royce automobiles.

In 1911, Rolls-Royce had introduced a front hood ornamentation in the form of a statuette called *The Spirit of Ecstasy* or, more commonly, the *Flying Lady*. It had been used continuously since that time. Federal trademark registration was first obtained in 1918 and, despite a ten-year lapse in such protection, trademark recognition was again procured in 1968.

Another distinctive feature of the Rolls-Royce automobile was its front grill—square-framed and vertically shuttered and called the Classic Grill. It had been introduced in 1906. A United States design patent had been obtained for the Classic Grill in 1914 but application for federal trademark registration had been denied in 1975.

A & A was in the business of selling plastic and fiberglass products, including specialty automobile parts. In March of 1972, A & A began selling and advertising its Elegant Beetle package, an assortment of auto parts designed to change the appearance of Volkswagen automobiles. Advertising stressed the likeness of the Volkswagen, as modified, to the Rolls-Royce.

The kit included both a simulated grill and hood ornament bearing resemblance, excepting minor details and the difference in fabrication, to the Classic Grill and Flying Lady.

Rolls-Royce became aware of the modification kits in mid-1972. A & A was notified of Rolls-Royce' objections in January 1973. A & A did not reply and Rolls-Royce did not attempt further contact until August 1975, when they sent a letter demanding cessation of the defendant's activities.

A & A refused Rolls-Royce's demand for voluntary termination of its *Elegant Beetle* sales. A & A sought to avoid liability for trademark infringement at the outset and contended that neither the *Classic Grill* nor the *Flying Lady* was capable of trademark recognition.

The British car maker didn't want money from A & A. It wanted the company to stop making the customization kits that jokingly copied the lines of Rolls-Royce models.

The court ruled that Rolls-Royce was entitled to relief for infringement of the federally registered Flying Lady, for infringement of the Flying Lady and the Classic Grill as Georgia-registered trademarks, for false designation of goods, and for deceptive trade practices. The court ordered A & A, among other things, to stop selling the kits and to destroy any unsold kits.

Rolls-Royce made its point.

Some companies file lawsuits against insolvent parties to defend a particular principle. Other companies file lawsuits in order to obtain the visceral pleasure of hauling their adversary into court. These are legitimate reasons to file a lawsuit. Just keep in mind why you're filing the lawsuit.

Once a course of action is selected, implement it expeditiously. Determine which employee or agent will speak for the company in the future on this matter and channel all future communications through that individual. Be sure to inform your employees what course of action you plan to pursue. If you fail to do this, you run the risk that an employee will unwittingly engage in conduct which is counter productive to your chosen course of action.

Using In-House Lawyers

One sure-fire way to control your legal costs is to hire your own in-house lawyer. Many businesses today have in-house lawyers or legal staffs. The proliferation of legal matters facing today's business person has led many businesses to conclude that their interests are best served by handling their legal affairs—or at least most of them—with their own lawyers.

While this approach creates a fixed cost (the salary and benefits of the in-house lawyer) as opposed to a variable cost (the outside lawyer's annual legal fees), the fixed cost can often be lower than the variable cost.

The economic advantage can be compelling. Assume, for example, that your business has 1,500 hours of legal work in a given year. If that legal work is performed by a senior associate or junior partner at a law firm (at the moderate rate of $135 per hour), the cost of that legal work will be $202,500. On the other hand, your company could employ an in-house lawyer for $100,000 per year to complete the same tasks. Even taking into account incidentals such as health insurance and other benefits—which might raise the cost of the in-house lawyer to $120,000—this still represents a substantial savings.

This scenario assumes that the in-house lawyer has a sufficient breadth of experience to be able to handle all of the legal issues in question. This is not always the case. Even if you hire an in-house lawyer, you may have to hire outside lawyers and law firms to address certain issues in specialized areas. Nevertheless, your legal bills will decrease as you reduce the number of matters which are referred to outside lawyers.

There are other advantages to using in-house lawyers. Continuity. Availability. Loyalty. Accountability. The in-house lawyer will in all likelihood work more than 1,500 hours per year. If the lawyer works 2,000 hours per year—which would still be less than billing 2,000 hours per year in a law firm—you have obtained the equivalent of 500 extra hours of legal protection from your investment.

TAMING THE LAWYERS

Conclusion

In this book, I have described certain tools with which you can reduce your legal costs and control your lawyers. Armed with the knowledge contained in the book and a firm resolve to implement some or all of the approaches in the book, you can gain greater control over your legal affairs and, with a bit of luck, perhaps even decrease the instances in which you need a lawyer.

Like any tool, however, these techniques are of no value unless they are used wisely and well. Only by applying the approaches in this book to your personal or business situation will you be able to produce the desired results.

The approaches discussed in this book operate in the context of the legal system itself. That system also deserves some of your attention and effort. The legal system belongs to you. You subsidize the courts with your taxes. You pay the lawyers, the mediators, the arbitrators, the court reporters and the expert witnesses. In many states, you elect the judges. In all states, you elect—and pay—the legislators who enact the laws.

In light of this, you and I ought to do everything we can to insure that the system functions fairly and efficiently. We cannot accomplish this goal by ceding control of our legal affairs to lawyers and the other members of the legal system. As individuals and business people, it is in our best interest to learn about the system, to monitor the activities of the lawyers, judges and legislators and to insure that they administer the legal system in a rational and just fashion.

As citizens, we have an obligation to protect the legal system from the inefficiencies and abuses which can develop when no one but the administrators pays attention to how the system operates.

It is my hope that this book will help that process. Demanding accountability from the lawyers is the first step. We should demand the same accountability from our judges and legislators. The system will only improve as a result of the involvement of responsible and informed citizens.

Appendicies

Appendix One

Sample Hourly Fee Bill

This an example of the kind of bill you should expect from your lawyer if you've agreed to an hourly fee arrangement. Other fee arrangements might result in different formats, but the basic elements of reporting activity and costs should remain consistent.

March 4, 1995

John Doe
XYZ Company
123 Main Street
Anywhere, CA 90123

File: Jones Co. vs. XYZ Corp.

DESCRIPTION OF SERVICES:

February 1, 1995 through February 28, 1995

DATE	ATTORNEY/ PARALEGAL	SERVICES	HOURS
2/3/95	JDS	Conference with Mr. Doe (.8). Discuss case with SLW (.3). Review Pleadings file (.4).	1.5
2/3/95	SLW	Discuss case with JDS (.3).	.3
2/4/95	JDS	Discuss case with PKJ (.6).	.6

2/4/95	PKJ	Discuss case with JDS (.6). Trip to XYZ to obtain files (.7). Review files obtained from XYZ (5.3).	
			6.6
2/8/95	SLW	Legal research regarding anticipatory breach of contract (6.3).	
			6.3
2/9/95	JDS	Prepare for deposition of M.Barker (4.7).	
			4.7
2/9/95	SLW	Legal research regarding motion for preliminary in- junction (6.1). Draft memomandum regarding anticipatory breach of contract (3.7).	
			9.8
2/10/95	JDS	Prepare for deposition of M. Barker (3.5). Conference with SLW, PKJ (.8).	
			4.3
2/10/95	SLW	Draft memorandum regarding motion for preliminary injunction (2.7). Conference with JDS, PKJ (.8).	
			3.5
2/10/95	PKJ	Conference with JDS, SLW (.8). Prepare documents for Barker deposition (6.8).	
			7.6

2/11/95	JDS	Prepare for deposition of M. Barker (7.3).	
			7.3

2/11/95	PKJ	Prepare documents for M. Barker deposition (5.4).	
			5.4

2/12/95	JDS	Prepare for deposition of M. Barker (.9). Deposition of M. Barker (8.3). Conference with SLW, PKJ (.8).	
			10.0

2/12/95	SLW	Deposition of M. Barker (8.3). Conference with JDS, PKJ (.8).	
			9.1

2/12/95	PKJ	Deposition of M. Barker (8.3). Conference with JDS, SLW (.8).	
			9.1

2/15/95	JDS	Review Johnson contract (.5). Draft interrogatories (2.3). Telephone call from Attorney Jackson (.2). Prepare memorandum to file (.4).	
			3.4

2/15/95	PKJ	Review and organize Johnson documents (5.6). Prepare memorandum to JDS (.8).	
			6.4

2/16/95	JDS	Draft interrogatories (1.9). Review Johnson documents (1.2). Review memorandum (.9). Conference with SLW (.7).	
			4.7

| 2/16/95 | SLW | Conference with JDS (.7). | |
| | | | .7 |

| 2/19/95 | JDS | Correspondence to Attorney Jackson (.3). Correspondence from Attorney Lee (.2). Telephone calls to Attorneys Jackson and Lee (.4). Telephone call to J. Doe (.2). | |
| | | | 1.1 |

| 2/24/95 | JDS | Conference with SLW (.4). | |
| | | | .4 |

| 2/24/95 | SLW | Conference with JDS (.4). Legal research regarding Motion for Summary Judgment (7.3). | |
| | | | 7.7 |

| 2/26/95 | SLW | Legal research regarding Motion for Summary Judgment (3.3). Conference with JDS (.1). Conference with PKJ (.4). Draft Motion for Summary Judgment (4.8). | |
| | | | 8.6 |

| 2/26/95 | PKJ | Conference with SLW (.4). Prepare documents in support of Motion for Summary Judgment (6.2). | |
| | | | 6.6 |

| 2/27/95 | SLW | Draft Motion for Summary Judgment and Brief in Support thereof (11.2). | |
| | | | 11.2 |

FEE SUMMARY

ATTORNEY/ PARALEGAL	HOURS	RATE	TOTAL
JDS	38.0	$185/Hour	$7,030.00
SLW	57.2	$115/Hour	6,578.00
PKJ	41.7	$55/Hour	2,293.50
TOTAL FEE			$15,901.50

EXPENSES

Copying
    In-House Copies 87.50
    Outside Copies 223.00
Postage 13.65
Courier Fees 45.00
Telecopier Charges 19.00
Long Distance Telephone Calls 27.50
Court Reporter Fees 635.00
Parking (M. Barker Deposition) 16.00

TOTAL EXPENSES $1,066.65

TOTAL THIS INVOICE $16,968.15

Appendix Two

Elements of Sample Litigation Plan

Before you begin lawsuit, you should request a litigation plan from your lawyer. These plans can include various elements and should be designed to reflect the facts involved in the case and your circumstances. However, any thorough plan should include the following elements.

1. FACTUAL SUMMARY
2. LEGAL ISSUES
3. ANALYSIS OF YOUR POTENTIAL LIABILITY OR AWARD
4. PROPOSED STRATEGY
5. SETTLEMENT STRATEGY AND RECOMMENDATION
6. ALTERNATIVES TO LITIGATION
7. LITIGATION STRATEGY
8. ESTIMATED DURATION OF LITIGATION
9. ESTIMATED COST OF EACH OPTION
10. PROPOSED LINE ITEM BUDGET

TAMING THE LAWYERS

Appendix Three

Sample Litigation Status Report

This is an example of the kind of letter you should expect from your law-yer—when a lawsuit has reached a predetermined chronological point or a significant procedural development.

March 4, 1995

John Doe
Executive Vice-President
XYZ Corporation
123 Main Street
Anywhere, CA 90123

RE: Jones Co. vs. XYZ Corp.

Dear John:

I am writing to apprise you of developments in the above-referenced case during the past month.

BACKGROUND

As you know, this is a lawsuit filed by the Jones Company ("Jones") against XYZ claiming that XYZ breached its contract with Jones. The contract stated that Jones was to supply XYZ with 50,000 six-foot cardboard likenesses of Bill and Hillary Clinton. XYZ had ordered the props for its annual sales convention, but the first couple's popu-larity plummeted when the President revealed shortly after his inau-guration that the middle class tax cut he had promised during the campaign would instead be a middle class tax increase. XYZ can-celed the order two months before the delivery date, but Jones claims that production had already begun and refused to cancel the order. When XYZ refused to take delivery, Jones sued XYZ for breach of contract.

CURRENT STATUS

We have filed an answer and counterclaim to Jones' lawsuit. The lawsuit is in the early stages of discovery.

RECENT ACTIVITY

During the past month, we have reviewed all of XYZ's documents regarding the case. We have performed legal research regarding Jones' legal theory (anticipatory breach of contract), as well as the issue of whether we can move for Summary Judgment. We took the deposition of Jones' Branch Manager, Matt Barker. We also prepared interrogatories to be sent to Jones.

ANTICIPATED ACTIVITY

In the next month, we plan to complete our interrogatories and requests for production of documents. Upon receipt of those documents, we will evaluate XYZ's position. Counsel for Jones has stated he will serve us with discovery requests sometime this month. We also hope to determine whether a Motion for Summary Judgment is appropriate.

LONG TERM STRATEGY

We believe that we can position XYZ to dispose of this case on a Motion for Summary Judgment by establishing that XYZ notified Jones of the cancellation before production actually began and that Jones had not incurred any costs at that point. We believe we can do this by obtaining production records from Jones, as well as through the testimony of Jones' Branch Manager (Matt Barker) and Chief Printer (John Olson).

If the facts developed do not support a Motion for Summary Judgment, we will attempt to prove that Jones failed to mitigate its damages.

COST SUMMARY

Including the bill of March 4, 1995, this case has cost $24,635 in fee and $1,785.50 in expenses for a total of $$26,420.50. We believe it will cost an additional $35,000 to complete discovery and $10,000 to file and argue a Motion for Summary Judgment if the facts support such a motion. If no motion can be filed, we will prepare for trial. Of course, all of these figures are estimates.

SETTLEMENT PROSPECTS

Jones has stated it will not settle for anything less than the full purchase price ($750,000) plus its attorney's fees. We have made no settlement offers due to the early stage of the case.

RECOMMENDATIONS

We believe XYZ should complete its discovery to determine whether a Motion for Summary Judgment is warranted. If not, XYZ should explore settlement possibilities before proceeding to trial.

Yours Very Truly,

J.D. Smith, Esq.

TAMING THE LAWYERS

Appendix Four

Ten Questions to Ask Your Prospective Lawyer

Before you hire an attorney, you interview several candidates. Before talking about your case—or potential case—in great detail, you should establish some background facts. Here are ten questions that will help you do this.

1. Describe your current practice.

2. Are you a generalist or a specialist?

3. What experience have you had with this type of legal problem?

4. What is your philosophy concerning the most effective way to handle this type of lawsuit?

5. Do you have experience in this industry?

6. What are your fee structures and how do you bill?

7. Tell me about your firm. What size is it? What is your position within it?

8. What are your "paper credentials"?

9. How do you propose to handle this case?

10. Why should I hire you?

TAMING THE LAWYERS

Appendix Five

The Cardinal Rules

Throughout this book, I have established some cardinal rules for managing legal issues and taming lawyers. Here, in one place, are my hard-earned conclusions.

1. NOBODY (ESPECIALLY THE LAWYERS) IS QUITE SURE EXACTLY WHAT THE LAW IS.

2. LAWYERS ARE TRAINED TO IDENTIFY PROBLEMS RATHER THAN SOLUTIONS.

3. IF YOU CAN RESOLVE YOUR DISPUTE WITHOUT GETTING THE LAWYERS INVOLVED, DO SO.

4. THE LONGER A LAWSUIT LASTS, THE MORE MONEY IT COSTS.

5. THE SELECTION OF YOUR LAWYER IS THE MOST IMPORTANT DECISION YOU WILL MAKE IN THE COURSE OF THE LEGAL ACTION.

6. HIRE THE LAWYER, NOT THE LAW FIRM.

7. LIKE MOST RAMBUNCTIOUS CREATURES, LAWYERS SHOULD BE KEPT ON A SHORT LEASH.

8. HIRED GUNS OFTEN MISFIRE.

9. SETTLE EARLY, NOT LATE.

TAMING THE LAWYERS

Index

20% OFF
MERRITT PUBLISHING BOOKS

Merritt features a full line of books on key topics for today's smart consumers and small businesses. Times are changing fast – find out how our books can help keep you **ahead** of the times.

☐**Yes!** Please send me a **FREE** Merritt Publishing Catalog, plus a 20% discount coupon good towards any book purchase from the catalog.

Name _____

Company _____

Address _____

City _____ State _____ Zip _____

Phone _____

Merritt Publishing • Post Office Box 955 • Dept. SWAL • Santa Monica, CA 90406-0955 • **1-800-638-7597**

SWAL

20% OFF
MERRITT PUBLISHING BOOKS

Merritt features a full line of books on key topics for today's smart consumers and small businesses. Times are changing fast – find out how our books can help keep you **ahead** of the times.

☐**Yes!** Please send me a **FREE** Merritt Publishing Catalog, plus a 20% discount coupon good towards any book purchase from the catalog.

Name _____

Company _____

Address _____

City _____ State _____ Zip _____

Phone _____

Merritt Publishing • Post Office Box 955 • Dept. SWAL • Santa Monica, CA 90406-0955 • **1-800-638-7597**

SWAL

BUSINESS REPLY MAIL
FIRST-CLASS MAIL   PERMIT NO. 243   SANTA MONICA CA

POSTAGE WILL BE PAID BY ADDRESSEE

MERRITT PUBLISHING

POST OFFICE BOX 955

SANTA MONICA CA 90406-9943

SWAL

BUSINESS REPLY MAIL
FIRST-CLASS MAIL   PERMIT NO. 243   SANTA MONICA CA

POSTAGE WILL BE PAID BY ADDRESSEE

MERRITT PUBLISHING

POST OFFICE BOX 955

SANTA MONICA CA 90406-9943

SWAL